PHILOSOPHICAL PAPERS

F. P. RAMSEY

EDITED BY

D. H. MELLOR

Faculty of Philosophy,
University of Cambridge

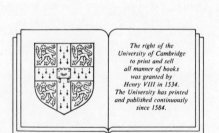

*The right of the
University of Cambridge
to print and sell
all manner of books
was granted by
Henry VIII in 1534.
The University has printed
and published continuously
since 1584.*

CAMBRIDGE UNIVERSITY PRESS

Cambridge
New York   Port Chester
Melbourne   Sydney

Published by the Press Syndicate of the University of Cambridge
The Pitt Building, Trumpington Street, Cambridge CB2 1RP
40 West 20th Street, New York, NY 10011, USA
10 Stamford Road, Oakleigh, Melbourne 3166, Australia

© Cambridge University Press 1990

First published 1990

Printed in Great Britain
at the University Press, Cambridge

British Library cataloguing in publication data
Ramsey, F. P. (Frank Plumpton), *1093–1930*
Philosophical papers.
1. Philosophy
I. Title II. Mellor, D. H. (David Hugh), *1938–*
511.3

Library of Congress cataloguing in publication data applied for

ISBN 0 521 37480 4 hard covers
ISBN 0 521 37621 1 paperback

M T LTD.

CONTENTS

v

CONTENTS

PREFACE

The papers in this volume have all been published before: details are given in the Bibliography. But only the following were prepared for publication by Ramsey himself: Chapter 2, 'Universals', and its Postscript, 'Note on the Preceding Paper' (part of 'Universals and the "Method of Analysis"'); Chapter 3, 'Facts and Propositions'; Chapter 8, 'The Foundations of Mathematics'; and Chapter 9, 'Mathematical Logic'.

All but one of the other papers were first prepared for publication after Ramsey's death in 1930 by his friend and editor R. B. Braithwaite, who included them in *The Foundations of Mathematics and other Logical Essays* (hereafter *FM*), the collection of Ramsey's papers published in 1931. The most finished of these is Chapter 4, 'Truth and Probability', written at the end of 1926. Braithwaite says in his introduction to *FM* that Ramsey once contemplated publishing this paper separately, and it lacks only an intended but unwritten final section on probability in science. The Postscript to this chapter comprises three notes, 'Reasonable Degree of Belief', 'Statistics' and 'Chance', written in the spring of 1928, and one, 'Probability and Partial Belief', written in the summer of 1929.

The other notes and papers first published in *FM* were also, with one exception, written in the summer of 1929. The exception is Chapter 10, *FM*'s 'Epilogue', a paper read in 1925 to a Cambridge discussion society (the so-called Apostles). Of the others, 'Causal Qualities' is really a postscript to 'Theories', the present Chapter 6, to which

PREFACE

I have therefore appended it. The note on 'Philosophy' is reprinted here as an introductory Chapter 1.

The other paper first published in *FM*, 'General Propositions and Causality', refers to a paper, 'Universals of Law and of Fact', written in the spring of 1928, and not published in *FM*. When, after *FM* went out of print, I edited a new collection of Ramsey's papers, *Foundations: Essays in Philosophy, Logic, Mathematics and Economics*, published in 1978, I put these two papers together into a chapter on 'Law and Causality', which is reprinted here as Chapter 7.

The other differences between *Foundations* and *FM* were: the inclusion of Ramsey's two major papers on economics, 'A Contribution to the Theory of Taxation' and 'A Mathematical Theory of Saving'; and the omission of G. E. Moore's Preface, Braithwaite's Introduction and Note on Symbolism, Ramsey's review of Wittgenstein's *Tractatus Logico-Philosophicus*, Parts II-IV of 'On a Problem of Formal Logic', and the notes reprinted here as Postscripts to Chapters 2, 4 and 6.

Now that *Foundations* is also out of print, this third collection of Ramsey's papers has been edited with the specific aim of making his previously published work on philosophy more accessible to practitioners and students of that subject. The work on economics and mathematics has therefore been discarded, and the philosophical papers published in *FM* but omitted from *Foundations* have been restored, together with the Note on Symbolism. All these papers are here reprinted in their original form, with no changes except those entailed by their reordering and by the correction of a few typographical errors.

In preparing and introducing this new collection I have received valuable encouragement and advice from Professors Braithwaite, Richard Jeffrey of Princeton University, and Isaac Levi of Columbia University, Dr. Nils-Eric Sahlin of

Lund University and my colleague Professor T. J. Smiley.
I remain indebted also to Professors L. Mirsky's and Richard
Stone's introductions to Ramsey's mathematics and economics
in *Foundations*, and to the contributions of Professor Braithwaite and others to my (1978) radio portrait of Ramsey, on
which I have drawn in the introduction that follows.
Finally, thanks are due to Messrs. Routledge & Kegan Paul,
the publishers of *FM* and of *Foundations*, for agreeing to this
publication, to Cambridge University Press for undertaking
it, and to Jamie Whyte for compiling the new Index.

D. H. M.

Cambridge
June 1989

INTRODUCTION

In the first three decades of this century Cambridge University contained several remarkable philosophers, of whom G. E. Moore, Bertrand Russell, A. N. Whitehead and Ludwig Wittgenstein are now perhaps the best known, together with John Maynard Keynes, who was a philosopher of probability as well as an economist. But they were not the only notable philosophers in Cambridge at that time: there were also, among others, J. E. McTaggart, W. E. Johnson, C. D. Broad, and R. B. Braithwaite. And above all, there was Frank Plumpton Ramsey, Fellow of King's College and University Lecturer in Mathematics. He was born on 22nd February, 1903, and so was only 26 when he died on 19th January, 1930; yet in his short life he produced the most profound and original work, in logic, mathematics and economics, as well as in philosophy: work that is still extraordinarily, and increasingly, influential.

It is not feasible within the confines of this Introduction to describe in detail either Ramsey's work or its major and manifold effects on the subjects it deals with. For an introduction to the work itself, readers may refer to Nils-Eric Sahlin's *The Philosophy of F. P. Ramsey* (1990); and for some recent evidence of its impact on philosophy, to *Prospects for Pragmatism: Essays in Memory of F. P. Ramsey* (1980), a collection which I edited for the fiftieth anniversary of Ramsey's death.

The papers that follow may indeed seem to need no introduction, so clearly does Ramsey express himself even in his least finished notes. But his clarity can deceive, because his seemingly simple formulations are apt to conceal the depth and precision of his thought. Sometimes also, as G. E. Moore remarked in his preface to *FM*, Ramsey ' fails to explain things as clearly as he could have done, simply because he does not see that any explanation is needed: he does not realise that what to him seems perfectly clear and straight-forward may to others, less gifted, offer many puzzles '.

For both these reasons some introduction is called for, if only to remind readers how much Ramsey repays close and repeated reading. It may also be desirable to indicate something of the present interest and influence of Ramsey's work. And although this volume is confined to his philosophy, its readers may well wish to learn something about his achievements in other fields, as well as about him, and about his attitudes to philosophy and to life. Hence the scope and form of this Introduction, and the inclusion of Ramsey's note on ' Philosophy ' as Chapter 1, and of the Epilogue—of which Braithwaite said in his Introduction to *FM* that ' Ramsey did not change the attitude towards life that he has so happily and characteristically expressed in it '.

Ramsey came of a distinguished Cambridge family. His father, A. S. Ramsey, was also a professional mathematician and the President (i.e. Vice-Master) of Magdalene College, and his younger brother Michael went on to become Archbishop of Canterbury. It was through his family, and his befriending of such Fellows of Magdalene as C. K. Ogden and I. A. Richards, that while, and even before, he was an undergraduate reading mathematics at Trinity College, the young Ramsey began to meet the thinkers who stimulated his later work.

It was Russell and Wittgenstein who gave the first impetus to Ramsey's early metaphysics, logic and philosophy of mathematics. In 1925, two years after graduating in mathematics with the highest marks in his year, Ramsey produced ' The Foundations of Mathematics ' (Chapter 8). This paper is the culmination of the logicist programme of reducing mathematics to logic undertaken in Russell's and Whitehead's *Principia Mathematica* (1913). It is, as Braithwaite's Introduction to *FM* puts it, ' an attempt to reconstruct the system of *Principia Mathematica* so that its blemishes may be avoided but its excellencies retained '. In particular, it improves Russell's weak definition of mathematical propositions as purely general ones by requiring them also to be tautologies in the sense of Wittgenstein's *Tractatus Logico-Philosophicus* (1922); and it simplifies Russell's complex theory of types by drawing the now standard distinction between the logical and the semantic paradoxes and dealing with them separately.

In the next year, 1926, Ramsey followed up this remarkable work by producing ' Mathematical Logic ' (Chapter 9), a paper which defends Russell's logicist view of mathematics in more general terms ' against the formalism of Hilbert and the intuitionism of Brouwer '. And although that view has since lost favour, the version of it developed in Ramsey's ' Foundations of Mathematics ' is still of much more than merely historical interest (see Chihara 1980).

Ramsey's other paper on mathematical logic, ' On a Problem of Formal Logic ', published in 1928, solves a special case of the decision problem for first-order predicate calculus with equality. This paper was intended to further the solution of the general decision problem, but that problem was later shown to be insoluble (see Church 1956), and although Ramsey's solution of his special case is still of interest, it is really too technical to be worth reproducing in this collection.

It is however worth remarking how fruitful in other ways the mathematics of this paper has turned out to be. According to L. Mirsky's part of the Introduction to *Foundations*, it made ' a contribution of the first magnitude to, and probably lasting significance for, mathematical research '. But this fact was not recognised at the time: as Mirsky says, the two mathematical results Ramsey proves in this paper—both now called Ramsey's theorem—' only began to enter the consciousness of the general mathematical community during the last [two decades] when they became the source of inspiration of hundreds of papers constituting a body of work now known as " Ramsey theory " '.

All this is remarkable enough, but the genesis of Ramsey theory is even more so. It is not of course remarkable that Ramsey should publish work in mathematics, since he was a mathematician by trade as well as by training: becoming in 1926 a University lecturer in mathematics, a post he held until his death four years later. But his lectures in the Cambridge Faculty of Mathematics were mostly on the foundations of mathematics, not on mathematics itself. On mathematics, as opposed to its foundations, he only published nine pages: the first nine pages of ' On a Problem of Formal Logic '.

If Ramsey's work on logic and mathematics was prompted initially by Russell and Wittgenstein, his work on probability and economics was prompted by another Cambridge friend, Maynard Keynes. Keynes' *A Treatise on Probability* (1921), which is still influential, treats that subject as an extension of deductive logic, the logic of conclusive inference, to inductive logic, the logic of reasonable inconclusive inference. It does so by appealing to a primitive logical relation of partial entailment between propositions: a relation which, when measurable, enables a probability measure, knowable *a priori*, to say how strong an inference from one proposition to another would be. But in his 1922 review of the *Treatise*, and in his 1926 paper ' Truth and Probability ' (Chapter 4), Ramsey criticised the idea of partial entailment, and the theory based on it, so effectively that Keynes himself abandoned it; and when Carnap (e.g. 1950) and his followers revived it, they improved it greatly by using Ramsey's probability measure of the strength of the beliefs inferred to measure the partial entailment relation used to infer them.

The fact that Keynes did not resent Ramsey's demolition of his theory of probability is shown by his getting Ramsey a Fellowship at King's College Cambridge in 1924 at the ripe age of 21, and then encouraging him to work on problems in economics. There resulted two papers on economics, ' A Contribution to the Theory of Taxation ' and 'A Mathematical Theory of Saving ', which appeared in *The Economic Journal* in 1927 and 1928 respectively. The latter deals with how much of its income a nation should save; the former with the relative rates at which purchases of different commodities should be taxed in order to raise a given revenue with the least disutility to the consumer.

These economics papers are of no great philosophical interest, and for that reason they too have been omitted from this volume. But that is not to deny their importance in economics. Keynes, in his obituary of Ramsey in *The Economic Journal* for March 1930, called the paper on saving ' one of the most remarkable contributions to mathematical economics ever made ', and Richard Stone's introduction to them in *Foundations* describes them as ' generally recognised as the starting points of two flourishing branches of economics: optimal taxation and optimal accumulation '.

But this recognition of Ramsey's work was a long time coming in economics, as it was in mathematics. As Stone remarks, Ramsey's ideas on saving did not catch on until 1960, and his work on taxation not until 1970. And as with his economics and his mathematics, so indeed with most of Ramsey's work. It is remarkable how long most of it has taken to be caught up with and developed by others, and it is worth asking why.

The first and most obvious reason is that much of Ramsey's

work was hard to take in at first because it was so profound and so original. Then there are the factors noted earlier: Ramsey's failure to explain things that, although by no means clear to others, were clear enough to him; and his deceptively light and simple style, which makes his arguments look easy until one tries to think them through oneself. Compare for example the *Tractatus'* portentous 'Whereof one cannot speak, thereof one must be silent' with Ramsey's 'But what we can't say we can't say, and we can't whistle it either'. Ramsey's comment seems almost flippant, until we see that it sums up a deep objection to the whole of the *Tractatus*, whose approach Ramsey was instrumental in persuading Wittgenstein to abandon.

Something else that inhibited a proper and widespread appreciation of Ramsey's work was the fact that he himself never pushed it. As I. A. Richards, his friend and early mentor at Magdalene, put it in a radio programme about Ramsey (Mellor 1978): 'He never was a showman at all, not the faintest trace of trying to make a figure of himself. Very modest, gentle, and on the whole he refrained almost entirely from argumentative controversy . . . He felt too clear in his own mind, I think, to want to refute other people'; a fact confirmed by Mrs Lettice Ramsey, his widow, by Braithwaite and by other friends.

It is not really surprising therefore that, after Ramsey died, more forceful figures should have overshadowed his reputation, and distracted attention from his work. That certainly happened in philosophy, which in the nineteen-thirties and forties in Cambridge was dominated by Wittgenstein. Braithwaite admitted as much in the broadcast mentioned above: 'Now with regard to why his views of probability weren't accepted more, I'm sorry, I think I am myself to blame to a certain extent: because I edited the works and I thought they were very interesting; but this was the moment when Wittgenstein had descended on Cambridge, and all of us took the next ten years trying to digest Wittgenstein.' With the benefit of hindsight, one might well feel that Cambridge in the thirties, indeed the whole philosophical community, would have been at least as well employed trying to digest Ramsey; and indeed that, but for Ramsey's early death, Wittgenstein's own work, on which Ramsey had a strong influence, would have developed more profitably than it did and been digested less uncritically than it was.

Whatever the reason, the fact remains that most of Ramsey's work was not picked up at once, and only much later was most of it rediscovered. Take the problem, tackled in ' Truth and Probability ', of how to use our actions to measure the strength of our beliefs. The problem is that actions are caused not by beliefs alone, but by combinations of beliefs and desires, and any action can be caused by more than one such combination. But how then can any action be used to measure any one particular belief? Ramsey's paper shows how, by showing how our choices between gambles can be made to yield measures both of our desires (subjective utilities) and of our beliefs (subjective probabilities): thus laying foundations for the serious use of these quantitative concepts in economics and statistics as well as in philosophy.

This paper was written in 1926 and published in *FM* in 1931. But utility theory only really caught on after its rediscovery by Von Neumann and Morgenstern in their 1944 book *The Theory of Games and Economic Behavior*; and not for years was it realised how much of their work had been anticipated, and in some ways bettered, by Ramsey. And as with utility, so with subjective probability: not until some of Ramsey's ideas were rediscovered by L. J. Savage in his book, *The Foundations of Statistics*, published in 1954, did statitisticians begin to take them seriously.

Unfortunately, taking Ramsey's ideas seriously doesn't

always mean getting them right. A striking example is the common assumption that 'Truth and Probability', like modern Bayesian decision theory (e.g. Jeffrey's *The Logic of Decision* 1965), tells us to 'act in the way we think most likely to realize the objects of our desires' whether or not those thoughts and desires are either reasonable or right. It does no such thing: it claims only that the psychological theory which says that we do in fact act in this way is 'a useful approximation to the truth'. Ramsey's claim is purely descriptive, the appearance of prescription arising only from misreading his first-person 'should' in sentences like 'the more confident I am . . . the less distance I should be willing to go . . . to check my opinion' as 'ought to' instead of 'would'.

What Ramsey really anticipates are not the subjective and amoral prescriptions of modern decision theory, but modern functionalist views of the mind (see Block 1980), which take beliefs, desires and other such attitudes to be definable by their effects on our actions, by their causes (e.g. our perceptions), and by their interactions (e.g. the belief that p satisfying the desire that p). Ramsey's theory of degrees of belief in 'Truth and Probability' is a very—and a very early—paradigm of a functionalist account of an aspect of the mind.

In his 1927 paper on 'Facts and Propositions', moreover, Ramsey also suggests a solution to a different problem about belief, which still plagues functionalism: namely, how to define the contents of beliefs, conceived as their truth conditions. The problem here is that the conditions in which a belief is true cannot be defined by how, combined with various desires, it makes us act, since that will be the same whether it is true or not. But what a belief's truth will affect is whether the actions which it combines with our desires to cause will succeed: i.e. whether they will realise the objects of those desires. In short, a belief's truth conditions are the conditions in which every action A that would combine with some desire to cause would succeed in realising that desire's object. Or, as Ramsey puts it, ' any set of actions [(A)] for whose utility p is a necessary and sufficient condition might be called a belief that p, and so would be true if p, i.e. if they [the actions] are useful '.

Ramsey devotes most of ' Facts and Propositions ' to sketching what he calls a ' pragmatist ' (i.e. functionalist) account of what he says ' may be called by any of the terms judgment, belief, or assertion '. But this paper is now better known for its denial that truth presents a separate problem: because, for example ' " He is always right " could be expressed by " For all a, R, b, if he asserts aRb, then aRb ", to which " is true " would be an obviously superfluous addition '. Many have tried since to refute this redundancy theory of truth, but Ramsey is really only echoing Aristotle: to assert truly is just to assert of what is, that it is. And if something like Tarski's later semantic theory of truth (e.g. Tarski 1944) fails to follow, that is only because Ramsey ascribes truth primarily to beliefs, not to sentences. For, as Ramsey says, what we need to explain is not the truth of the belief that aRb —let alone that of the unasserted sentence ' aRb '—but what it is to have such beliefs, and what in particular gives them their contents and hence their truth conditions: an issue that is still very much alive (see e.g. Loar's *Mind and Meaning* 1981).

An earlier work of Ramsey's which is even more sadly neglected is his 1925 paper on ' Universals ' (Chapter 2). In this he disputes the ' fundamental division of objects into two classes, particular and universal ', a division that is usually denied only by nominalists, and then only by denying that there are any universals. Ramsey has a deeper point, and his ground for it is his argument that there is no essential difference, in an atomic proposition ϕa, between the incompleteness of a and that of ϕ. Again, attempts have since been made to refute this contention (e.g. by Dummett in *Frege*, 1973, ch. 4); but most of the recently revived work on universals (e.g. Armstrong's *Nominalism & Realism* 1978) has just ignored it. Yet Ramsey's account alone answers such basic questions as: why we quantify over particulars first (Ramsey: because that's what makes them particulars); how particulars and universals can combine, without vicious regress, to form atomic facts; and why it takes at least one of each to do so. So provided the metaphysics of universals continues to recover from its long and emasculating subjection to semantics, I predict that this paper too will eventually come into its own.

A late work of Ramsey's that has also had less impact than it should is his 1929 note on ' Theories ' (Chapter 6), which treats a theory's theoretical terms as existentially bound variables, thus generating what is now called its ' Ramsey sentence '. But although this account of theories has been noted with approval (e.g. by Carnap 1966, ch. 26), the explanations it provides of several otherwise puzzling features of them have not. For example, on Ramsey's account, parts of a theory, containing theoretical variables within the scope of its quantifiers, are not ' strictly propositions by themselves ', and their meaning ' can only be given when we know to what stock of " propositions " . . . [they] are to be added '. But this holism of theoretical meaning means, among other things, that rival theories of the same empirical phenomena may well be ' incommensurable ': i.e. such that their ' adherents . . . could quite well dispute, although neither affirmed anything the other denied '. Yet not until Kuhn's *The Structure of Scientific Revolutions* (1962) did this phenomenon of theoretical incommensurability attract much attention. And since then, because Ramsey's simple explanation of it has been largely overlooked, it has been much overrated, both as a puzzle and in its supposed implications:

e.g. for deductive accounts of theoretical explanation (Hempel 1965, ch. 12), which on Ramsey's account it doesn't affect at all—since, as he notes, it has no effect on reasoning within the scope of a single theory's quantifiers.

This is not of course to deny that incommensurability makes it harder to say which of two rival theories in science one should believe. And this and other difficulties of justifying belief in scientific theories have led Popper (e.g. 1972, ch. 3) and his followers to deny that knowledge entails belief. Not so Ramsey, who retains the more usual conception that, to be known, propositions must at least be believed. But his brisk and memorable note on ' Knowledge ' (Chapter 5), written in 1929, does anticipate other recent writers (e.g. Nozick 1981, ch. 3) in severing the link between knowledge and justification, thus escaping the classic dilemma of having to admit either an endless regress of things known* or some self-justifying foundations for knowledge. For knowledge, according to Ramsey, is not justified true belief, but true belief ' obtained by a reliable process ': in the crucial case of memory, the process being ' the causal process connecting what happens with my remembering it '.

So knowledge for Ramsey relies on causation: and causation relies on laws of nature, which are a species of generalisation. As to what generalisations are, Ramsey in 1927, in ' Facts and Propositions ', followed Wittgenstein's *Tractatus* in equating ' For all x, fx ' with the conjunction of all instances of ' fx '; and gave a remarkable answer to the obvious objection that to get ' For all x, fx ' from (say) '$fa\&fb\&fc$ ', one must add ' a, b, c are everything '. His answer was that this addition can be deleted, because, if true, it is a necessary truth: since if it is false then something, d, differs numerically from a, b and c, and ' numerical identity and difference are necessary relations '.

To the further question, of how laws differ from other true

generalisations, Ramsey gave not one remarkable answer but two. ' Universals of Law and of Fact ' (Chapter 7A) contains his earlier answer, which has recently been given renewed currency by Lewis (1973). This says that ' laws [are] consequences of those [general] propositions which we should take as axioms if we knew everything and organised it as simply as possible in a deductive system '. This account of laws enables a strong defence of a Humean view of them (see e.g. Armstrong 1983), and still has wide appeal: seeming, for example, to underlie the deference many philosophers pay to microphysics, as being the most likely source of axioms for Ramsey's system.

Ramsey himself, however, abandoned this account of laws within a year. His later theory, given in ' General Propositions and Causality ' (Chapter 7B), is at once more subtle and less finished, and much less amenable to summary. But of all Ramsey's philosophical papers, I think this is the one from which we still have most to learn. Roughly, it distinguishes laws from merely accidentally true generalisations, not by their content but by their role, for example in our assessment of action. We cannot assess a man's action ' except by considering what would have happened if he had acted differently; and this kind of unfulfilled conditional cannot be interpreted as a material implication, but depends essentially on variable hypotheticals '. To differ over these conditionals is not to differ over the facts that make generalisations true or false. It is to differ over a general ' system with which the speaker meets the future ', comprising those generalisations to which he gives this lawlike status. These ' variable hypotheticals are not judgments but rules for judging " If I meet a ϕ, I shall regard it as a ψ ". This cannot be *negated* but it can be *disagreed* with by one who does not adopt it.'

Such disagreement is of course objectively debatable: for instance, too many past ϕs may have been known to be ψ for this to be a sensible rule. But even apart from that, Ramsey sees the need for his theory ' to explain the peculiar importance and objectivity ascribed to causal laws ', and how in particular ' the deduction of effect from cause is conceived to be so radically different from that of cause from effect '. This asymmetry Ramsey explains by the temporal asymmetry of the cause-effect relation, and that in turn by the fact ' that any present volition of ours is (for us) irrelevant to any past event. To another (or to ourselves in the future) it can serve as a sign of the past, but to us now what we do affects only the probability of the future.' Thus our past is distinguished from our future as the region of space-time about which we can have knowledge that will never depend on our knowledge of our own present intentions. That distinction in turn determines the direction of time and of the cause-effect relation, and hence how we can use the generalisations we call causal laws to help us decide how to act ourselves, and how to assess the actions of others.

This theory of Ramsey's is of course only a starting point for progress towards an adequate account of the relations between time, knowledge, action, causation and laws of nature. Yet I am sure it is the right one, and from it some progress has been made (e.g. Dummett 1964, Mellor 1981). But we have a long way to go, even to catch up with all the implications of Ramsey's thought.

And as with Ramsey on causation, so with the rest of his work in philosophy. My object in republishing it now is not to enshrine it but, as Braithwaite said in his Introduction to *FM*, ' to stimulate others to think about the hardest things in the world with some of that singleness of mind which characterised Frank Ramsey '—and to help them to do so by giving them the inestimable benefit of Ramsey's own ideas.

D. H. MELLOR

REFERENCES

Armstrong, D. M. (1978) *Nominalism & Realism*, Cambridge University Press.
(1983) *What is a Law of Nature* , Cambridge University Press.

Block, N., ed. (1980) *Readings in Philosophy of Psychology Volume 1*, Methuen, London.

Carnap, R. (1950) *Logical Foundations of Probability*, University of Chicago Press.
(1966) *Philosophical Foundations of Physics*, Basic Books, New York.

Chihara, C. S. (1980) ' Ramsey's Theory of Types: Suggestions for a Return to Fregean Sources ', in D. H. Mellor, ed. (1980), pp. 21–47.

Church, A. (1956), *Introduction to Mathematical Logic*, Princeton University Press.

Dummett, M. (1964) ' Bringing About the Past ', in his *Truth and Other Enigmas* (1978), Duckworth, London.
(1973) *Frege: Philosophy of Language*, Duckworth, London.

Hempel, C. G., (1965) *Aspects of Scientific Explanation*, Free Press, New York.

Jeffrey, R. C. (1965), *The Logic of Decision*, University of Chicago Press.

Keynes, J. M. (1921), *A Treatise on Probability*, Macmillan, London.

Lewis, D. K. (1973), *Counterfactuals*, Blackwell, Oxford.

Kuhn, T. S. (1962), *The Structure of Scientific Revolutions*, University of Chicago Press.

Loar, B. (1981) *Mind and Meaning*, Cambridge University Press.

Mellor, D. H. (1978), ' Better than the Stars ', Broadcast on BBC Radio 3, 27th February, 1978.
ed. (1980), *Prospects for Pragmatism*, Cambridge University Press.
(1981), *Real Time*, Cambridge University Press.

REFERENCES

Nozick, R. (1981), *Philosophical Explanations*, Clarendon Press, Oxford.

Popper, K. R. (1972), *Objective Knowledge*, Oxford University Press.

Sahlin, N.-E. (1990), *The Philosophy of F. P. Ramsey*, Cambridge University Press.

Savage, L. J. (1954), *Foundations of Statistics*, Wiley, New York.

Tarski, A., (1944), ' The Semantic Conception of Truth ', in *Readings in Philosophical Analysis*, ed. H. Feigl and W. Sellars (1949), Appleton-Century-Crofts, New York, pp. 52–84.

von Neumann, J. and Morgenstern, O. (1944), *Theory of Games and Economic Behaviour*, Princeton University Press.

Whitehead, A. N. and Russell, B. (1913) *Principia Mathematica*, Cambridge University Press.

Wittgenstein, L. (1922), *Tractatus Logico-Philosophicus*, Routledge and Kegan Paul, London.

NOTE ON SYMBOLISM

In some of these essays Ramsey uses the symbolism of A. N. Whitehead and Bertrand Russell's *Principia Mathematica*. Its most important features are :—

p, q, r used for *propositions.*

a, b, c used for *individuals.*

f, g, ϕ, χ, ψ used for *propositional functions.*

[These are sometimes written $\phi\hat{x}$, $\psi(\hat{x}, \hat{y}, \hat{z})$, etc., to show how many arguments they take.]

Then ϕa [sometimes written $\phi(a)$], $\psi(a, b, c)$, etc., are propositions.

x, y, z used for *variables* in expressions like

$(x) . \phi x$ meaning *For every x, ϕx is true.*

$(\exists x) . \phi x$ meaning *There is an x for which ϕx is true.*

Logical constants :—

$\sim$ meaning *not.*

$\vee$ meaning *or.*

. meaning *and.*

$\supset$ meaning *implies* [$\supset_x$ *implies for every x*].

$\equiv$ meaning *is equivalent to* [$\equiv_x$ *is equivalent to for every x*].

Other expressions sometimes used in this book :—

$\hat{x}(\phi x)$ meaning *the class of ϕ's.*

ϵ meaning *is a member of the class.*

$\subset$ meaning *is contained in* (relation between classes).

Nc meaning *the cardinal number of.*

$(\imath x)(\phi x)$ meaning *the one and only thing satisfying ϕ.*

E ! $(\imath x)$ (ϕx) meaning *One and only one thing satisfies ϕ.*

Points, colons, etc., . : :. are used for bracketing.

Ramsey also uses the following symbols not used by Whitehead and Russell :—

A stroke ‾ above the proposition or function to denote its contradictory $[\bar{p} = \sim p]$.

(a) meaning *the class whose only member is a.*

Occasionally Ramsey uses ordinary mathematical notations [$m \equiv n$ (mod l) means *m and n when divided by l have the same remainder*], and in discussing probability J. M. Keynes' symbolism p/h meaning *the probability of proposition p given proposition h.*

R. B. B.

PHILOSOPHY (1929)

Philosophy must be of some use and we must take it seriously; it must clear our thoughts and so our actions. Or else it is a disposition we have to check, and an inquiry to see that this is so ; i.e. the chief proposition of philosophy is that philosophy is nonsense. And again we must then take seriously that it is nonsense, and not pretend, as Wittgenstein does, that it is important nonsense !

In philosophy we take the propositions we make in science and everyday life, and try to exhibit them in a logical system with primitive terms and definitions, etc. Essentially a philosophy is a system of definitions or, only too often, a system of descriptions of how definitions might be given.

I do not think it is necessary to say with Moore that the definitions explain what we have hitherto meant by our propositions, but rather that they show how we intend to use them in future. Moore would say they were the same, that philosophy does not change what anyone meant by ' This is a table '. It seems to me that it might ; for meaning is mainly potential, and a change might therefore only be manifested on rare and critical occasions. Also sometimes philosophy should clarify and distinguish notions previously vague and confused, and clearly this is meant to fix our future meaning only.[1] But this is clear, that the definitions are to give at least our future meaning, and not merely to give any pretty way of obtaining a certain structure.

I used to worry myself about the nature of philosophy through excessive scholasticism. I could not see how we could understand a word and not be able to recognize whether a

[1] But in so far as our past meaning was not utterly confused, philosophy will naturally give that, too. E.g. that paradigm of philosophy, Russell's theory of descriptions.

proposed definition of it was or was not correct. I did not realize the vagueness of the whole idea of understanding, the reference it involves to a multitude of performances any of which may fail and require to be restored. Logic issues in tautologies, mathematics in identities, philosophy in definitions; all trivial but all part of the vital work of clarifying and organizing our thought.

If we regard philosophy as a system of definitions (and elucidations of the use of words which cannot be nominally defined), the things that seem to me problems about it are these:

(1) What definitions do we feel it up to *philosophy* to provide, and what do we leave to the sciences or feel it unnecessary to give at all?

(2) When and how can we be content without a definition but merely with a description of how a definition might be given? [This point is mentioned above.]

(3) How can philosophical enquiry be conducted without a perpetual *petitio principii*?

(1) Philosophy is not concerned with special problems of definition but only with general ones: it does not propose to define particular terms of art or science, but to settle e.g. problems which arise in the definition of any such term or in the relation of any term in the physical world to the terms of experience.

Terms of art and science, however, must be defined, but not necessarily nominally; e.g. we define mass by explaining how to measure it, but this is not a nominal definition; it merely gives the term 'mass' in a theoretical structure a clear relation to certain experimental facts. The terms we do not need to define are those which we know we could define if need arose, like 'chair', or those which like 'clubs' (the suit of cards) we can translate easily into visual or some other language, but cannot conveniently expand in words.

(2) The solution to what we called in (1) a 'general problem of definition' is naturally a description of definitions, from which we learn how to form the actual definition in any particular case. That we so often seem to get no actual *definitions*, is because the solution of the problem is often that nominal definition is inappropriate, and that what is wanted is an explanation of the use of the symbol.

But this does not touch what may be supposed to be the real difficulty under this head (2) ; for what we have said applies only to the case in which the word to be defined being merely described (because treated as one of a class), its definition or explanation is also, of course, merely described, but described in such a way that when the actual word is given its actual definition can be derived. But there are other cases in which the word to be defined being given, we are given in return no definition of it but a statement that its meaning involves entities of such-and-such sorts in such-and-such ways, i.e. a statement which *would* give us a definition if we had names for these entities.

As to the use of this, it is plainly to fit the term in connection with variables, to put it as a value of the right complex variable ; and it presupposes that we can have variables without names for all their values. Difficult questions arise as to whether we must always be *able* to name all the values, and if so what kind of ability this means, but clearly the phenomenon is in some way possible in connection with sensations for which our language is so fragmentary. For instance, ' Jane's voice ' is a description of a characteristic of sensations for which we have no name. We could perhaps name it, but can we identify and name the different inflexions of which it consists ?

An objection often made to these descriptions of definitions of sensory characteristics is that they express what we should find on analysis, but that this kind of analysis changes the sensation analysed by developing the conplexity which it pretends merely to discover. That attention can change our experience is indubitable, but it seems to me possible that sometimes it reveals a pre-existing complexity (i.e. enables us to symbolize this adequately), for this is compatible with any change in incidental facts, anything even except a creation of the complexity.

Another difficulty with regard to descriptions of definitions is that if we content ourselves with them we may get simply nonsense by introducing nonsensical variables, e.g. described variables such as 'particular' or theoretical ideas such as 'point'. We might for instance say that by 'patch' we mean an infinite class of points ; if so we should be giving up philosophy for theoretical psychology. For in philosophy we analyse *our* thought, in which patch could not be replaced by infinite class of points : we could not determine a particular infinite class extensionally ; 'This patch is red' is not short for '*a* is red and *b* is red etc. . . .' where *a*, *b*, etc., are points. (How would it be if just *a* were not red ?) Infinite classes of points could only come in when we look at the mind from outside and construct a theory of it, in which its sensory field consists of classes of coloured points about which it thinks.

Now if we made this theory about our own mind we should have to regard it as accounting for certain *facts*, e.g. that this patch is red ; but when we are thinking of other people's minds we have no facts, but are altogether in the realm of theory, and can persuade ourselves that these theoretical constructions exhaust the field. We then turn back on our own minds, and say that what are really happening there are simply these theoretical processes. The clearest instance of this is, of course, materialism. But many other philosophies, e.g. Carnap's, make just the same mistake.

(3) Our third question was how we could avoid *petitio principii*, the danger of which arises somewhat as follows :—

In order to clarify my thought the proper method seems to be simply to think out with myself ' What do I mean by that ? ' ' What are the separate notions involved in this term ? ' ' Does this really follow from that ? ' etc., and to test identity of meaning of a proposed definiens and the definiendum by real and hypothetical examples. This we can often do without thinking about the nature of meaning itself ; we can tell whether we mean the same or different things by ' horse ' and ' pig ' without thinking at all about meaning in general. But in order to settle more complicated questions of the sort we obviously need a logical structure, a system of logic, into which to bring them. These we may hope to obtain by a relatively easy previous application of the same methods ; for instance, it should not be difficult to see that for either not-p or not-q to be true is just the same thing as for not both p and q to be true. In this case we construct a logic, and do all our philosophical analysis entirely *unselfconsciously*, thinking all the time of the facts and not about our thinking about them, deciding what we mean without any reference to the nature of meanings. [Of course we could also think about the nature of meaning in an unselfconscious way; i.e. think of a case of meaning before us without reference to our meaning *it*.] This is one method and it may be the right one ; but I think it is wrong and leads to an impasse, and I part company from it in the following way.

It seems to me that in the process of clarifying our thought we come to terms and sentences which we cannot elucidate in the obvious manner by defining their meaning. For instance, variable hypotheticals and theoretical terms we cannot define, but we can explain the way in which they are used, and in this explanation we are forced to look not only at the objects which we are talking about, but at our own mental states.

As Johnson would say, in this part of logic we cannot neglect the epistemic or subjective side.

Now this means that we cannot get clear about these terms and sentences without getting clear about meaning, and we seem to get into the situation that we cannot understand e.g. what we say about time and the external world without first understanding meaning and yet we cannot understand meaning without first understanding certainly time and probably the external world which are involved in it. So we cannot make our philosophy into an ordered progress to a goal, but have to take our problems as a whole and jump to a simultaneous solution ; which will have something of the nature of a hypothesis, for we shall accept it not as the consequence of direct argument, but as the only one we can think of which satisfies our several requirements.

Of course, we should not strictly speak of argument, but there is in philosophy a process analogous to ' linear inference ' in which things become successively clear ; and since, for the above reason, we cannot carry this through to the end, we are in the ordinary position of scientists of having to be content with piecemeal improvements : we can make several things clearer, but we cannot make anything clear.

I find this self-consciousness inevitable in philosophy except in a very limited field. We are driven to philosophize because we do not know clearly what we mean ; the question is always ' What do I mean by x ? ' And only very occasionally can we settle this without reflecting on meaning. But it is not only an obstacle, this necessity of dealing with meaning ; it is doubtless an essential clue to the truth. If we neglect it I feel we may get into the absurd position of the child in the following dialogue : ' Say breakfast.' ' Can't.' ' What can't you say ? ' ' Can't say breakfast.'

But the necessity of self-consciousness must not be used as a justification for nonsensical hypotheses ; we are doing philosophy not theoretical psychology, and our analyses of our statements, whether about meaning or anything else, must be such as we can understand.

The chief danger to our philosophy, apart from laziness and woolliness, is *scholasticism*, the essence of which is treating what is vague as if it were precise and trying to fit it into an exact logical category. A typical piece of scholasticism is Wittgenstein's view that all our everyday propositions are completely in order and that it is impossible to think illogically. (This last is like saying that it is impossible to break the rules of bridge because if you break them you are not playing bridge but, as Mrs C. says, not-bridge.) Another is the argumentation about acquaintance with before leading to the conclusion that we perceive the past. A simple consideration of the automatic telephone shows that we could react differently to AB and BA without perceiving the past, so that the argument is substantially unsound. It turns on a play with ' acquaintance ' which means, first, capacity to symbolize and, secondly, sensory perception. Wittgenstein seems to equivocate in just the same way with his notion of ' given.'

UNIVERSALS (1925)

The purpose of this paper is to consider whether there is a fundamental division of objects into two classes, particulars and universals. This question was discussed by Mr Russell in a paper printed in the Aristotelian Society's Proceedings for 1911. His conclusion that the distinction was ultimate was based upon two familiar arguments, directed against the two obvious methods of abolishing the distinction by holding either that universals are collections of particulars, or that particulars are collections of their qualities. These arguments, perfectly sound as far as they go, do not however seem to me to settle the whole question. The first, which appears again in *The Problems of Philosophy*, shows as against the nominalists that such a proposition as ' This sense-datum is white ' must have as one constituent something, such as whiteness or similarity, which is not of the same logical type as the sense-datum itself. The second argument, also briefly expounded in McTaggart's *The Nature of Existence*, proves that a man cannot be identified with the sum of his qualities. But although a man cannot be one of his own qualities, that is no reason why he should not be a quality of something else. In fact material objects *are* described by Dr Whitehead as ' true Aristotelian adjectives ' ; so that we cannot regard these two arguments as rendering the distinction between particular and universal secure against all criticism.

What then, I propose to ask, is the difference between a particular and a universal ? What can we say about one which will not also be true of the other ? If we follow Mr Russell we shall have to investigate three kinds of distinction, psychological, physical and logical. First we have the difference between a percept and a concept, the objects of two different kinds of mental acts ; but this is unlikely to be a distinction of any fundamental importance, since a difference in two mental acts may not correspond to any difference whatever in their objects. Next we have various distinctions between objects based on their relations to space and time ; for instance, some objects can only be in one place at a time, others, like the colour red, can be in many. Here again, in spite of the importance of the subject, I do not think we can have reached the essence of the matter. For when, for instance, Dr Whitehead says that a table is an adjective, and Mr Johnson that it is a substantive, they are not arguing about how many places the table can be in at once, but about its logical nature. And so it is with logical distinctions that our inquiry must mainly deal.

According to Mr Russell the class of universals is the sum of the class of predicates and the class of relations ; but this doctrine has been denied by Dr Stout.[1] But Dr Stout has been already sufficiently answered.[2] So I shall only discuss the more usual opinion to which Mr Russell adheres.

According to him terms are divided into individuals or particulars, qualities and relations, qualities and relations being grouped together as universals ; and sometimes qualities are even included among relations as one-termed relations in distinction from two-, three-, or many-termed relations. Mr Johnson also divides terms into substantives and adjectives, including relations as transitive adjectives ; and he regards the distinction between substantive and adjective as explaining that between particular and universal. But between these authorities, who agree so far, there is still an important

[1] "The Nature of Universals and Propositions," *Proc. British Academy*, 1921–22 (reprinted in *Studies in Philosophy and Psychology*, 1930).
[2] See the symposium between G. E. Moore, G. F. Stout & G. Dawes Hicks in *Aristotelian Society Supplementary Volume III*, 1923.

difference. Mr Johnson holds that although the nature of a substantive is such that it can only function in a proposition as subject and never as predicate, yet an adjective can function either as predicate or as a subject of which a secondary adjective can be predicated. For example, in 'Unpunctuality is a fault' the subject is itself an adjective—the quality of unpunctuality. There is thus a want of symmetry between substantives and adjectives, for while a predicate must be an adjective, a subject may be either a substantive or an adjective, and we must define a substantive as a term which can only be a subject, never a predicate.

Mr Russell, on the other hand, in his lectures on Logical Atomism,[1] has denied this. He says that about an adjective there is something incomplete, some suggestion of the form of a proposition ; so that the adjective-symbol can never stand alone or be the subject of a proposition, but must be completed into a proposition in which it is the predicate. Thus, he says, the appropriate symbol for redness is not the word ' red ' but the function ' x is red ', and red can only come into a proposition through the values of this function. So Mr Russell would say ' Unpunctuality is a fault ' really means something like ' For all x, if x is unpunctual, x is reprehensible ' ; and the adjective unpunctuality is not the subject of the proposition but only comes into it as the predicate of those of its parts which are of the form ' x is unpunctual '. This doctrine is the basis of new work in the Second Edition of *Principia Mathematica*.

Neither of these theories seems entirely satisfactory, although neither could be disproved. Mr Russell's view does, indeed, involve difficulties in connection with our cognitive relations to universals, for which reason it was rejected in the First Edition of *Principia*; but these difficulties seem to me, as now to Mr Russell, by no means insurmountable. But I could

[1] *The Monist*, 1918 and 1919.

not discuss them here without embarking upon innumerable questions irrelevant to the main points which I wish to make. Neither theory, then, can be disproved, but to both objections can be raised which may seem to have some force. For instance, Mr Russell urges that a relation between two terms cannot be a third term which comes between them, for then it would not be a relation at all, and the only genuinely relational element would consist in the connections between this new term and the two original terms. This is the kind of consideration from which Mr Bradley deduced his infinite regress, of which Mr Russell apparently now approves. Mr Johnson might reply that for him the connectional or structural element is not the relation but the characterizing and coupling ties ; but these ties remain most mysterious objects. It might also be objected that Mr Johnson does not make particulars and universals different enough, or take into account the peculiar incompleteness of adjectives which appears in the possibility of prefixing to them the auxiliary ' being '; ' being red ', ' being a man ' do not seem real things like a chair and a carpet. Against Mr Russell it might be asked how there can be such objects as his universals, which contain the form of a proposition and so are incomplete. In a sense, it might be urged, all objects are incomplete ; they cannot occur in facts except in conjunction with other objects, and they contain the forms of propositions of which they are constituents. In what way do universals do this more than anything else ?

Evidently, however, none of these arguments are really decisive, and the position is extremely unsatisfactory to any one with real curiosity about such a fundamental question. In such cases it is a heuristic maxim that the truth lies not in one of the two disputed views but in some third possibility which has not yet been thought of, which we can only discover

11

by rejecting something assumed as obvious by both the disputants.

Both the disputed theories make an important assumption which, to my mind, has only to be questioned to be doubted. They assume a fundamental antithesis between subject and predicate, that if a proposition consists of two terms copulated, these two terms must be functioning in different ways, one as subject, the other as predicate. Thus in ' Socrates is wise ', Socrates is the subject, wisdom the predicate. But suppose we turn the proposition round and say ' Wisdom is a characteristic of Socrates ', then wisdom, formerly the predicate, is now the subject. Now it seems to me as clear as anything can be in philosophy that the two sentences ' Socrates is wise ', ' Wisdom is a characteristic of Socrates ' assert the same fact and express the same proposition. They are not, of course, the same sentence, but they have the same meaning, just as two sentences in two different languages can have the same meaning. Which sentence we use is a matter either of literary style, or of the point of view from which we approach the fact. If the centre of our interest is Socrates we say ' Socrates is wise ', if we are discussing wisdom we may say ' Wisdom is a characteristic of Socrates ' ; but whichever we say we mean the same thing. Now of one of these sentences ' Socrates ' is the subject, of the other ' wisdom ' ; and so which of the two is subject, which predicate, depends upon what particular sentence we use to express our proposition, and has nothing to do with the logical nature of Socrates or wisdom, but is a matter entirely for grammarians. In the same way, with a sufficiently elastic language any proposition can be so expressed that any of its terms is the subject. Hence there is no essential distinction between the subject of a proposition and its predicate, and no fundamental classification of objects can be based upon such a distinction.

I do not claim that the above argument is immediately conclusive ; what I claim is that it throws doubt upon the whole basis of the distinction between particular and universal as deduced from that between subject and predicate, and that the question requires a new examination. It is a point which has often been made by Mr Russell that philosophers are very liable to be misled by the subject-predicate construction of our language. They have supposed that all propositions must be of the subject-predicate form, and so have been led to deny the existence of relations. I shall argue that nearly all philosophers, including Mr Russell himself, have been misled by language in a far more far-reaching way than that ; that the whole theory of particulars and universals is due to mistaking for a fundamental characteristic of reality what is merely a characteristic of language.

Let us, therefore, examine closely this distinction of subject and predicate, and for simplicity let us follow Mr Johnson and include relations among predicates and their terms among subjects. The first question we have to ask is this : what propositions are they that have a subject or subjects and a predicate ? Is this the case with all propositions or only with some ? Before, however, we go on to answer this question, let us remind ourselves that the task on which we are engaged is not merely one of English grammar ; we are not school children analysing sentences into subject, extension of the subject, complement and so on, but are interested not so much in sentences themselves, as in what they mean, from which we hope to discover the logical nature of reality. Hence we must look for senses of subject and predicate which are not purely grammatical, but have a genuine logical significance.

Let us begin with such a proposition as ' Either Socrates is wise or Plato is foolish '. To this, it will probably be agreed, the conception of subject and predicate is inapplicable ;

it may be applicable to the two parts ' Socrates is wise ', ' Plato is foolish ', but the whole ' Either Socrates is wise or Plato is foolish ' is an alternative proposition and not one with a subject or predicate. But to this someone may make the following objection : In such a proposition we can take any term we please, say Socrates, to be the subject. The predicate will then be ' being wise unless Plato is foolish ' or the propositional function ' $\hat{x}$ is wise or Plato is foolish '. The phrase ' being wise unless Plato is foolish ' will then stand for a complex universal which is asserted to characterize Socrates. Such a view, though very frequently held, seems to me nevertheless certainly mistaken. In order to make things clearer let us take a simpler case, a proposition of the form ' aRb ' ; then this theory will hold that there are three closely related propositions ; one asserts that the relation R holds between the terms a and b, the second asserts the possession by a of the complex property of ' having R to b ', while the third asserts that b has the complex property that a has R to it. These must be three different propositions because they have different sets of constituents, and yet they are not three propositions, but one proposition, for they all say the same thing, namely that a has R to b. So the theory of complex universals is responsible for an incomprehensible trinity, as senseless as that of theology. This argument can be strengthened by considering the process of definition, which is as follows. For certain purposes ' aRb ' may be an unnecessarily long symbol, so that it is convenient to shorten it into ' ϕb.' This is done by definition, $\phi x = aRx$, signifying that any symbol of the form ϕx is to be interpreted as meaning what is meant by the corresponding symbol aRx, for which it is an abbreviation. In more complicated cases such an abbreviation is often extremely useful, but it could always be dispensed with if time and paper permitted. The believer in complex universals is now confronted with a dilemma : is

'ϕ', thus defined, a name for the complex property of x which consists in a having R to x? If so, then ϕx will be the assertion that x has this property; it will be a subject-predicate proposition whose subject is x and predicate ϕ; and this is not identical with the relational proposition aRx. But as ϕx is by hypothesis defined to be short for aRx this is absurd. For if a definition is not to be interpreted as signifying that the definiendum and the definiens have the same meaning, the process of definition becomes unintelligible and we lose all justification for interchanging definiens and definiendum at will, on which depends its whole utility. Suppose on the other hand 'ϕ', as defined above, is not a name for the complex property; then how can the complex property ever become an object of our contemplation, and how can we ever speak of it, seeing that 'ϕ', its only possible name, is not a name for it at all but short for something else? And then what reason can there be to postulate the existence of this thing?

In spite of this *reductio ad absurdum* of the theory, it may still be worth while to inquire into its origin, and into why it is held by so many people, including formerly myself, without its occurring to them to doubt it. The chief reason for this is I think to be found in linguistic convenience; it gives us one object which is 'the meaning' of 'ϕ'. We often want to talk of 'the meaning of "ϕ"', and it is simpler to suppose that this is a unique object than to recognize that it is a much more complicated matter, and that 'ϕ' has a relation of meaning not to one complex object but to the several simple objects which are named in its definition. There is, however, another reason why this view is so popular, and that is the imaginary difficulty which would otherwise be felt in the use of a variable propositional function. How, it might be asked, are we to interpret such a statement as 'a has all the properties of b', except on the supposition that there are properties ? The answer is that it is to be interpreted as being the logical product of all propositions which can be constructed in the following way : take a proposition in which a occurs, say ϕa, change a into b and obtain ϕb, and then form the proposition $\phi b \,.\, \supset \,.\, \phi a$. It is not really quite so simple as that, but a more accurate account of it would involve a lot of tiresome detail, and so be out of place here ; and we can take it as a sufficient approximation that 'a has all the properties of b' is the joint assertion of all propositions of the form $\phi b \,.\, \supset \,.\, \phi a$, where there is no necessity for ϕ to be the name of a universal, as it is merely the rest of a proposition in which a occurs. Hence the difficulty is entirely imaginary. It may be observed that the same applies to any other case of apparent variables some of whose values are incomplete symbols, and this may explain the tendency to assert that some of Mr Russell's incomplete symbols are not really incomplete but the names of properties or predicates.

I conclude, therefore, that complex universals are to be rejected; and that such a proposition as 'Either Socrates is wise or Plato foolish' has neither subject nor predicate. Similar arguments apply to any compound proposition, that is any proposition containing such words as 'and', 'or', 'not', 'all', 'some' ; and hence if we are to find a logical distinction between subject and predicate anywhere it will be in atomic propositions, as Mr Russell calls them, which could be expressed by sentences containing none of the above words, but only names and perhaps a copula.

The distinction between subject and predicate will then arise from the several names in an atomic proposition functioning in different ways ; and if this is not to be a purely grammatical distinction it must correspond to a difference in the functioning of the several objects in an atomic fact, so that what we have primarily to examine is the construction of the atomic fact out of its constituents. About this three views might be suggested ; first there is that of Mr Johnson according to whom the constituents are connected together by what he calls the characterizing tie. The nature of this entity is rather obscure, but I think we can take it as something which is not a constituent of the fact but represented in language by the copula 'is', and we can describe this theory as holding that the connection is made by a real copula. Next there is the theory of Mr Russell that the connection is made by one of the constituents ; that in every atomic fact there must be one constituent which is in its own nature incomplete or connective and, as it were, holds the other constituents together. This constituent will be a universal, and the others particulars. Lastly there is Mr Wittgenstein's theory that neither is there a copula, nor one specially connected constitutent, but that, as he expresses it, the objects hang one in another like the links of a chain.

From our point of view it is the second of these theories that demands most attention ; for the first and third do not really explain any difference in the mode of functioning of subject and predicate, but leave this a mere dogma. Only on Mr Russell's theory will there be an intelligible difference between particular and universal, grounded on the necessity for there to be in each fact a copulating term or universal, corresponding to the need for every sentence to have a verb. So it is Mr Russell's theory that we must first consider.

The great difficulty with this theory lies in understanding how one sort of object can be specially incomplete. There is a sense in which any object is incomplete ; namely that it can only occur in a fact by connection with an object or objects of suitable type ; just as any name is incomplete, because to form a proposition we have to join to it certain other names of suitable type. As Wittgenstein says: "The thing is independent, in so far as it can occur in all *possible*

17

circumstances, but this form of independence is a form of connection with the atomic fact, a form of dependence. (It is impossible for words to occur in two different ways, alone and in the proposition)."[1]   And Johnson : " Ultimately a universal means an adjective that may characterize a particular, and a particular means a substantive that may be characterized by a universal."[2]   Thus we may admit that 'wise' involves the form of a proposition, but so does ' Socrates ', and it is hard to see any ground for distinguishing between them. This is the substance of Mr Johnson's criticism that Mr Russell will not let the adjective stand alone, and in treating ' s is p ' as a function of two variables takes the arguments to be not s and p, but s and ' $\hat{x}$ is p '.

In reply to this criticism Mr Russell would, I imagine, use two lines of argument, whose validity we must examine. The first would dwell on the great convenience in mathematical logic of his functional symbolism, of which he might say there was no explanation except that this symbolism corresponded to reality more closely than any other.   His second line of argument would be that everyone can feel a difference between particulars and universals ; that the prevalence of nominalism showed that the reality of universals was always suspected, and that this was probably because they did in fact differ from particulars by being less independent, less self-contained.   Also that this was the only account of the difference between particulars and universals which made them really different kinds of objects, as they evidently were, and not merely differently related to us or to our language.   For instance, Mr Johnson describes the particular as presented to thought for its character to be determined in thought, and others might say a particular was what was meant by the grammatical subject of a sentence ; and on these

[1] *Tractatus Logico-Philosophicus*, 2·0122.
[2] *Logic Part I*, p. 11.

views what was particular, what universal would depend on unessential characteristics of our psychology or our language.

Let us take these lines of argument in reverse order, beginning with the felt difference between particular and universal, and postponing the peculiar symbolic convenience of propositional functions. Anyone, it may be said, sees a difference between Socrates and wisdom. Socrates is a real independent entity, wisdom a quality and so essentially a quality of something else. The first thing to remark about this argument is that it is not really about objects at all. 'Socrates is wise' is not an atomic proposition, and the symbols 'Socrates' and 'wise' are not the names of objects but incomplete symbols. And according to Wittgenstein, with whom I agree, this will be the case with any other instance that may be suggested, since we are not acquainted with any genuine objects or atomic propositions, but merely infer them as presupposed by other propositions. Hence the distinction we feel is one between two sorts of incomplete symbols, or logical constructions, and we cannot infer without further investigation that there is any corresponding distinction between two sorts of names or objects.

We can, I think, easily obtain a clearer idea of the difference between these two sorts of incomplete symbols (Wittgenstein calls them 'expressions') typified by 'Socrates' and 'wise'. Let us consider when and why an expression occurs, as it were, as an isolated unit. For instance 'aRb' does not naturally divide into 'a' and 'Rb', and we want to know why anyone should so divide it and isolate the expression 'Rb'. The answer is that if it were a matter of this proposition alone, there would be no point in dividing it in this way, but that the importance of expressions arises, as Wittgenstein points out, just in connection with generalization. It is not 'aRb' but '$(x) . xRb$' which makes Rb prominent. In writing $(x) . xRb$ we use the expression Rb to collect

19

together the set of propositions xRb which we want to assert to be true ; and it is here that the expression Rb is really essential because it is this which is common to this set of propositions. If now we realize that this is the essential use of expressions, we can see at once what is the difference between Socrates and wise. By means of the expression ' Socrates ' we collect together all the propositions in which it occurs, that is, all the propositions which we should ordinarily say were about Socrates, such as ' Socrates is wise ', ' Socrates is just ', ' Socrates is neither wise nor just '. These propositions are collected together as the values of ' ϕ Socrates ', where ϕ is a variable.

Now consider the expression ' wise '; this we use to collect together the propositions ' Socrates is wise ', ' Plato is wise ', and so on, which are values of ' x is wise '. But this is not the only collection we can use ' wise ' to form ; just as we used ' Socrates ' to collect all the propositions in which it occurred, we can use ' wise ' to collect all those in which it occurs, including not only ones like ' Socrates is wise ' but also ones like ' Neither Socrates nor Plato is wise ', which are not values of ' x is wise ' but only of the different function ' ϕ wise ', where ϕ is variable. Thus whereas Socrates gives only one collection of propositions, wise gives two : one analogous to that given by Socrates, namely the collection of all propositions in which wise occurs ; and the other a narrower collection of propositions of the form ' x is wise '.

This is obviously the explanation of the difference we feel between Socrates and wise which Mr Russell expresses by saying that with wise you have to bring in the form of a proposition. Since all expressions must be completed to form a proposition, it was previously hard to understand how wise could be more incomplete than Socrates. Now we can see that the reason for this is that whereas with ' Socrates ' we only have the idea of completing it in any manner into a proposition, with ' wise ' we have not only this but also an idea of completing it in a special way, giving us not merely any proposition in which wise occurs but also one in which it occurs in a particular way, which we may call its occurrence as predicate, as in ' Socrates is wise '.

What is this difference due to, and is it a real difference at all ? That is to say, can we not do with ' Socrates ' what we do with 'wise', and use it to collect a set of propositions narrower than the whole set in which it occurs ? Is this impossible, or is it merely that we never in fact do it ? These are the questions we must now try to answer. The way to do it would seem to be the following. Suppose we can distinguish among the properties of Socrates a certain subset which we can call qualities, the idea being roughly that only a simple property is a quality. Then we could form in connection with ' Socrates ' two sets of propositions just as we can in connection with ' wise '. There would be the wide set of propositions in which ' Socrates ' occurs at all, which we say assert properties of Socrates, but also there would be the narrower set which assert qualities of Socrates. Thus supposing justice and wisdom to be qualities, ' Socrates is wise ', ' Socrates is just ' would belong to the narrower set and be values of a function ' Socrates is q '. But ' Socrates is neither wise nor just ' would not assert a quality of Socrates but only a compound characteristic or property, and would only be a value of the function ' ϕ Socrates ', not of ' Socrates is q '.

But although such a distinction between qualities and properties may be logically possible, we do not seem ever to carry it out systematically. Some light may be thrown on this fact by a paragraph in Mr Johnson's *Logic* in which he argues that, whereas "we may properly construct a compound adjective out of simple adjectives, yet the nature of any term functioning as a substantive is such that it is impossible to construct a genuine compound substantive ".[1] Thus from the two propositions ' Socrates is wise ', ' Socrates is just ' we can form the proposition ' Neither is Socrates wise nor is Socrates just ', or, for short, ' Socrates is neither wise nor just ' ; which still, according to Mr Johnson, predicates an adjective of Socrates, is a value of ' ϕ Socrates ' and would justify ' $(\exists \phi)$. ϕ Socrates ', or ' Socrates has some property '. If, on the other hand, we take the two propositions ' Socrates is wise ', ' Plato is wise ' and form from them ' Neither Socrates is wise nor Plato is wise ' ; this is not a value of ' x is wise ' and would not justify ' $(\exists x)$. x is wise ', or ' Someone is wise '. So inasmuch as ' Socrates is neither wise nor just ' justifies ' Socrates has some adjective ' we can say that ' neither wise nor just ' is a compound adjective ; but since ' Neither Socrates nor Plato is wise ' does not justify ' something is wise ', ' neither Socrates nor Plato ' cannot be a compound substantive any more than nobody is a compound man.

If, however, we could form a range of qualities as opposed to properties, ' Socrates is neither wise nor just ' would not justify ' Socrates has some quality ' and ' neither wise nor just ' would not be a quality. Against this Mr Johnson says that there is no universally valid criterion by which we can distinguish qualities from other properties ; and this is certainly a very plausible contention when we are talking, as we are now, of qualities and properties of logical constructions such as Socrates. For the distinction is only really clear in connection with genuine objects ; then we can say that ϕ represents a quality when ϕa is a two-termed atomic proposition, and this would distinguish qualities from other propositional functions or properties. But when the subject a is a logical construction and ϕa a compound proposition of

[1] *Part II*, p. 61.

which we do not know the analysis, it is hard to know what would be meant by asking if ϕ were simple, and calling it, if simple, a quality. It would clearly have to be a matter not of absolute but of relative simplicity.

Yet it is easy to see that, in theory, an analogous distinction can certainly be made for incomplete symbols also. Take any incomplete symbol 'a'; this will be defined not in isolation but in conjunction with any symbol of a certain sort x. Thus we might define ax to mean aRx. Then this incomplete symbol 'a' will give us two ranges of propositions: the range ax obtained by completing it in the way indicated in its definition ; and the general range of propositions in which a occurs at all, that is to say, all truth-functions of the propositions of the preceding range and constant propositions not containing a. Thus in the two famous cases of descriptions and classes, as treated in *Principia Mathematica*, the narrower range will be that in which the description or class has primary occurrence, the wider range that in which it has any sort of occurrence primary or secondary, where the terms ' primary ' and ' secondary ' occurrence have the meanings explained in *Principia*. In brief with regard to any incomplete symbol we can distinguish its primary and secondary occurrences, and this is fundamentally the same distinction which we found to be characteristic of the adjective. So that any incomplete symbol is really an adjective, and those which appear substantives only do so in virtue of our failing whether through inability or neglect to distinguish their primary and secondary occurrences. As a practical instance let us take the case of material objects ; these we are accustomed to regard as substantives, that is to say we use them to define ranges of propositions in one way only, and make no distinction between their primary and secondary occurrences. At least no one made such a distinction until Dr Whitehead declared that material objects are adjectives of the events in which they are situated, so that the primary occurrence of a material object A is in a proposition ' A is situated in E '. From such propositions as this we can construct all other propositions in which A occurs. Thus ' A is red ' will be ' For all E, A is situated in E implies redness is situated in E ', in which A has secondary occurrence. So the distinction between primary and secondary occurrence is not merely demonstrated as logically necessary, but for this case effected practically.

The conclusion is that, as regards incomplete symbols, the fundamental distinction is not between substantive and adjective but between primary and secondary occurrence ; and that a substantive is simply a logical construction between, whose primary and secondary occurrences we fail to distinguish. So that to be a substantive is not an objective but a subjective property in the sense that it depends not indeed on any one mind but on the common elements in all men's minds and purposes.

This is my first conclusion, which is I think of some importance in the philosophy of nature and of mind; but it is not the conclusion which I most want to stress, and it does not answer the question with which I began my paper. For it is a conclusion about the method and possibility of dividing certain logical constructions into substantives and adjectives, it being in connection with these logical constructions that the idea of substantive and adjective traditionally originated. But the real question at issue is the possibility of dividing not logical constructions but genuine objects into particulars and universals, and to answer this we must go back and pick up the thread of the argument, where we abandoned it for this lengthy digression about logical constructions.

We saw above that the distinction between particular and universal was derived from that between subject and predicate which we found only to occur in atomic propositions. We

then examined the three theories of atomic propositions
or rather of atomic facts, Mr Johnson's theory of a tie,
Mr Russell's that the copulation is performed by universals,
of which there must be one and only one in each atomic fact,
and Mr Wittgenstein's that the objects hang in one another
like the links of a chain. We observed that of these theories
only Mr Russell's really assigned a different function to
subject and predicate and so gave meaning to the distinction
between them, and we proceeded to discuss this theory. We
found that to Mr Johnson's criticisms Mr Russell had two
possible answers ; one being to argue that his theory alone
took account of the difference we feel there to be between
Socrates and wisdom, the other that his notation was far
more convenient than any other and must therefore correspond more closely to the facts. We then took the first of
these arguments, and examined the difference between
Socrates and wisdom. This we found to consist in the fact
that whereas Socrates determined only one range of propositions in which it occurred, wise determined two such ranges,
the complete range ' f wise ', and the narrower range ' x is
wise '. We then examined the reason for this difference
between the two incomplete symbols Socrates and wise, and
decided that it was of a subjective character and depended
on human interests and needs.

What we have now to consider is whether the difference
between Socrates and wise has any such bearing on the
composition of atomic facts as Mr Russell alleges it to
have. This we can usefully combine with the consideration
of Mr Russell's other possible argument from the superior
convenience of his symbolism. The essence of this symbolism,
as Mr Johnson has observed, consists in not letting the
adjective stand alone, but making it a propositional function
by attaching it to a variable x. A possible advantage of this
procedure at once suggests itself in terms of our previous

treatment of the difference between substantive and adjective ; namely, that attaching the variable x helps us to make the distinction we require to make in the case of the adjective, but not in the case of the substantive, between the values of ϕx and those of f $(\phi \hat{z})$ where f is variable. Only so, it might be said, can we distinguish (x) . ϕx from (f) . $f(\phi \hat{z})$. But very little consideration is required to see that this advantage is very slight and of no fundamental importance. We could easily make the distinction in other ways ; for instance by determining that if the variable came after the ϕ it should mean what we now express by ϕx, but if before the ϕ what we express by $f(\phi \hat{z})$; or simply by deciding to use the letters ' x ', ' y ', ' z ', in one case, ' f ', ' g ', ' h ', in the other.

But, although this supposed advantage in the functional symbolism is imaginary, there is a reason which renders it absolutely indispensable. Take such a property as ' either having R to a, or having S to b '; it would be absolutely impossible to represent this by a simple symbol ' ϕ '. For how then could we define ϕ ? We could not put $\phi = Ra$. $\vee$. Sb because we should not know whether the blanks were to be filled with the same or different arguments, and so whether ϕ was to be a property or relation. Instead we must put ϕx . $= .$ xRa . $\vee$. xSb ; which explains not what is meant by ϕ by itself but that followed by any symbol x it is short for xRa . $\vee$. xSb. And this is the reason which makes inevitable the introduction of propositional functions. It simply means that in such a case ' ϕ ' is not a name but an incomplete symbol and cannot be defined in isolation or allowed to stand by itself.

But this conclusion about xRa . $\vee$. xSb will not apply to all propositional functions. If ϕa is a two-termed atomic proposition, ' ϕ ' is a name of the term other than a, and can perfectly well stand by itself ; so, it will be asked, why do we write ' ϕx ' instead of ' ϕ ' in this case also ? The reason for this lies in a fundamental characteristic of mathematical logic, its extensionality, by which I mean its primary interest in classes and relations in extension. Now if in any proposition whatever we change any individual name into a variable, the resulting propositional function defines a class ; and the class may be the same for two functions of quite different forms, in one of which ' ϕ ' is an incomplete symbol, in the other a name. So mathematical logic, being only interested in functions as a means to classes, sees no need to distinguish these two sorts of functions, because the difference between them, though all-important to philosophy, will not correspond to any difference between the classes they define. So because some ϕ's are incomplete and cannot stand alone, and all ϕ's are to be treated alike in order to avoid useless complication, the only solution is to allow none to stand alone.

Such is the justification of Mr Russell's practice ; but it is also the refutation of his theory, which fails to appreciate the distinction between those functions which are names and those which are incomplete symbols, a distinction which, as remarked above, though immaterial for mathematics is essential for philosophy. I do not mean that Mr Russell would now deny this distinction ; on the contrary it is clear from the Second Edition of *Principia* that he would accept it; but I think that his present theory of universals is the relic of his previous failure to appreciate it.

It will be remembered that we found two possible arguments for his theory of universals. One was from the efficiency of the functional notation ; this clearly lapses because, as we have seen, the functional notation merely overlooks an essential distinction which happens not to interest the mathematician, and the fact that some functions cannot stand alone is no argument that all cannot. The other argument was from the difference we feel between Socrates and wise, which corresponds to a difference in his logical system between individuals and functions. Just as Socrates determines one range of propositions, but wise two, so a determines the one range ϕa, but $\phi \hat{z}$ the two ranges ϕx and $f(\phi \hat{z})$. But what is this difference between individuals and functions due to? Again simply to the fact that certain things do not interest the mathematician. Anyone who was interested not only in classes of things, but also in their qualities, would want to distinguish from among the others those functions which were names; and if we called the objects of which they are names qualities, and denoted a variable quality by q, we should have not only the range ϕa but also the narrower range qa, and the difference analogous to that between ' Socrates ' and ' wisdom ' would have disappeared. We should have complete symmetry between qualities and individuals ; each could have names which could stand alone, each would determine two ranges of propositions, for a would determine the ranges qa and ϕa, where q and ϕ are variables, and q would determine the ranges qx and fq, where x and f are variables.

So were it not for the mathematician's biassed interest he would invent a symbolism which was completely symmetrical as regards individuals and qualities ; and it becomes clear that there is no sense in the words individual and quality ; all we are talking about is two different types of objects, such that two objects, one of each type, could be sole constituents of an atomic fact. The two types being in every way symmetrically related, nothing can be meant by calling one type the type of individuals and the other that of qualities, and these two words are devoid of connotation.

To this, however, various objections might be made which must be briefly dealt with. First it might be said that the two terms of such an atomic fact must be connected by the characterizing tie and/or the relation of characterization, which are asymmetrical, and distinguish their relata into individuals and qualities. Against this I would say that the relation of characterization is simply a verbal fiction. ' q characterizes a ' means no more and no less than ' a is q ', it is merely a lengthened verbal form ; and since the relation of characterization is admittedly not a constituent of ' a is q ' it cannot be anything at all. As regards the tie, I cannot understand what sort of a thing it could be, and prefer Wittgenstein's view that in the atomic fact the objects are connected together without the help of any mediator. This does not mean that the fact is simply the collection of its constituents but that it consists in their union without any mediating tie. There is one more objection suggested by Mr Russell's treatment in the new edition of *Principia*. He there says that all atomic propositions are of the forms $R_1(x)$, $R_2(x, y)$, $R_3(x, y, z)$, etc., and so can *define* individuals as terms which can occur in propositions with any number of terms ; whereas of course an n-termed relation could only occur in a proposition with $n + 1$ terms. But this assumes his theory as to the constitution of atomic facts, that each must contain a term of a special kind, called a universal ; a theory we found to be utterly groundless. The truth is that we know and can know nothing whatever about the forms of atomic propositions ; we do not know whether some or all objects can occur in more than one form of atomic proposition ; and there is obviously no way of deciding any such question. We cannot even tell that there are not atomic facts consisting of two terms of the same type. It might be thought that this would involve us in a vicious circle contradiction, but a little reflection will show that it does not, for the contradictions due to letting a function be its own argument only arise when we take for argument a function containing a negation which is therefore an incomplete symbol not the name of an object.

In conclusion let us describe from this new point of view the procedure of the mathematical logician. He takes any type of objects whatever as the subject of his reasoning, and calls them individuals, meaning by that simply that he has chosen this type to reason about, though he might equally well have chosen any other type and called them individuals. The results of replacing names of these individuals in propositions by variables he then calls functions, irrespective of whether the constant part of the function is a name or an incomplete symbol, because this does not make any difference to the class which the function defines. The failure to make this distinction has led to these functional symbols, some of which are names and some incomplete, being treated all alike as names of incomplete objects or properties, and is responsible for that great muddle the theory of universals. Of all philosophers Wittgenstein alone has seen through this muddle and declared that about the forms of atomic propositions we can know nothing whatever.

2

NOTE ON THE PRECEDING PAPER (1926)

. . . When I wrote my article I was sure that it was impossible to discover atomic propositions by actual analysis. Of this I am now very doubtful, and I cannot therefore be sure that they may not be discovered to be all of one or other of a series of forms which can be expressed by $R_1(x)$, $R_2(x, y)$, $R_3(x, y, z)$, etc., in which case we could, as Mr Russell has suggested, define individuals as terms which can occur in propositions of any of these forms, universals as terms which can only occur in one form. This I admit may be found to be the case, but as no one can as yet be certain what sort of atomic propositions there are, it cannot be positively asserted; and there is no strong presumption in its favour, for I think that the argument of my article establishes that nothing of the sort can be known *a priori*.

And this is a matter of some importance, for philosophers such as Mr Russell have thought that, although they did not know into what ultimate terms propositions are analysable, these terms must nevertheless be divisible into universals and particulars, categories which are used in philosophical investigations as if it were certain *a priori* that they would be applicable. This certainly seems to be derived primarily from the supposition that there must be a difference between ultimate objects analogous to one felt to subsist between such terms as Socrates and wise; and to see if this can reasonably be maintained, we must discover what difference there is between Socrates and wise analogous to the distinction made in Mr Russell's system between particulars and universals.

If we consider the development of Mr Russell's system of logic, as expounded in the Introduction to the Second Edition of *Principia Mathematica*, we can see what difference there is in his treatment of particulars and universals. We find that universals always occur as propositional functions, which serve to determine ranges of propositions, especially the range of values of the function ϕx, and the range of functions of the function $f(\phi \hat{x})$ (where f is variable). Individuals also serve to determine ranges of propositions, but in this case there is only one principal range, the range of functions of the individual ϕa (ϕ variable). We could make a narrower range, as Mr Russell points out, by using a variable quality, but we have no need to do so. Now this is the only difference between the way individuals and universals function in his system, and as we find that there is a precisely similar difference between Socrates and wise, it is probable that we have here the essence of the matter. Wise, like a ϕx in Mr Russell's system, determines the narrower range of propositions ' x is wise' and the wider one 'f wise', where the last range includes all propositions whatever in which wise occurs. Socrates, on the other hand, is only used to determine the wider range of propositions in which it occurs in any manner ; we have no precise way of singling out any narrower range. We cannot do it by limiting it to propositions in which Socrates occurs as subject, because in any proposition in which he occurs he can be regarded as the subject : we can always regard the proposition as saying ' It is true of Socrates that — '. The point is that with Socrates the narrower range is missing. . . .

Nevertheless this difference between Socrates and wise is illusory, because it can be shown to be theoretically possible to make a similar narrower range for Socrates, though we have never needed to do this. Nevertheless, once this fact is observed, the difference between Socrates and wise lapses, and we begin, like Dr Whitehead, to call Socrates an adjective. If you think all or nearly all propositions about material objects are truth-functions of propositions about their location in events, then, on my view, you will regard material objects as adjectives of events. For that is the real meaning of the distinction between adjective and substantive. I do not say that the distinction has arisen from explicit reflection about the difference in regard to ranges of propositions, but that this difference obscurely felt is the source of the distinction. My view is strikingly confirmed by the case of Dr Whitehead, who, having made material objects analogous to wise in the way in question, then declared that they were adjectives.

3

FACTS AND PROPOSITIONS (1927)

The problem with which I propose to deal is the logical
analysis of what may be called by any of the terms judgment,
belief, or assertion. Suppose I am at this moment judging
that Cæsar was murdered : then it is natural to distinguish
in this fact on the one side either my mind, or my present
mental state, or words or images in my mind, which we will
call the mental factor or factors, and on the other side either
Cæsar, or Cæsar's murder, or Cæsar and murder, or the
proposition Cæsar was murdered, or the fact that Cæsar was
murdered, which we will call the objective factor or factors ;
and to suppose that the fact that I am judging that Cæsar
was murdered consists in the holding of some relation or
relations between these mental and objective factors. The
questions that arise are in regard to the nature of the two
sets of factors and of the relations between them, the
fundamental distinction between these elements being hardly
open to question.

Let us begin with the objective factor or factors ; the
simplest view is that there is one such factor only, a
proposition, which may be either true or false, truth and falsity
being unanalysable attributes. This was at one time the view
of Mr Russell, and in his essay " On the Nature of Truth and
Falsehood "[1] he explains the reasons which led him to
abandon it. These were, in brief, the incredibility of the
existence of such objects as ' that Cæsar died in his bed ',
which could be described as objective falsehoods, and the
mysterious nature of the difference, on this theory, between
truth and falsehood. He therefore concluded, in my opinion

[1] In *Philosophical Essays*, 1910.

rightly, that a judgment has no single object, but is a multiple relation of the mind or mental factors to many objects, those, namely, which we should ordinarily call constituents of the proposition judged.

There is, however, an alternative way of holding that a judgment has a single object, which it would be well to consider before we pass on. In the above-mentioned essay Mr Russell asserts that a perception, which unlike a judgment he regards as infallible, has a single object, for instance, the complex object ' knife-to-left-of-book '. This complex object can, I think, be identified with what many people (and Mr Russell now) would call the *fact* that the knife is to the left of the book ; we could, for instance, say that we perceived this fact. And just as if we take any true proposition such as that Cæsar did not die in his bed, we can form a corresponding phrase beginning with ' the fact that ' and talk about the fact that he did not die in his bed, so Mr Russell supposed that to any true proposition there corresponded a complex object.

Mr Russell, then, held that the object of a perception was a fact, but that in the case of a judgment the possibility of error made such a view untenable, since the object of a judgment that Cæsar died in his bed could not be the fact that he died in his bed, as there was no such fact. It is, however, evident that this difficulty about error could be removed by postulating for the case of judgment two different relations between the mental factors and the fact, one occurring in true judgments, the other in false. Thus, a judgment that Cæsar was murdered and a judgment that Cæsar was not murdered would have the same object, the fact that Cæsar was murdered, but differ in respect of the relations between the mental factor and this object. Thus, in *The Analysis of Mind* [1] Mr Russell speaks of beliefs as either pointing

---

[1] p. 272. It should be observed that in *The Analysis of Mind* a ' belief ' is what we call a mental factor, not the whole complex of mental factors and relations and objective factors.

towards or pointing away from facts. It seems to me, however, that any such view either of judgment or of perception would be inadequate for a reason which, if valid, is of great importance. Let us for simplicity take the case of perception and, assuming for the sake of argument that it is infallible, consider whether 'He perceives that the knife is to the left of the book' can really assert a dual relation between a person and a fact. Suppose that I who make the assertion cannot myself see the knife and book, that the knife is really to the right of the book, but that through some mistake I suppose that it is on the left and that he perceives it to be on the left, so that I assert falsely 'He perceives that the knife is to the left of the book'. Then my statement, though false, is significant, and has the same meaning as it would have if it were true ; this meaning cannot therefore be that there is a dual relation between the person and something (a fact) of which 'that the knife is to the left of the book' is the name, because there is no such thing. The situation is the same as that with descriptions ; 'The King of France is wise' is not nonsense, and so 'the King of France', as Mr Russell has shown, is not a name but an incomplete symbol, and the same must be true of 'the King of Italy'. So also 'that the knife is to the left of the book', whether it is true or false, cannot be the name of a fact.

But, it will be asked, why should it not be a description of a fact ? If I say 'He perceives that the knife is to the left of the book', I mean that he perceives a fact which is not named but described as of a certain sort, and the difficulty will disappear when my assertion is analysed according to Mr Russell's theory of descriptions. Similarly, it will be said, 'the death of Cæsar' is a description of an event, and 'the fact that Cæsar died' is only an alternative expression for 'the death of Cæsar'.

Such an objection is plausible but not, in my opinion, valid.

The truth is that a phrase like ' the death of Cæsar ' can be used in two different ways ; ordinarily, we use it as the description of an event, and we could say that ' the death of Cæsar ' and ' the murder of Cæsar ' were two different descriptions of the same event. But we can also use ' the death of Cæsar ' in a context like ' He was aware of the death of Cæsar ' meaning ' He was aware that Cæsar had died ' : here (and this is the sort of case which occurs in the discussion of cognition) we cannot regard ' the death of Cæsar ' as the description of an event ; if it were, the whole proposition would be ' There is an event E of a certain sort such that he is aware of E ', and would be still true if we substituted another description of the same event, e.g. ' the murder of Cæsar '. That is, if his awareness has for its object an event described by ' the death of Cæsar ', then, if he is aware of the death of Cæsar, he must also be aware of the murder of Cæsar, for they are identical. But, in fact, he could quite well be aware that Cæsar had died without knowing that he had been murdered, so that his awareness must have for its object not merely an event but an event and a character also.

The connection between the event which was the death of Cæsar and the fact that Cæsar died is, in my opinion, this : ' That Cæsar died ' is really an existential proposition, asserting the existence of an event of a certain sort, thus resembling ' Italy has a King ', which asserts the existence of a man of a certain sort. The event which is of that sort is called the death of Cæsar, and should no more be confused with the fact that Cæsar died than the King of Italy should be confused with the fact that Italy has a King.

We have seen, then, that a phrase beginning ' the fact that ' is not a name, and also not a description ; it is, therefore, neither a name nor a description of any genuine constituent of a proposition, and so a proposition about ' the fact that aRb ' must be analysed into (1) the proposition aRb, (2) some further proposition about *a*, *R*, *b*, and other things ; and an analysis of cognition in terms of relations to facts cannot be accepted as ultimate. We are driven, therefore, to Mr Russell's conclusion that a judgment [1] has not one object but many, to which the mental factor is multiply related ; but to leave it at that, as he did, cannot be regarded as satisfactory. There is no reason to suppose the multiple relation simple ; it may, for instance, result from the combination of dual relations between parts of the mental factor and the separate objects ; and it is desirable that we should try to find out more about it, and how it varies when the form of proposition believed is varied. Similarly, a theory of descriptions which contented itself with observing that ' The King of France is wise ' could be regarded as asserting a possibly complex multiple relation between kingship, France, and wisdom, would be miserably inferior to Mr Russell's theory, which explains exactly what relation it is.

But before we proceed further with the analysis of judgment, it is necessary to say something about truth and falsehood, in order to show that there is really no separate problem of truth but merely a linguistic muddle. Truth and falsity are ascribed primarily to propositions. The proposition to which they are ascribed may be either explicitly given or described. Suppose first that it is explicitly given ; then it is evident that ' It is true that Cæsar was murdered ' means no more than that Cæsar was murdered, and ' It is false that Cæsar was murdered ' means that Cæsar was not murdered. They are phrases which we sometimes use for emphasis or for stylistic reasons, or to indicate the position occupied by the statement in our argument. So also we can say ' It is a fact that he was murdered ' or ' That he was murdered is contrary to fact '.

In the second case in which the proposition is described and

[1] And, in our view, any other form of knowledge or opinion *that* something is the case.

not given explicitly we have perhaps more of a problem, for we get statements from which we cannot in ordinary language eliminate the words ' true ' and ' false '. Thus if I say ' He is always right ', I mean that the propositions he asserts are always true, and there does not seem to be any way of expressing this without using the word ' true '. But suppose we put it thus ' For all p, if he asserts p, p is true ', then we see that the propositional function p is true is simply the same as p, as e.g. its value ' Cæsar was murdered is true ' is the same as ' Cæsar was murdered '. We have in English to add ' is true ' to give the sentence a verb, forgetting that ' p ' already contains a (variable) verb. This may perhaps be made clearer by supposing for a moment that only one form of proposition is in question, say the relational form aRb ; then ' He is always right ' could be expressed by ' For all a, R, b, if he asserts aRb, then aRb ', to which ' is true ' would be an obviously superfluous addition. When all forms of proposition are included the analysis is more complicated but not essentially different ; and it is clear that the problem is not as to the nature of truth and falsehood, but as to the nature of judgment or assertion, for what is difficult to analyse in the above formulation is ' He asserts aRb '.

It is, perhaps, also immediately obvious that if we have analysed judgment we have solved the problem of truth ; for taking the mental factor in a judgment (which is often itself called a judgment), the truth or falsity of this depends only on what proposition it is that is judged, and what we have to explain is the meaning of saying that the judgment is a judgment that a has R to b, i.e. is true if aRb, false if not. We can, if we like, say that it is true if there exists a corresponding fact that a has R to b, but this is essentially not an analysis but a periphrasis, for ' The fact that a has R to b exists ' is no different from ' a has R to b '.

In order to proceed further, we must now consider the

39

mental factors in a belief. Their nature will depend on the sense in which we are using the ambiguous term belief : it is, for instance, possible to say that a chicken believes a certain sort of caterpillar to be poisonous, and mean by that merely that it abstains from eating such caterpillars on account of unpleasant experiences connected with them. The mental factors in such a belief would be parts of the chicken's behaviour, which are somehow related to the objective factors, viz. the kind of caterpillar and poisonousness. An exact analysis of this relation would be very difficult, but it might well be held that in regard to this kind of belief the pragmatist view was correct, i.e. that the relation between the chicken's behaviour and the objective factors was that the actions were such as to be useful if, and only if, the caterpillars were actually poisonous. Thus any set of actions for whose utility p is a necessary and sufficient condition might be called a belief that p, and so would be true if p, i.e. if they are useful.[1]

But without wishing to depreciate the importance of this kind of belief, it is not what I wish to discuss here. I prefer to deal with those beliefs which are expressed in words, or possibly images or other symbols, consciously asserted or denied ; for these beliefs, in my view, are the most proper subject for logical criciticm.

The mental factors of such a belief I take to be words, spoken aloud or to oneself or merely imagined, connected together and accompanied by a feeling or feelings of belief or disbelief, related to them in a way I do not propose to discuss.[2] I shall suppose for simplicity that the thinker with

[1] It is useful to believe aRb would mean that it is useful to do things which are useful if, and only if, aRb ; which is evidently equivalent to aRb.

[2] I speak throughout as if the differences between belief, disbelief, and mere consideration lay in the presence or absence of ' feelings ' ; but any other word may be substituted for ' feeling ' which the reader prefers, e.g. ' specific quality ' or ' act of assertion ' and ' act of denial '.

whom we are concerned uses a systematic language without irregularities and with an exact logical notation like that of *Principia Mathematica*. The primitive signs in such a language can be divided into names, logical constants, and variables. Let us begin with names; each name means an object, meaning being a dual relation between them. Evidently name, meaning, relation, and object may be really all complex, so that the fact that the name means the object is not ultimately of the dual relational form but far more complicated.[1] Nevertheless, just as in the study of chess nothing is gained by discussing the atoms of which the chessmen are composed, so in the study of logic nothing is gained by entering into the ultimate analysis of names and the objects they signify. These form the elements of the thinker's beliefs in terms of which the various logical relations of one belief to another can all be stated, and their internal constitution is immaterial.

By means of names alone the thinker can form what we may call atomic sentences, which from our formal standpoint offer no very serious problem. If *a*, *R*, and *b* are things which are simple in relation to his language, i.e. of the types of instances of which he has names, he will believe that *aRb* by having names for *a*, *R*, and *b* connected in his mind and accompanied by a feeling of belief. This statement is, however, too simple, since the names must be united in a way appropriate to *aRb* rather than to *bRa*; this can be explained by saying that the name of *R* is not the word ' *R* ', but the relation we make between ' *a* ' and ' *b* ' by writing ' *aRb* '. The sense in which this relation unites ' *a* ' and ' *b* ' then determines whether it is a belief that *aRb* or that *bRa*. There are various other difficulties of the same sort, but I propose to pass on to the more interesting problems which arise when we consider

---

[1] This is most obvious in the case of names, which generally consist of letters, so that their complexity is evident.

more complicated beliefs which require for their expression not only names but logical constants as well, so that we have to explain the mode of significance of such words as ' not ' and ' or '.

One possible explanation [1] is that they, or some of them, e.g. ' not ' and ' and ' in terms of which the others can be defined, are the names of relations, so that the sentences in which they occur are similar to atomic ones except that the relations they assert are logical instead of material. On this view every proposition is ultimately affirmative, asserting a simple relation between simple terms, or a simple quality of a simple term. Thus, ' This is not-red ' asserts a relation of negation between this and redness, and ' This is not not-red ' another relation of negation between this, redness and the first relation of negation.

This view requires such a different attitude to logic from mine that it is difficult for me to find a common basis from which to discuss it. There are, however, one or two things I should like to say in criticism: first, that I find it very unsatisfactory to be left with no explanation of formal logic except that it is a collection of ' necessary facts '. The conclusion of a formal inference must, I feel, be in some sense contained in the premisses and not something new ; I cannot believe that from one fact, e.g. that a thing is red, it should be possible to infer an infinite number of different facts, such as that it is not not-red, and that it is both red and not not-red. These, I should say, are simply the same fact expressed by other words ; nor is it inevitable that there should be all these different ways of saying the same thing. We might, for instance, express negation not by inserting a word ' not ', but by writing what we negate upside down. Such a symbolism is only inconvenient because we are not trained to perceive complicated symmetry about a horizontal axis, but if we

[1] See, especially, J. A. Chadwick, " Logical Constants," *Mind*, 1927.

adopted it we should be rid of the redundant ' not-not ', for the result of negating the sentence ' p ' twice would be simply the sentence ' p ' itself.

It seems to me, therefore, that ' not ' cannot be a name (for if it were, ' not-not-p ' would have to be about the object not and so different in meaning from ' p '), but must function in a radically different fashion. It follows that we must allow negations and disjunctions to be ultimately different from positive assertions and not merely the assertions of different but equally positive relationships. We must, therefore, abandon the idea that every proposition asserts a relation between terms, an idea that seems as difficult to discard as the older one that a proposition always asserts a predicate of a subject.

Suppose our thinker is considering a single atomic sentence, and that the progress of his meditation leads either to his believing it or his disbelieving it. These may be supposed to consist originally in two different feelings related to the atomic sentence, and in such a relation mutually exclusive ; the difference between assertion and denial thus consisting in a difference of feeling and not in the absence or presence of a word like ' not '. Such a word will, however, be almost indispensable for purposes of communication, belief in the atomic sentence being communicated by uttering it aloud, disbelief by uttering it together with the word ' not '. By a sort of association this word will become part of the internal language of our thinker, and instead of feeling disbelief towards ' p ' he will sometimes feel belief towards ' not-p '.

If this happens we can say that disbelieving ' p ' and believing ' not-p ' are equivalent occurrences, but to determine what we mean by this ' equivalent ' is, to my mind, the central difficulty of the subject. The difficulty exists on any theory, but is particularly important on mine, which holds that the significance of ' not ' consists not in a meaning relation to an object, but in this equivalence between disbelieving 'p' and believing 'not-p'.

It seems to me that the equivalence between believing 'not-p' and disbelieving 'p' is to be defined in terms of causation, the two occurrences having in common many of their causes and many of their effects. There would be many occasions on which we should expect one or other to occur, but not know which, and whichever occurred we should expect the same kind of behaviour in consequence. To be equivalent, we may say, is to have in common certain causal properties, which I wish I could define more precisely. Clearly they are not at all simple ; there is no uniform action which believing 'p' will always produce. It may lead to no action at all, except in particular circumstances, so that its causal properties will only express what effects result from it when certain other conditions are fulfilled. And, again, only certain sorts of causes and effects must be admitted ; for instance, we are not concerned with the factors determining, and the results determined by, the rhythm of the words.

Feeling belief towards the words 'not-p' and feeling disbelief towards the words 'p' have then in common certain causal properties. I propose to express this fact by saying that the two occurrences express the same attitude, the attitude of disbelieving p or believing not-p. On the other hand, feeling belief towards 'p' has different causal properties, and so expresses a different attitude, the attitude of believing p. It is evident that the importance of beliefs and disbeliefs lies not in their intrinsic nature, but in their causal properties, i.e. their causes and more especially their effects. For why should I want to have a feeling of belief towards names 'a', 'R', and 'b', when aRb, and of disbelief when not-aRb, except because the effects of these feelings are more often satisfactory than those of the alternative ones.

If then I say about someone whose language I do not

know ' He is believing that not-aRb ', I mean that there is occurring in his mind such a combination of a feeling and words as expresses the attitude of believing not-aRb, i.e. has certain causal properties, which can *in this simple case*,[1] be specified as those belonging to the combination of a feeling of disbelief and names for a, R, and b, or, in the case of one who uses the English language, to the combination of a feeling of belief, names for a, R, and b, and an odd number of ' not ' 's. Besides this, we can say that the causal properties are connected with a, R, and b in such a way that the only things which can have them must be composed of names of a, R, and b. (This is the doctrine that the meaning of a sentence must result from the meaning of the words in it.)

When we are dealing with one atomic proposition only, we are accustomed to leave to the theory of probability the intermediate attitudes of partial belief, and consider only the extremes of full belief and full disbelief. But when our thinker is concerned with several atomic propositions at once, the matter is more complicated, for we have to deal not only with completely definite attitudes, such as believing p and disbelieving q, but also with relatively indefinite attitudes, such as believing that either p or q is true but not knowing which. Any such attitude can, however, be defined in terms of the truth-possibilities of atomic propositions with which it agrees and disagrees. Thus, if we have n atomic propositions, with regard to their truth and falsity there are 2^n mutually exclusive possibilities, and a possible attitude is given by taking any set of these and saying that it is one of this set which is, in fact, realized, not one of the remainder. Thus, to believe p or q is to express agreement with the possibilities p true and q true, p false and q true, p true and q false, and

---

[1] In the more complicated cases treated below a similar specification seems to me impossible except by reference to a particular language. There are ways in which it can apparently be done, but I think they are illusory.

45

disagreement with the remaining possibility p false and q false. To say that feeling belief towards a sentence expresses such an attitude is to say that it has certain causal properties which vary with the attitude, i.e. with which possibilities are knocked out and which, so to speak, are still left in. Very roughly the thinker will act in disregard of the possibilities rejected, but how to explain this accurately I do not know.

In any ordinary language such an attitude can be expressed by a feeling of belief towards a complicated sentence formed out of the atomic sentences by logical conjunctions; which attitude it is, depending not on the feeling but on the form of the sentence. We can therefore say elliptically that the sentence expresses the attitude, and that the meaning of a sentence is agreement and disagreement with such and such truth-possibilities, meaning by that that one who asserts or believes the sentence so agrees and disagrees.

In most logical notations the meaning of the sentence is determined by logical operation signs that occur in it, such as ' not ' and ' and '. These mean in the following way : ' not-p ', whether ' p ' be atomic or not, expresses agreement with the possibilities with which ' p ' expresses disagreement and vice versa. ' p and q ' expresses agreement with such possibilities as both ' p ' and ' q ' express agreement with, and disagreement with all others. By these rules the meaning of any sentence constructed from atomic sentences by means of ' not ' and ' and ' is completely determined, the meaning of ' not ' being thus a law determining the attitude expressed by ' not-p ' in terms of that expressed by ' p '.

This could, of course, only be used as a *definition* of ' not ' in a symbolism based directly on the truth-possibilities. Thus in the notation explained on page 95 of Mr Wittgenstein's *Tractatus Logico-Philosophicus*, we could define ' not-p ' as the symbol obtained by interchanging the T's and blanks in the last column of 'p '. Ordinarily, however, we always use a different sort of symbolism in which ' not ' is a primitive sign which cannot be defined without circularity ; but even in this symbolism we can ask how ' " nicht " means not ' is to be analysed, and it is this question which the above remarks are intended to answer. In our ordinary symbolism the truth-possibilities are most conveniently expressed as conjunctions of atomic propositions and their negatives, and any proposition will be expressible as a disjunction of the truth-possibilities with which it agrees.

If we apply the logical operations to atomic sentences in an indiscriminate manner, we shall sometimes obtain composite sentences which express no attitude of belief. Thus ' p or not-p ' excludes no possibility and so expresses no attitude of belief at all. It should be regarded not as a significant sentence, but a sort of degenerate case,[1] and is called by Mr Wittgenstein a *tautology*. It can be added to any other sentence without altering its meaning, for ' q : p or not-p ' agrees with just the same possibilities as ' q '. The propositions of formal logic and pure mathematics are in this sense tautologies, and that is what is meant by calling them ' necessary truths '.

Similarly ' p and not-p ' excludes every possibility and expresses no possible attitude : it is called a *contradiction*.

In terms of these ideas we can explain what is meant by logical, mathematical, or formal inference or implication. The inference from ' p ' to ' q ' is formally guaranteed when ' If p, then q ' is a tautology, or when the truth-possibilities with which ' p ' agrees are contained among those with which ' q ' agrees. When this happens, it is always possible to express ' p ' in the form ' q and r ', so that the conclusion ' q ' can be said to be already contained in the premiss.

Before passing on to the question of general propositions

---

[1] In the mathematical sense in which two lines or two points form a degenerate conic.

I must say something about an obvious difficulty. We supposed above that the meanings of the names in our thinker's language might be really complex, so that what was to him an atomic sentence might after translation into a more refined language appear as nothing of the sort. If this were so it might happen that some of the combinations of truth and falsity of his atomic propositions were really self-contradictory. This has actually been supposed to be the case with ' blue ' and ' red ', and Leibniz and Wittgenstein have regarded ' This is both blue and red ' as being self-contradictory, the contradiction being concealed by defective analysis. Whatever may be thought of this hypothesis, it seems to me that formal logic is not concerned with it, but presupposes that all the truth-possibilities of atomic sentences are really possible, or at least treats them as being so. No one could say that the inference from ' This is red ' to ' This is not blue ' was formally guaranteed like the syllogism. If I may revert to the analogy of chess, this assumption might perhaps be compared to the assumption that the chessmen are not so strongly magnetized as to render some positions on the board mechanically impossible, so that we need only consider the restrictions imposed by the rules of the game, and can disregard any others which might conceivably arise from the physical constitution of the men.

We have so far confined ourselves to atomic propositions and those derived from them by any finite number of truth-operations, and unless our account is to be hopelessly incomplete we must now say something about general propositions such as are expressed in English by means of the words ' all ' and ' some ', or in the notation of *Principia Mathematica* by apparent variables. About these I adopt the view of Mr Wittgenstein [1] that ' For all x, fx ' is to be regarded as equivalent to the logical product of all the values of ' fx ',

[1] And also, apparently, of Mr Johnson. See his *Logic Part II*, p. 59.

i.e. to the combination fx_1 and fx_2 and fx_3 and . . ., and that 'There is an x such that fx' is similarly their logical sum. In connection with such symbols we can distinguish first the element of generality, which comes in in specifying the truth-arguments, which are not, as before, enumerated, but determined as all values of a certain propositional function ; and secondly the truth-function element which is the logical product in the first case and the logical sum in the second.

What is novel about general propositions is simply the specification of the truth-arguments by a propositional function instead of by enumeration. Thus general propositions, just like molecular ones, express agreement and disagreement with the truth-possibilities of atomic propositions, but they do this in a different and more complicated way. Feeling belief towards 'For all x, fx' has certain causal properties which we call its expressing agreement only with the possibility that all the values of fx are true. For a symbol to have these casual properties it is not necessary, as it was before, for it to contain names for all the objects involved combined into the appropriate atomic sentences, but by a peculiar law of psychology it is sufficient for it to be constructed in the above way by means of a propositional function.

As before, this must not be regarded as an attempt to define 'all' and 'some', but only as a contribution to the analysis of 'I believe *that all* (or *some*)'.

This view of general propositions has the great advantage that it enables us to extend to them Mr Wittgenstein's account of logical inference, and his view that formal logic consists of tautologies. It is also the only view which explains how 'fa' can be inferred from 'For all x, fx', and 'There is an x such that fx' from 'fa'. The alternative theory that 'There is an x such that fx' should be regarded as an atomic proposition of the form '$F(f)$' (f has application) leaves this entirely obscure ;

it gives no intelligible connection between *a* being red and red having application, but abandoning any hope of explaining this relation is content merely to label it ' necessary.'

Nevertheless, I anticipate that objection will be made on the following lines : firstly, it will be said that *a* cannot enter into the meaning of ' For all *x*, *fx* ', because I can assert this without ever having heard of *a*. To this I answer that this is an essential part of the utility of the symbolism of generality, that it enables us to make assertions about things we have never heard of and so have no names for. Besides, that *a* is involved in the meaning of ' For all *x*, *fx* ' can be seen from the fact that if I say " For all *x*, *fx*,' and someone replies ' not-*fa* ', then, even though I had not before heard of *a*, he would undoubtedly be contradicting me.

The second objection that will be made is more serious ; it will be said that this view of general propositions makes what things there are in the world not, as it really is, a contingent fact, but something presupposed by logic or at best a proposition of logic. Thus it will be urged that even if I could have a list of everything in the world ' *a* ', ' *b* ', ... ' *z* ', ' For all *x*, *fx* ' would still not be equivalent to ' *fa. fb* ... *fz* ', but rather to ' *fa. fb* ... .*fz* and *a*, *b* . . . *z* are everything '. To this Mr Wittgenstein would reply that ' *a*, *b* . . . *z* are every-thing ' is nonsense, and could not be written at all in his improved symbolism for identity. A proper discussion of this answer would involve the whole of his philosophy, and is, therefore, out of the question here ; all that I propose to do is to retort with a *tu quoque* ! The objection would evidently have no force if ' *a*, *b* ... *z* are everything ' were, as with suit-able definitions I think it can be made to be, a tautology ; for then it could be left out without altering the meaning. The objectors will therefore claim that it is not a tautology, or in their terminology not a necessary proposition ; and this they will presumably hold with regard to any proposition of the sort, i.e. they will say that to assert of a set of things that they are or are not everything cannot be either necessarily true or necessarily false. But they will, I conceive, admit that numerical identity and difference are necessary relations, that ' There is an x such that fx ' necessarily follows from 'fa', and that whatever follows necessarily from a necessary truth is itself necessary. If so, their position cannot be maintained ; for suppose a, b, c are in fact not everything, but that there is another thing d. Then that d is not identical with a, b, or c is a necessary fact ; therefore it is necessary that there is an x such that x is not identical with a, b, or c, or that a, b, c are not the only things in the world. This is therefore, even on the objector's view, a necessary and not a contingent truth.

In conclusion, I must emphasise my indebtedness to Mr Wittgenstein, from whom my view of logic is derived. Everything that I have said is due to him, except the parts which have a pragmatist tendency,[1] which seem to me to be needed in order to fill up a gap in his system. But whatever may be thought of these additions of mine, and however this gap should be filled in, his conception of formal logic seems to me indubitably an enormous advance on that of any previous thinker.

My pragmatism is derived from Mr Russell ; and is, of course, very vague and undeveloped. The essence of pragmatism I take to be this, that the meaning of a sentence is to be defined by reference to the actions to which asserting it would lead, or, more vaguely still, by its possible causes and effects. Of this I feel certain, but of nothing more definite.

[1] And the suggestion that the notion of an atomic proposition may be relative to a language.

4

TRUTH AND PROBABILITY (1926)

To say of what is that it is not, or of what is not that it is, is false, while to say of what is that it is and of what is not that it is not is true.—*Aristotle.*

When several hypotheses are presented to our mind which we believe to be mutually exclusive and exhaustive, but about which we know nothing further, we distribute our belief equally among them . . . . This being admitted as an account of the way in which we *actually do* distribute our belief in simple cases, the whole of the subsequent theory follows as a deduction of the way in which we must distribute it in complex cases *if we would be consistent.—W. F. Donkin.*

The object of reasoning is to find out, from the consideration of what we already know, something else which we do not know. Consequently, reasoning is good if it be such as to give a true conclusion from true premises, and not otherwise.—*C. S. Peirce.*

Truth can never be told so as to be understood, and not be believed.— *W. Blake.*

FOREWORD

In this essay the Theory of Probability is taken as a branch of logic, the logic of partial belief and inconclusive argument; but there is no intention of implying that this is the only or even the most important aspect of the subject. Probability is of fundamental importance not only in logic but also in statistical and physical science, and we cannot be sure beforehand that the most useful interpretation of it in logic will be appropriate in physics also. Indeed the general difference of opinion between statisticians who for the most part adopt the frequency theory of probability and logicians who mostly reject it renders it likely that the two schools are really discussing different things, and that the word ' probability ' is used by logicians in one sense and by statisticians in another. The conclusions we shall come to as to the meaning of probability in logic must not, therefore, be taken as prejudging its meaning in physics.

CONTENTS

(1) The Frequency Theory

In the hope of avoiding some purely verbal controversies, I propose to begin by making some admissions in favour of the frequency theory. In the first place this theory must be conceded to have a firm basis in ordinary language, which often uses ' probability ' practically as a synonym for proportion ; for example, if we say that the probability of recovery from smallpox is three-quarters, we mean, I think, simply that that is the proportion of smallpox cases which recover. Secondly, if we start with what is called the calculus of probabilities, regarding it first as a branch of pure mathematics, and then looking round for some interpretation of the formulae which shall show that our axioms are consistent and our subject not entirely useless, then much the simplest and least controversial interpretation of the calculus is one in terms of frequencies. This is true not only of the ordinary mathematics of probability, but also of the symbolic calculus developed by Mr. Keynes ; for if in his a/h, a and h are taken to be not propositions but propositional functions or class-concepts which define finite classes, and a/h is taken to mean the proportion of members of h which are also members of a, then all his propositions become arithmetical truisms.

54

Besides these two inevitable admissions, there is a third
and more important one, which I am prepared to make
temporarily although it does not express my real opinion. It is
this. Suppose we start with the mathematical calculus, and
ask, not as before what interpretation of it is most convenient
to the pure mathematicism, but what interpretation gives
results of greatest value to science in general, then it may be
that the answer is again an interpretation in terms of
frequency; that probability as it is used in statistical theories,
especially in statistical mechanics—the kind of probability
whose logarithm is the entropy—is really a ratio between the
numbers of two classes, or the limit of such a ratio. I do
not myself believe this, but I am willing for the present
to concede to the frequency theory that probability as used
in modern science is really the same as frequency.

But, supposing all this admitted, it still remains the case
that we have the authority both of ordinary language and
of many great thinkers for discussing under the heading of
probability what appears to be quite a different subject,
the logic of partial belief. It may be that, as some sup-
porters of the frequency theory have maintained, the logic
of partial belief will be found in the end to be merely the
study of frequencies, either because partial belief is definable as, or by reference to, some sort of frequency,
or because it can only be the subject of logical treatment
when it is grounded on experienced frequencies. Whether these
contentions are valid can, however, only be decided as a
result of our investigation into partial belief, so that I propose to ignore the frequency theory for the present and
begin an inquiry into the logic of partial belief. In this,
I think, it will be most convenient if, instead of straight
away developing my own theory, I begin by examining
the views of Mr Keynes, which are so well known and in
essentials so widely accepted that readers probably feel

that there is no ground for re-opening the subject *de novo* until they have been disposed of.

(2) Mr Keynes' Theory

Mr Keynes[1] starts from the supposition that we make probable inferences for which we claim objective validity ; we proceed from full belief in one proposition to partial belief in another, and we claim that this procedure is objectively right, so that if another man in similar circumstances entertained a different degree of belief, he would be wrong in doing so. Mr Keynes accounts for this by supposing that between any two propositions, taken as premiss and conclusion, there holds one and only one relation of a certain sort called probability relations ; and that if, in any given case, the relation is that of degree a, from full belief in the premiss, we should, if we were rational, proceed to a belief of degree a in the conclusion.

Before criticising this view, I may perhaps be allowed to point out an obvious and easily corrected defect in the statement of it. When it is said that the degree of the probability relation is the same as the degree of belief which it justifies, it seems to be presupposed that both probability relations, on the one hand, and degrees of belief on the other can be naturally expressed in terms of numbers, and then that the number expressing or measuring the probability relation is the same as that expressing the appropriate degree of belief. But if, as Mr. Keynes holds, these things are not always expressible by numbers, then we cannot give his statement that the degree of the one is the same as the degree of the other such a simple interpretation, but must suppose him to mean only that there is a one-one correspondence between probability relations and the degrees of belief which

---

[1] J. M. Keynes, *A Treatise on Probability* (1921).

they justify. This correspondence must clearly preserve the relations of greater and less, and so make the manifold of probability relations and that of degrees of belief similar in Mr Russell's sense. I think it is a pity that Mr Keynes did not see this clearly, because the exactitude of this correspondence would have provided quite as worthy material for his scepticism as did the numerical measurement of probability relations. Indeed some of his arguments against their numerical measurement appear to apply quite equally well against their exact correspondence with degrees of belief ; for instance, he argues that if rates of insurance correspond to subjective, i.e. actual, degrees of belief, these are not rationally determined, and we cannot infer that probability relations can be similarly measured. It might be argued that the true conclusion in such a case was not that, as Mr Keynes thinks, to the non-numerical probability relation corresponds a non-numerical degree of rational belief, but that degrees of belief, which were always numerical, did not correspond one to one with the probability relations justifying them. For it is, I suppose, conceivable that degrees of belief could be measured by a psychogalvanometer or some such instrument, and Mr Keynes would hardly wish it to follow that probability relations could all be derivatively measured with the measures of the beliefs which they justify.

But let us now return to a more fundamental criticism of Mr. Keynes' views, which is the obvious one that there really do not seem to be any such things as the probability relations he describes. He supposes that, at any rate in certain cases, they can be perceived ; but speaking for myself I feel confident that this is not true. I do not perceive them, and if I am to be persuaded that they exist it must be by argument ; moreover I shrewdly suspect that others do not perceive them either, because they are able to come to so very little agreement as to which of them relates any two given propositions.

All we appear to know about them are certain general propositions, the laws of addition and multiplication ; it is as if
everyone knew the laws of geometry but no one could tell
whether any given object were round or square ; and I find
it hard to imagine how so large a body of general knowledge
can be combined with so slender a stock of particular facts.
It is true that about some particular cases there is agreement,
but these somehow paradoxically are always immensely complicated ; we all agree that the probability of a coin coming
down heads is $\frac{1}{2}$, but we can none of us say exactly what is
the evidence which forms the other term for the probability
relation about which we are then judging. If, on the other
hand, we take the simplest possible pairs of propositions such
as ' This is red ' and ' That is blue ' or ' This is red ' and
' That is red ', whose logical relations should surely be
easiest to see, no one, I think, pretends to be sure what is the
probability relation which connects them. Or, perhaps, they
may claim to see the relation but they will not be able to say
anything about it with certainty, to state if it is more or
less than $\frac{1}{3}$, or so on. They may, of course, say that it is
incomparable with any numerical relation, but a relation
about which so little can be truly said will be of little scientific
use and it will be hard to convince a sceptic of its
existence. Besides this view is really rather paradoxical ;
for any believer in induction must admit that between ' This is
red ' as conclusion and ' This is round ', together with a billion
propositions of the form ' a is round and red ' as evidence,
there is a finite probability relation ; and it is hard to suppose
that as we accumulate instances there is suddenly a point,
say after 233 instances, at which the probability relation
becomes finite and so comparable with some numerical relations.

It seems to me that if we take the two propositions ' a
is red ', ' b is red ', we cannot really discern more than four

simple logical relations between them ; namely identity of form, identity of predicate, diversity of subject, and logical independence of import. If anyone were to ask me what probability one gave to the other, I should not try to answer by contemplating the propositions and trying to discern a logical relation between them, I should, rather, try to imagine that one of them was all that I knew, and to guess what degree of confidence I should then have in the other. If I were able to do this, I might no doubt still not be content with it but might say ' This is what I should think, but, of course, I am only a fool ' and proceed to consider what a wise man would think and call that the degree of probability. This kind of self-criticism I shall discuss later when developing my own theory ; all that I want to remark here is that no one estimating a degree of probability simply contemplates the two propositions supposed to be related by it ; he always considers *inter alia* his own actual or hypothetical degree of belief. This remark seems to me to be borne out by observation of my own behaviour ; and to be the only way of accounting for the fact that we can all give estimates of probability in cases taken from actual life, but are quite unable to do so in the logically simplest cases in which, were probability a logical relation, it would be easiest to discern.

Another argument against Mr Keynes' theory can, I think. be drawn from his inability to adhere to it consistently even in discussing first principles. There is a passage in his chapter on the measurement of probabilities which reads as follows :—

" Probability is, *vide* Chapter II (§ 12), relative in a sense to the principles of *human* reason. The degree of probability, which it is rational for *us* to entertain, does not presume perfect logical insight, and is relative in part to the secondary propositions which we in fact know ; and it is not dependent upon whether more perfect logical insight is or is not conceivable. It is the degree of probability to which those logical processes lead, of which our minds are capable ; or, in the language of Chapter II, which those secondary propositions justify, which we in fact know. If we do not take this view of probability, if we do not limit it in this way and make it, to this extent, relative to human powers, we are altogether adrift in the unknown ; for we cannot ever know what degree of probability would be justified by the perception of logical relations which we are, and must always be, incapable of comprehending." [1]

This passage seems to me quite unreconcilable with the view which Mr Keynes adopts everywhere except in this and another similar passage. For he generally holds that the degree of belief which we are justified in placing in the conclusion of an argument is determined by what relation of probability unites that conclusion to our premisses. There is only one such relation and consequently only one relevant true secondary proposition, which, of course, we may or may not know, but which is necessarily independent of the human mind. If we do not know it, we do not know it and cannot tell how far we ought to believe the conclusion. But often, he supposes, we do know it ; probability relations are not ones which we are incapable of comprehending. But on this view of the matter the passage quoted above has no meaning : the relations which justify probable beliefs are probability relations, and it is nonsense to speak of them being justified by logical relations which we are, and must always be, incapable of comprehending.

The significance of the passage for our present purpose lies in the fact that it seems to presuppose a different view of probability, in which indefinable probability relations play no part, but in which the degree of rational belief depends on a variety of logical relations. For instance, there might be between the premiss and conclusion the relation

[1] p. 32, his italics.

that the premiss was the logical product of a thousand instances of a generalization of which the conclusion was one other instance, and this relation, which is not an indefinable probability relation but definable in terms of ordinary logic and so easily recognizable, might justify a certain degree of belief in the conclusion on the part of one who believed the premiss. We should thus have a variety of ordinary logical relations justifying the same or different degrees of belief. To say that the probability of a given h was such-and-such would mean that between a and h was some relation justifying such-and-such a degree of belief. And on this view it would be a real point that the relation in question must not be one which the human mind is incapable of comprehending.

This second view of probability as depending on logical relations but not itself a new logical relation seems to me more plausible than Mr Keynes' usual theory ; but this does not mean that I feel at all inclined to agree with it. It requires the somewhat obscure idea of a logical relation justifying a degree of belief, which I should not like to accept as indefinable because it does not seem to be at all a clear or simple notion. Also it is hard to say what logical relations justify what degrees of belief, and why ; any decision as to this would be arbitrary, and would lead to a logic of probability consisting of a host of so-called ' necessary ' facts, like formal logic on Mr Chadwick's view of logical constants.[1] Whereas I think it far better to seek an explanation of this ' necessity ' after the model of the work of Mr Wittgenstein, which enables us to see clearly in what precise sense and why logical propositions are necessary, and in a general way why the system of formal logic consists of the propositions it does consist of, and what is their common characteristic. Just as natural science tries to explain and

[1] J. A. Chadwick, " Logical Constants," *Mind*, 1927.

account for the facts of nature, so philosophy should try, in a sense, to explain and account for the facts of logic ; a task ignored by the philosophy which dismisses these facts as being unaccountably and in an indefinable sense ' necessary '.

Here I propose to conclude this criticism of Mr Keynes' theory, not because there are not other respects in which it seems open to objection, but because I hope that what I have already said is enough to show that it is not so completely satisfactory as to render futile any attempt to treat the subject from a rather different point of view.

(3) DEGREES OF BELIEF

The subject of our inquiry is the logic of partial belief, and I do not think we can carry it far unless we have at least an approximate notion of what partial belief is, and how, if at all, it can be measured. It will not be very enlightening to be told that in such circumstances it would be rational to believe a proposition to the extent of $\frac{2}{3}$, unless we know what sort of a belief in it that means. We must therefore try to develop a purely psychological method of measuring belief. It is not enough to measure probability ; in order to apportion correctly our belief to the probability we must also be able to measure our belief.

It is a common view that belief and other psychological variables are not measurable, and if this is true our inquiry will be vain ; and so will the whole theory of probability conceived as a logic of partial belief; for if the phrase ' a belief two-thirds of certainty ' is meaningless, a calculus whose sole object is to enjoin such beliefs will be meaningless also. Therefore unless we are prepared to give up the whole thing as a bad job we are bound to hold that beliefs can to some extent be measured. If we were to follow the analogy of Mr Keynes' treatment of probabilities we should say that some beliefs were measurable and some not ; but this does not seem to me likely to be a correct account of the matter : I do not see how we can sharply divide beliefs into those which have a position in the numerical scale and those which have not. But I think beliefs do differ in measurability in the following two ways. First, some beliefs can be measured more accurately than others ; and, secondly, the measurement of beliefs is almost certainly an ambiguous process leading to a variable answer depending on how exactly the measurement is conducted. The degree of a belief is in this respect like the time interval between two events ; before Einstein it was supposed that all the ordinary ways of measuring a time interval would lead to the same result if properly performed. Einstein showed that this was not the case ; and time interval can no longer be regarded as an exact notion, but must be discarded in all precise investigations. Nevertheless, time interval and the Newtonian system are sufficiently accurate for many purposes and easier to apply.

I shall try to argue later that the degree of a belief is just like a time interval ; it has no precise meaning unless we specify more exactly how it is to be measured. But for many purposes we can assume that the alternative ways of measuring it lead to the same result, although this is only approximately true. The resulting discrepancies are more glaring in connection with some beliefs than with others, and these therefore appear less measurable. Both these types of deficiency in measurability, due respectively to the difficulty in getting an exact enough measurement and to an important ambiguity in the definition of the measurement process, occur also in physics and so are not difficulties peculiar to our problem ; what is peculiar is that it is difficult to form any idea of how the measurement is to be conducted, how a unit is to be obtained, and so on.

Let us then consider what is implied in the measurement of beliefs. A satisfactory system must in the first place assign to any belief a magnitude or degree having a definite position in an order of magnitudes ; beliefs which are of the same degree as the same belief must be of the same degree as one another, and so on. Of course this cannot be accomplished without introducing a certain amount of hypothesis or fiction. Even in physics we cannot maintain that things that are equal to the same thing are equal to one another unless we take ' equal ' not as meaning ' sensibly equal ' but a fictitious or hypothetical relation. I do not want to discuss the metaphysics or epistemology of this process, but merely to remark that if it is allowable in physics it is allowable in psychology also. The logical simplicity characteristic of the relations dealt with in a science is never attained by nature alone without any admixture of fiction.

But to construct such an ordered series of degrees is not the whole of our task ; we have also to assign numbers to these degrees in some intelligible manner. We can of course easily explain that we denote full belief by 1, full belief in the contradictory by 0, and equal beliefs in the proposition and its contradictory by $\frac{1}{2}$. But it is not so easy to say what is meant by a belief $\frac{2}{3}$ of certainty, or a belief in the proposition being twice as strong as that in its contradictory. This is the harder part of the task, but it is absolutely necessary ; for we do calculate numerical probabilities, and if they are to correspond to degrees of belief we must discover some definite way of attaching numbers to degrees of belief. In physics we often attach numbers by discovering a physical process of addition [1] : the measure-numbers of lengths are not assigned arbitrarily subject only to the proviso that the greater length shall have the greater measure ; we determine them further by deciding on a

[1] See N. Campbell, *Physics The Elements* (1920), p. 277.

64

physical meaning for addition ; the length got by putting together two given lengths must have for its measure the sum of their measures. A system of measurement in which there is nothing corresponding to this is immediately recognized as arbitrary, for instance Mohs' scale of hardness[1] in which 10 is arbitrarily assigned to diamond, the hardest known material, 9 to the next hardest, and so on. We have therefore to find a process of addition for degrees of belief, or some substitute for this which will be equally adequate to determine a numerical scale.

Such is our problem ; how are we to solve it ? There are, I think, two ways in which we can begin. We can, in the first place, suppose that the degree of a belief is something perceptible by its owner ; for instance that beliefs differ in the intensity of a feeling by which they are accompanied, which might be called a belief-feeling or feeling of conviction, and that by the degree of belief we mean the intensity of this feeling. This view would be very inconvenient, for it is not easy to ascribe numbers to the intensities of feelings; but apart from this it seems to me observably false, for the beliefs which we hold most strongly are often accompanied by practically no feeling at all ; no one feels strongly about things he takes for granted.

We are driven therefore to the second supposition that the degree of a belief is a causal property of it, which we can express vaguely as the extent to which we are prepared to act on it. This is a generalization of the well-known view, that the differentia of belief lies in its causal efficacy, which is discussed by Mr Russell in his *Analysis of Mind.* He there dismisses it for two reasons, one of which seems entirely to miss the point. He argues that in the course of trains of thought we believe many things which do not lead to action. This objection is however beside the mark, because

[1] Ibid., p. 271.

it is not asserted that a belief is an idea which does actually lead to action, but one which would lead to action in suitable circumstances ; just as a lump of arsenic is called poisonous not because it actually has killed or will kill anyone, but because it would kill anyone if he ate it. Mr Russell's second argument is, however, more formidable. He points out that it is not possible to suppose that beliefs differ from other ideas only in their effects, for if they were otherwise identical their effects would be identical also. This is perfectly true, but it may still remain the case that the nature of the difference between the causes is entirely unknown or very vaguely known, and that what we want to talk about is the difference between the effects, which is readily observable and important.

As soon as we regard belief quantatively, this seems to me the only view we can take of it. It could well be held that the difference between believing and not believing lies in the presence or absence of introspectible feelings. But when we seek to know what is the difference between believing more firmly and believing less firmly, we can no longer regard it as consisting in having more or less of certain observable feelings ; at least I personally cannot recognize any such feelings. The difference seems to me to lie in how far we should act on these beliefs : this may depend on the degree of some feeling or feelings, but I do not know exactly what feelings and I do not see that it is indispensable that we should know. Just the same thing is found in physics ; men found that a wire connecting plates of zinc and copper standing in acid deflected a magnetic needle in its neighbourhood. Accordingly as the needle was more or less deflected the wire was said to carry a larger or a smaller current. The nature of this ' current ' could only be conjectured : what were observed and measured were simply its effects.

It will no doubt be objected that we know how strongly

we believe things, and that we can only know this if we can measure our belief by introspection. This does not seem to me necessarily true ; in many cases, I think, our judgment about the strength of our belief is really about how we should act in hypothetical circumstances. It will be answered that we can only tell how we should act by observing the present belief-feeling which determines how we should act ; but again I doubt the cogency of the argument. It is possible that what determines how we should act determines us also directly or indirectly to have a correct opinion as to how we should act, without its ever coming into consciousness.

Suppose, however, I am wrong about this and that we can decide by introspection the nature of belief, and measure its degree ; still, I shall argue, the kind of measurement of belief with which probability is concerned is not this kind but is a measurement of belief *qua* basis of action. This can I think be shown in two ways. First, by considering the scale of probabilities between 0 and 1, and the sort of way we use it, we shall find that it is very appropriate to the measurement of belief as a basis of action, but in no way related to the measurement of an introspected feeling. For the units in terms of which such feelings or sensations are measured are always, I think, differences which are just perceptible : there is no other way of obtaining units. But I see no ground for supposing that the interval between a belief of degree $\frac{1}{3}$ and one of degree $\frac{1}{2}$ consists of as many just perceptible changes as does that between one of $\frac{2}{3}$ and one of $\frac{5}{6}$, or that a scale based on just perceptible differences would have any simple relation to the theory of probability. On the other hand the probability of $\frac{1}{3}$ is clearly related to the kind of belief which would lead to a bet of 2 to 1, and it will be shown below how to generalize this relation so as to apply to action in general. Secondly, the quantitative aspects of beliefs as the basis of action are evidently more important than the intensities of belief-feelings.

The latter are no doubt interesting, but may be very variable from individual to individual, and their practical interest is entirely due to their position as the hypothetical causes of beliefs *qua* bases of action.

It is possible that some one will say that the extent to which we should act on a belief in suitable circumstances is a hypothetical thing, and therefore not capable of measurement. But to say this is merely to reveal ignorance of the physical sciences which constantly deal with and measure hypothetical quantities ; for instance, the electric intensity at a given point is the force which would act on a unit charge if it were placed at the point.

Let us now try to find a method of measuring beliefs as bases of possible actions. It is clear that we are concerned with dispositional rather than with actualized beliefs ; that is to say, not with beliefs at the moment when we are thinking of them, but with beliefs like my belief that the earth is round, which I rarely think of, but which would guide my action in any case to which it was relevant.

The old-established way of measuring a person's belief is to propose a bet, and see what are the lowest odds which he will accept. This method I regard as fundamentally sound ; but it suffers from being insufficiently general, and from being necessarily inexact. It is inexact partly because of the diminishing marginal utility of money, partly because the person may have a special eagerness or reluctance to bet, because he either enjoys or dislikes excitement or for any other reason, e.g. to make a book. The difficulty is like that of separating two different co-operating forces. Besides, the proposal of a bet may inevitably alter his state of opinion ; just as we could not always measure electric intensity by actually introducing a charge and seeing what force it was subject to, because the introduction of the charge would change the distribution to be measured.

In order therefore to construct a theory of quantities of belief which shall be both general and more exact, I propose to take as a basis a general psychological theory, which is now universally discarded, but nevertheless comes, I think, fairly close to the truth in the sort of cases with which we are most concerned. I mean the theory that we act in the way we think most likely to realize the objects of our desires, so that a person's actions are completely determined by his desires and opinions. This theory cannot be made adequate to all the facts, but it seems to me a useful approximation to the truth particularly in the case of our self-conscious or professional life, and it is presupposed in a great deal of our thought. It is a simple theory and one which many psychologists would obviously like to preserve by introducing unconscious desires and unconscious opinions in order to bring it more into harmony with the facts. How far such fictions can achieve the required result I do not attempt to judge : I only claim for what follows approximate truth, or truth in relation to this artificial system of psychology, which like Newtonian mechanics can, I think, still be profitably used even though it is known to be false.

It must be observed that this theory is not to be identified with the psychology of the Utilitarians, in which pleasure had a dominating position. The theory I propose to adopt is that we seek things which we want, which may be our own or other people's pleasure, or anything else whatever, and our actions are such as we think most likely to realize these goods. But this is not a precise statement, for a precise statement of the theory can only be made after we have introduced the notion of quantity of belief.

Let us call the things a person ultimately desires ' goods ', and let us at first assume that they are numerically measurable and additive. That is to say that if he prefers for its own sake an hour's swimming to an hour's reading, he will prefer two hours' swimming to one hour's swimming and one hour's reading. This is of course absurd in the given case but this may only be because swimming and reading are not ultimate goods, and because we cannot imagine a second hour's swimming precisely similar to the first, owing to fatigue, etc.

Let us begin by supposing that our subject has no doubts about anything, but certain opinions about all propositions. Then we can say that he will always choose the course of action which will lead in his opinion to the greatest sum of good.

It should be emphasized that in this essay good and bad are never to be understood in any ethical sense but simply as denoting that to which a given person feels desire and aversion.

The question then arises how we are to modify this simple system to take account of varying degrees of certainty in his beliefs. I suggest that we introduce as a law of psychology that his behaviour is governed by what is called the mathematical expectation ; that is to say that, if p is a proposition about which he is doubtful, any goods or bads for whose realization p is in his view a necessary and sufficient condition enter into his calculations multiplied by the same fraction, which is called the ' degree of his belief in p '. We thus define degree of belief in a way which presupposes the use of the mathematical expectation.

We can put this in a different way. Suppose his degree of belief in p is $\frac{m}{n}$; then his action is such as he would choose it to be if he had to repeat it exactly n times, in m of which p was true, and in the others false. [Here it may be necessary to suppose that in each of the n times he had no memory of the previous ones.]

This can also be taken as a definition of the degree of belief, and can easily be seen to be equivalent to the previous definition. Let us give an instance of the sort of case which might occur. I am at a cross-roads and do not know the way ; but I rather think one of the two ways is right. I propose therefore to go that way but keep my eyes open for someone to ask ; if now I see someone half a mile away over the fields, whether I turn aside to ask him will depend on the relative inconvenience of going out of my way to cross the fields or of continuing on the wrong road if it is the wrong road. But it will also depend on how confident I am that I am right ; and clearly the more confident I am of this the less distance I should be willing to go from the road to check my opinion. I propose therefore to use the distance I would be prepared to go to ask, as a measure of the confidence of my opinion ; and what I have said above explains how this is to be done. We can set it out as follows : suppose the disadvantage of going x yards to ask is $f(x)$, the advantage of arriving at the right destination is r, that of arriving at the wrong one w. Then if I should just be willing to go a distance d to ask, the degree of my belief that I am on the right road is given by

$$p = 1 - \frac{f(d)}{r - w}.$$

For such an action is one it would just pay me to take, if I had to act in the same way n times, in np of which I was on the right way but in the others not.

For the total good resulting from not asking each time

$$= npr + n(1 - p)w$$
$$= nw + np(r - w),$$

that resulting from asking at distance x each time

$$= nr - nf(x). \qquad \text{[I now always go right.]}$$

This is greater than the preceding expression, provided

$$f(x) < (r - w)\,(1 - p),$$

∴ the critical distance d is connected with p, the degree of belief, by the relation $f(d) = (r - w)\,(1 - p)$

$$\text{or } p = 1 - \frac{f(d)}{r - w} \qquad \text{as asserted above.}$$

It is easy to see that this way of measuring beliefs gives results agreeing with ordinary ideas; at any rate to the extent that full belief is denoted by 1, full belief in the contradictory by 0, and equal belief in the two by $\frac{1}{2}$. Further, it allows validity to betting as means of measuring beliefs. By proposing a bet on p we give the subject a possible course of action from which so much extra good will result to him if p is true and so much extra bad if p is false. Supposing the bet to be in goods and bads instead of in money, he will take a bet at any better odds than those corresponding to his state of belief; in fact his state of belief is measured by the odds he will just take; but this is vitiated, as already explained, by love or hatred of excitement, and by the fact that the bet is in money and not in goods and bads. Since it is universally agreed that money has a diminishing marginal utility, if money bets are to be used, it is evident that they should be for as small stakes as possible. But then again the measurement is spoiled by introducing the new factor of reluctance to bother about trifles.

Let us now discard the assumption that goods are additive and immediately measurable, and try to work out a system with as few assumptions as possible. To begin with we shall suppose, as before, that our subject has certain beliefs about everything; then he will act so that what he believes to be the total consequences of his action will be the best possible. If then we had the power of the Almighty, and could persuade our subject of our power, we could, by offering him options, discover how he placed in order of merit all possible courses of the world. In this way all possible worlds would be put in an order of value, but we should have no definite way of representing them by numbers. There would be no meaning in the assertion that the difference in value between α and β was equal to that between γ and δ. [Here and elsewhere we use Greek letters to represent the different possible totalities of events between which our subject chooses—the ultimate organic unities.]

Suppose next that the subject is capable of doubt ; then we could test his degree of belief in different propositions by making him offers of the following kind. Would you rather have world α in any event; or world β if p is true, and world γ if p is false? If, then, he were certain that p was true, he would simply compare α and β and choose between them as if no conditions were attached ; but if he were doubtful his choice would not be decided so simply. I propose to lay down axioms and definitions concerning the principles governing choices of this kind. This is, of course, a very schematic version of the situation in real life, but it is, I think, easier to consider it in this form.

There is first a difficulty which must be dealt with ; the propositions like p in the above case which are used as conditions in the options offered may be such that their truth or falsity is an object of desire to the subject. This will be found to complicate the problem, and we have to assume that there are propositions for which this is not the case, which we shall call ethically neutral. More precisely an atomic proposition p is called ethically neutral if two possible worlds differing only in regard to the truth of p are always of equal value ; and a non-atomic proposition p is called ethically neutral if all its atomic truth-arguments [1] are ethically neutral.

We begin by defining belief of degree $\frac{1}{2}$ in an ethically neutral proposition. The subject is said to have belief of degree $\frac{1}{2}$ in such a proposition p if he has no preference between the options (1) α if p is true, β if p is false, and (2) α if p is false, β if p is true, but has a preference between α and β simply. We suppose by an axiom that if this is true of any

---

[1] I assume here Wittgenstein's theory of propositions ; it would probably be possible to give an equivalent definition in terms of any other theory.

one pair α, β it is true of all such pairs.[1] This comes roughly to defining belief of degree $\frac{1}{2}$ as such a degree of belief as leads to indifference between betting one way and betting the other for the same stakes.

Belief of degree $\frac{1}{2}$ as thus defined can be used to measure values numerically in the following way. We have to explain what is meant by the difference in value between α and β being equal to that between γ and δ; and we define this to mean that, if p is an ethically neutral proposition believed to degree $\frac{1}{2}$, the subject has no preference between the options (1) α if p is true, δ if p is false, and (2) β if p is true, γ if p is false.

This definition can form the basis of a system of measuring values in the following way :—

Let us call any set of all worlds equally preferable to a given world a value : we suppose that if world α is preferable to β any world with the same value as α is preferable to any world with the same value as β and shall say that the value of α is greater than that of β. This relation ' greater than ' orders values in a series. We shall use α henceforth both for the world and its value.

Axioms.

(1) There is an ethically neutral proposition p believed to degree $\frac{1}{2}$.

(2) If p, q are such propositions and the option

α if p, δ if not-p is equivalent to β if p, γ if not-p

then α if q, δ if not-q is equivalent to β if q, γ if not-q.

Def. In the above case we say $\alpha\beta = \gamma\delta$.

Theorems. If $\alpha\beta = \gamma\delta$,

$$\text{then } \beta\alpha = \delta\gamma, \ \alpha\gamma = \beta\delta, \ \gamma\alpha = \delta\beta.$$

---

[1] α and β must be supposed so far undefined as to be compatible with both p and not-p.

(2a) If $\alpha\beta = \gamma\delta$, then $\alpha > \beta$ is equivalent to $\gamma > \delta$

and $\alpha = \beta$ is equivalent to $\gamma = \delta$.

(3) If option A is equivalent to option B and B to C then A to C.

Theorem. If $\alpha\beta = \gamma\delta$ and $\beta\eta = \zeta\gamma$,

then $\alpha\eta = \zeta\delta$.

(4) If $\alpha\beta = \gamma\delta$, $\gamma\delta = \eta\zeta$, then $\alpha\beta = \eta\zeta$.

(5) (α, β, γ). E! $(\imath x)$ $(\alpha x = \beta\gamma)$.

(6) (α, β). E! $(\imath x)$ $(\alpha x = x\beta)$.

(7) Axiom of continuity :—Any progression has a limit (ordinal).

(8) Axiom of Archimedes.

These axioms enable the values to be correlated one-one with real numbers so that if α^1 corresponds to α, etc.

$$\alpha\beta = \gamma\delta . \equiv . \alpha^1 - \beta^1 = \gamma^1 - \delta^1.$$

Henceforth we use α for the correlated real number α^1 also.

Having thus defined a way of measuring value we can now derive a way of measuring belief in general. If the option of α for certain is indifferent with that of β if p is true and γ if p is false,[1] we can define the subject's degree of belief in p as the ratio of the difference between α and γ to that between β and γ ; which we must suppose the same for all α's, β's and γ's that satisfy the conditions. This amounts roughly

---

[1] Here β must include the truth of p, γ its falsity ; p need no longer be ethically neutral. But we have to assume that there is a world with any assigned value in which p is true, and one in which p is false.

to defining the degree of belief in p by the odds at which the subject would bet on p, the bet being conducted in terms of differences of value as defined. The definition only applies to partial belief and does not include certain beliefs; for belief of degree 1 in p, α for certain is indifferent with α if p and any β if not-p.

We are also able to define a very useful new idea—'the degree of belief in p given q'. This does not mean the degree of belief in 'If p then q', or that in 'p entails q', or that which the subject would have in p if he knew q, or that which he ought to have. It roughly expresses the odds at which he would now bet on p, the bet only to be valid if q is true. Such conditional bets were often made in the eighteenth century.

The degree of belief in p given q is measured thus. Suppose the subject indifferent between the options (1) α if q true, β if q false, (2) γ if p true and q true, δ if p false and q true, β if q false. Then the degree of his belief in p given q is the ratio of the difference between α and δ to that between γ and δ, which we must suppose the same for any α, β, γ, δ which satisfy the given conditions. This is not the same as the degree to which he would believe p, if he believed q for certain; for knowledge of q might for psychological reasons profoundly alter his whole system of beliefs.

Each of our definitions has been accompanied by an axiom of consistency, and in so far as this is false, the notion of the corresponding degree of belief becomes invalid. This bears some analogy to the situation in regard to simultaneity discussed above.

I have not worked out the mathematical logic of this in detail, because this would, I think, be rather like working out to seven places of decimals a result only valid to two. My logic cannot be regarded as giving more than the sort of way it might work.

From these definitions and axioms it is possible to prove the fundamental laws of probable belief (degrees of belief lie between 0 and 1) :

(1) Degree of belief in p + degree of belief in $\bar{p}$ = 1.

(2) Degree of belief in p given q + degree of belief in $\bar{p}$ given q = 1.

(3) Degree of belief in (p and q) = degree of belief in p × degree of belief in q given p.

(4) Degree of belief in (p and q) + degree of belief in (p and $\bar{q}$) = degree of belief in p.

The first two are immediate. (3) is proved as follows.

Let degree of belief in $p = x$, that in q given $p = y$.

Then ξ for certain $\equiv \xi + (1-x)t$ if p true, $\xi - xt$ if p false, for any t.

$\xi + (1-x)\, t$ if p true $\equiv$

$$\begin{cases} \xi + (1-x)\, t + (1-y)\, u \text{ if ' } p \text{ and } q \text{ ' true,} \\ \xi + (1-x)\, t - yu \text{ if } p \text{ true } q \text{ false ;} \end{cases} \quad \text{for any } u.$$

Choose u so that $\xi + (1-x)\, t - yu = \xi - xt$,

i.e. let $u = t/y \ (y \neq 0)$

Then ξ for certain $\equiv$

$$\begin{cases} \xi + (1-x)\, t + (1-y)\, t/y \text{ if } p \text{ and } q \text{ true} \\ \xi - xt \text{ otherwise,} \end{cases}$$

$\therefore$ degree of belief in ' p and q ' $= \dfrac{xt}{t + (1-y)\, t/y} = xy. \ (t \neq 0)$

If $y = 0$, take $t = 0$.

Then ξ for certain $\equiv \xi$ if p true, ξ if p false

$\qquad\qquad \equiv \xi + u$ if p true, q true ; $\quad \xi$ if p false, q
$\qquad\qquad\quad$ false ; $\quad \xi$ if p false

$\qquad\qquad \equiv \xi + u,\, pq$ true ; $\quad \xi,\, pq$ false

$\therefore$ degree of belief in $pq = 0$.

(4) follows from (2), (3) as follows :—

Degree of belief in $pq =$ that in $p \times$ that in q given p, by (3).
Similarly degree of belief in $p\bar{q} =$ that in $p \times$ that in $\bar{q}$ given p
$\therefore$ sum $=$ degree of belief in p, by (2).

These are the laws of probability, which we have proved to be necessarily true of any consistent set of degrees of belief. Any definite set of degrees of belief which broke them would be inconsistent in the sense that it violated the laws of preference between options, such as that preferability is a transitive asymmetrical relation, and that if α is preferable to β, β for certain cannot be preferable to α if p, β if not-p. If anyone's mental condition violated these laws, his choice would depend on the precise form in which the options were offered him, which would be absurd. He could have a book made against him by a cunning better and would then stand to lose in any event.

We find, therefore, that a precise account of the nature of partial belief reveals that the laws of probability are laws of consistency, an extension to partial beliefs of formal logic, the logic of consistency. They do not depend for their meaning on any degree of belief in a proposition being uniquely determined as the rational one ; they merely distinguish those sets of beliefs which obey them as consistent ones.

Having any definite degree of belief implies a certain measure of consistency, namely willingness to bet on a given proposition at the same odds for any stake, the stakes being measured in terms of ultimate values. Having degrees of belief obeying the laws of probability implies a further measure of consistency, namely such a consistency between the odds acceptable on different propositions as shall prevent a book being made against you.

Some concluding remarks on this section may not be out of place. First, it is based fundamentally on betting, but this will not seem unreasonable when it is seen that all our lives we are in a sense betting. Whenever we go to the station we are betting that a train will really run, and if we had not a sufficient degree of belief in this we should decline the bet and stay at home. The options God gives us are always conditional on our guessing whether a certain proposition is true. Secondly, it is based throughout on the idea of mathematical expectation; the dissatisfaction often felt with this idea is due mainly to the inaccurate measurement of goods. Clearly mathematical expectations in terms of money are not proper guides to conduct. It should be remembered, in judging my system, that in it value is actually defined by means of mathematical expectation in the case of beliefs of degree $\frac{1}{2}$, and so may be expected to be scaled suitably for the valid application of the mathematical expectation in the case of other degrees of belief also.

Thirdly, nothing has been said about degrees of belief when the number of alternatives is infinite. About this I have nothing useful to say, except that I doubt if the mind is capable of contemplating more than a finite number of alternatives. It can consider questions to which an infinite number of answers are possible, but in order to consider the answers it must lump them into a finite number of groups. The difficulty becomes practically relevant when discussing induction, but even then there seems to me no need to introduce it. We can discuss whether past experience gives a high probability to the sun's rising to-morrow without bothering about what probability it gives to the sun's rising each morning for evermore. For this reason I cannot but feel that Mr Ritchie's discussion of the problem [1] is unsatisfactory ; it is true that we can agree that inductive generalizations need have no finite probability, but particular expectations entertained on inductive grounds undoubtedly do have a high numerical probability in the minds of all of us. We all are more certain that the sun will rise to-morrow than that I shall not throw 12 with two dice first time, i.e. we have a belief of higher degree than $\frac{35}{36}$ in it. If induction ever needs a logical justification it is in connection with the probability of an event like this.

(4) The Logic of Consistency

We may agree that in some sense it is the business of logic to tell us what we ought to think ; but the interpretation of this statement raises considerable difficulties. It may be said that we ought to think what is true, but in that sense we are told what to think by the whole of science and not merely by logic. Nor, in this sense, can any justification be found for partial belief ; the ideally best thing is that we should have beliefs of degree 1 in all true propositions and beliefs of degree 0 in all false propositions. But this is too high a standard to expect of mortal men, and we must agree that some degree of doubt or even of error may be humanly speaking justified.

[1] A. D. Ritchie, "Induction and Probability," *Mind*, 1926, p. 318. ' The conclusion of the foregoing discussion may be simply put. If the problem of induction be stated to be " How can inductive generalizations acquire a large numerical probability ? " then this is a pseudo-problem, because the answer is " They cannot ". This answer is not, however, a denial of the validity of induction but is a direct consequence of the nature of probability. It still leaves untouched the real problem of induction which is " How can the probability of an induction be increased ? " and it leaves standing the whole of Keynes' discussion on this point.'

Many logicians, I suppose, would accept as an account of their science the opening words of Mr Keynes' *Treatise on Probability* : " Part of our knowledge we obtain direct ; and part by argument. The Theory of Probability is concerned with that part which we obtain by argument, and it treats of the different degrees in which the results so obtained are conclusive or inconclusive." Where Mr Keynes says ' the Theory of Probability ', others would say Logic. It is held, that is to say, that our opinions can be divided into those we hold immediately as a result of perception or memory, and those which we derive from the former by argument. It is the business of Logic to accept the former class and criticize merely the derivation of the second class from them.

Logic as the science of argument and inference is traditionally and rightly divided into deductive and inductive ; but the difference and relation between these two divisions of the subject can be conceived in extremely different ways. According to Mr Keynes valid deductive and inductive arguments are fundamentally alike ; both are justified by logical relations between premiss and conclusion which differ only in degree. This position, as I have already explained, I cannot accept. I do not see what these inconclusive logical relations can be or how they can justify partial beliefs. In the case of conclusive logical arguments I can accept the account of their validity which has been given by many authorities, and can be found substantially the same in Kant, De Morgan, Peirce and Wittgenstein. All these authors agree that the conclusion of a formally valid argument is contained in its premisses ; that to deny the conclusion while accepting the premisses would be self-contradictory ; that a formal deduction does not increase our knowledge, but only brings out clearly what we already know in another form ; and that we are bound to accept its validity on pain of being inconsistent with ourselves. The logical relation which justifies the inference is that the sense or import of the conclusion is contained in that of the premisses.

But in the case of an inductive argument this does not happen in the least; it is impossible to represent it as resembling a deductive argument and merely weaker in degree; it is absurd to say that the sense of the conclusion is partially contained in that of the premisses. We could accept the premisses and utterly reject the conclusion without any sort of inconsistency or contradiction.

It seems to me, therefore, that we can divide arguments into two radically different kinds, which we can distinguish in the words of Peirce as (1) ' explicative, analytic, or deductive ' and (2) ' amplifiative, synthetic, or (loosely speaking) inductive '.[1] Arguments of the second type are from an important point of view much closer to memories and perceptions than to deductive arguments. We can regard perception, memory and induction as the three fundamental ways of acquiring knowledge; deduction on the other hand is merely a method of arranging our knowledge and eliminating inconsistencies or contradictions.

Logic must then fall very definitely into two parts: (excluding analytic logic, the theory of terms and propositions) we have the lesser logic, which is the logic of consistency, or formal logic; and the larger logic, which is the logic of discovery, or inductive logic.

What we have now to observe is that this distinction in no way coincides with the distinction between certain and partial beliefs; we have seen that there is a theory of consistency in partial beliefs just as much as of consistency in certain beliefs, although for various reasons the former is not so important as the latter. The theory of probability is in fact a generalization of formal logic; but in the process

[1] C. S. Peirce, *Chance Love and Logic*, p. 92.

of generalization one of the most important aspects of formal logic is destroyed. If p and $\bar{q}$ are inconsistent so that q follows logically from p, that p implies q is what is called by Wittgenstein a ' tautology ' and can be regarded as a degenerate case of a true proposition not involving the idea of consistency. This enables us to regard (not altogether correctly) formal logic including mathematics as an objective science consisting of objectively necessary propositions. It thus gives us not merely the ἀνάγκη λέγειν, that if we assert p we are bound in consistency to assert q also, but also the ἀνάγκη εἶναι, that if p is true, so must q be. But when we extend formal logic to include partial beliefs this direct objective interpetation is lost ; if we believe pq to the extent of $\frac{1}{3}$, and $p\bar{q}$ to the extent of $\frac{1}{3}$, we are bound in consistency to believe $\bar{p}$ also to the extent of $\frac{1}{3}$. This is the ἀνάγκη λέγειν ; but we cannot say that if pq is $\frac{1}{3}$ true and $p\bar{q}$ $\frac{1}{3}$ true, $\bar{p}$ also must be $\frac{1}{3}$ true, for such a statement would be sheer nonsense. There is no corresponding ἀνάγκη εἶναι. Hence, unlike the calculus of consistent full belief, the calculus of objective partial belief cannot be immediately interpreted as a body of objective tautology.

This is, however, possible in a roundabout way ; we saw at the beginning of this essay that the calculus of probabilities could be interpreted in terms of class-ratios ; we have now found that it can also be interpreted as a calculus of consistent partial belief. It is natural, therefore, that we should expect some intimate connection between these two interpretations, some explanation of the possibility of applying the same mathematical calculus to two such different sets of phenomena. Nor is an explanation difficult to find ; there are many connections between partial beliefs and frequencies. For instance, experienced frequencies often lead to corresponding partial beliefs, and partial beliefs lead to the expectation of corresponding frequencies in accordance with Bernouilli's

Theorem. But neither of these is exactly the connection we want ; a partial belief cannot in general be connected uniquely with any actual frequency, for the connection is always made by taking the proposition in question as an instance of a propositional function. What propositional function we choose is to some extent arbitrary and the corresponding frequency will vary considerably with our choice. The pretensions of some exponents of the frequency theory that partial belief means full belief in a frequency proposition cannot be sustained. But we found that the very idea of partial belief involves reference to a hypothetical or ideal frequency ; supposing goods to be additive, belief of degree $\frac{m}{n}$ is the sort of belief which leads to the action which would be best if repeated n times in m of which the proposition is true ; or we can say more briefly that it is the kind of belief most appropriate to a number of hypothetical occasions otherwise identical in a proportion $\frac{m}{n}$ of which the proposition in question is true. It is this connection between partial belief and frequency which enables us to use the calculus of frequencies as a calculus of consistent partial belief. And in a sense we may say that the two interpretations are the objective and subjective aspects of the same inner meaning, just as formal logic can be interpreted objectively as a body of tautology and subjectively as the laws of consistent thought.

We shall, I think, find that this view of the calculus of probability removes various difficulties that have hitherto been found perplexing. In the first place it gives us a clear justification for the axioms of the calculus, which on such a system as Mr Keynes' is entirely wanting. For now it is easily seen that if partial beliefs are consistent they will obey these axioms, but it is utterly obscure why Mr Keynes' mysterious logical relations should obey them.[1] We should be so curiously ignorant of the instances of these relations, and so curiously knowledgeable about their general laws.

Secondly, the Principle of Indifference can now be altogether dispensed with ; we do not regard it as belonging to formal logic to say what should be a man's expectation of drawing a white or a black ball from an urn ; his original expectations may within the limits of consistency be any he likes ; all we have to point out is that if he has certain expectations he is bound in consistency to have certain others. This is simply bringing probability into line with ordinary formal logic, which does not criticize premisses but merely declares that certain conclusions are the only ones consistent with them. To be able to turn the Principle of Indifference out of formal logic is a great advantage ; for it is fairly clearly impossible to lay down purely logical conditions for its validity, as is attempted by Mr Keynes. I do not want to discuss this question in detail, because it leads to hair-splitting and arbitrary distinctions which could be discussed for ever. But anyone who tries to decide by Mr Keynes' methods what are the proper alternatives to regard as equally probable in molecular mechanics, e.g. in Gibbs' phase-space, will soon be convinced that it is a matter of physics rather than pure logic. By using the multiplication formula, as it is used in inverse probability, we can on Mr Keynes' theory reduce all probabilities to quotients of *a priori* probabilities ; it is therefore in regard to these latter that the Principle of Indifference is of primary importance ; but here the question is obviously not one of formal logic. How can we on merely

[1] It appears in Mr Keynes' system as if the principal axioms—the laws of addition and multiplication—were nothing but definitions. This is merely a logical mistake ; his definitions are formally invalid unless corresponding axioms are presupposed. Thus his definition of multiplication presupposes the law that if the probability of *a* given *bh* is equal to that of *c* given *dk*, and the probability of *b* given *h* is equal to that of *d* given *k*, then will the probabilities of *ab* given *h* and of *cd* given *k* be equal.

logical grounds divide the spectrum into equally probable bands ?

A third difficulty which is removed by our theory is the one which is presented to Mr Keynes' theory by the following case. I think I perceive or remember something but am not sure ; this would seem to give me some ground for believing it, contrary to Mr Keynes' theory, by which the degree of belief in it which it would be rational for me to have is that given by the probability relation between the proposition in question and the things I know for certain. He cannot justify a probable belief founded not on argument but on direct inspection. In our view there would be nothing contrary to formal logic in such a belief ; whether it would be reasonable would depend on what I have called the larger logic which will be the subject of the next section ; we shall there see that there is no objection to such a possibility, with which Mr Keynes' method of justifying probable belief solely by relation to certain knowledge is quite unable to cope.

(5) THE LOGIC OF TRUTH

The validity of the distinction between the logic of consistency and the logic of truth has been often disputed ; it has been contended on the one hand that logical consistency is only a kind of factual consistency ; that if a belief in p is inconsistent with one in q, that simply means that p and q are not both true, and that this is a necessary or logical fact. I believe myself that this difficulty can be met by Wittgenstein's theory of tautology, according to which if a belief in p is inconsistent with one in q, that p and q are not both true is not a fact but a tautology. But I do not propose to discuss this question further here.

From the other side it is contended that formal logic or the logic of consistency is the whole of logic, and inductive logic either nonsense or part of natural science. This contention, which would I suppose be made by Wittgenstein, I feel more difficulty in meeting. But I think it would be a pity, out of deference to authority, to give up trying to say anything useful about induction.

Let us therefore go back to the general conception of logic as the science of rational thought. We found that the most generally accepted parts of logic, namely, formal logic, mathematics and the calculus of probabilities, are all concerned simply to ensure that our beliefs are not self-contradictory. We put before ourselves the standard of consistency and construct these elaborate rules to ensure its observance. But this is obviously not enough ; we want our beliefs to be consistent not merely with one another but also with the facts [1] : nor is it even clear that consistency is always advantageous ; it may well be better to be sometimes right than never right. Nor when we wish to be consistent are we always able to be : there are mathematical propositions whose truth or falsity cannot as yet be decided. Yet it may humanly speaking be right to entertain a certain degree of belief in them on inductive or other grounds : a logic which proposes to justify such a degree of belief must be prepared actually to go against formal logic ; for to a formal truth formal logic can only assign a belief of degree 1. We could prove in Mr Keynes' system that its probability is 1 on any evidence. This point seems to me to show particularly clearly that human logic or the logic of truth, which tells men how they should think, is not merely independent of but sometimes actually incompatible with formal logic.

In spite of this nearly all philosophical thought about human logic and especially induction has tried to reduce it in some way

[1] Cf. Kant : ' Denn obgleich eine Erkenntnis der logischen Form völlig gemäss sein möchte, dass ist sich selbst nicht widerspräche, so kann sie doch noch immer dem Gegenstande widersprechen.' *Kritik der reinen Vernunft*, First Edition, p. 59.

to formal logic. Not that it is supposed, except by a very few, that consistency will of itself lead to truth ; but consistency combined with observation and memory is frequently credited with this power.

Since an observation changes (in degree at least) my opinion about the fact observed, some of my degrees of belief after the observation are necessarily inconsistent with those I had before. We have therefore to explain how exactly the observation should modify my degrees of belief; obviously if p is the fact observed, my degree of belief in q after the observation should be equal to my degree of belief in q given p before, or by the multiplication law to the quotient of my degree of belief in pq by my degree of belief in p. When my degrees of belief change in this way we can say that they have been changed consistently by my observation.

By using this definition, or on Mr Keynes' system simply by using the multiplication law, we can take my present degrees of belief, and by considering the totality of my observations, discover from what initial degrees of belief my present ones would have arisen by this process of consistent change. My present degrees of belief can then be considered logically justified if the corresponding initial degrees of belief are logically justified. But to ask what initial degrees of belief are justified, or in Mr Keynes' system what are the absolutely *a priori* probabilities, seems to me a meaningless question ; and even if it had a meaning I do not see how it could be answered.

If we actually applied this process to a human being, found out, that is to say, on what *a priori* probabilities his present opinions could be based, we should obviously find them to be ones determined by natural selection, with a general tendency to give a higher probability to the simpler alternatives. But, as I say, I cannot see what could be meant by asking whether these degrees of belief were logically justified. Obviously the best thing would be to know for certain in advance what was true and what false, and therefore if any one system of initial beliefs is to receive the philosopher's approbation it should be this one. But clearly this would not be accepted by thinkers of the school I am criticising. Another alternative is to apportion initial probabilities on the purely formal system expounded by Wittgenstein, but as this gives no justification for induction it cannot give us the human logic which we are looking for.

Let us therefore try to get an idea of a human logic which shall not attempt to be reducible to formal logic. Logic, we may agree, is concerned not with what men actually believe, but what they ought to believe, or what it would be reasonable to believe. What then, we must ask, is meant by saying that it is reasonable for a man to have such and such a degree of belief in a proposition ? Let us consider possible alternatives.

First, it sometimes means something explicable in terms of formal logic : this possibility for reasons already explained we may dismiss. Secondly, it sometimes means simply that were I in his place (and not e.g. drunk) I should have such a degree of belief. Thirdly, it sometimes means that if his mind worked according to certain rules, which we may roughly call 'scientific method', he would have such a degree of belief. But fourthly it need mean none of these things ; for men have not always believed in scientific method, and just as we ask 'But am I necessarily reasonable', we can also ask 'But is the scientist necessarily reasonable ? ' In this ultimate meaning it seems to me that we can identify reasonable opinion with the opinion of an ideal person in similar circumstances. What, however, would this ideal person's opinion be ? As has previously been remarked, the highest ideal would be always to have a true opinion and be certain of it ; but this ideal is more suited to God than to man.[1]

We have therefore to consider the human mind and what is the most we can ask of it.[2] The human mind works essentially according to general rules or habits ; a process of thought not proceeding according to some rule would simply be a random sequence of ideas ; whenever we infer *A* from *B* we do so in virtue of some relation between them. We can therefore state the problem of the ideal as " What habits in a general sense would it be best for the human mind to have ? " This is a large and vague question which could hardly be answered unless the possibilities were first limited by a fairly definite conception of human nature. We could imagine some very useful habits unlike those possessed by any men. [It must be explained that I use habit in the most general possible sense to mean simply rule or law of behaviour, including instinct : I do not wish to distinguish acquired

---

[1] [Earlier draft of matter of preceding paragraph in some ways better.—F.P.R.

What is meant by saying that a degree of belief is reasonable ? First and often that it is what I should entertain if I had the opinions of the person in question at the time but was otherwise as I am now, e.g. not drunk. But sometimes we go beyond this and ask : ' Am I reasonable ? ' This may mean, do I conform to certain enumerable standards which we call scientific method, and which we value on account of those who practise them and the success they achieve. In this sense to be reasonable means to think like a scientist, or to be guided only be ratiocination and induction or something of the sort (i.e. reasonable means reflective). Thirdly, we may go to the root of why we admire the scientist and criticize not primarily an individual opinion but a mental habit as being conducive or otherwise to the discovery of truth or to entertaining such degrees of belief as will be most useful. (To include habits of doubt or partial belief.) Then we can criticize an opinion according to the habit which produced it. This is clearly right because it all depends on this habit ; it would not be reasonable to get the right conclusion to a syllogism by remembering vaguely that you leave out a term which is common to both premisses.

We use reasonable in sense 1 when we say of an argument of a scientist this does not seem to me reasonable ; in sense 2 when we *contrast* reason and superstition or instinct ; in sense 3 when we *estimate* the value of new methods of thought such as soothsaying.]

[2] What follows to the end of the section is almost entirely based on the writings of C. S. Peirce. [Especially his "Illustrations of the Logic of Science", *Popular Science Monthly*, 1877 and 1878, reprinted in *Chance Love and Logic* (1923).]

rules or habits in the narrow sense from innate rules or instincts, but propose to call them all habits alike.] A completely general criticism of the human mind is therefore bound to be vague and futile, but something useful can be said if we limit the subject in the following way.

Let us take a habit of forming opinion in a certain way ; e.g. the habit of proceeding from the opinion that a toadstool is yellow to the opinion that it is unwholesome. Then we can accept the fact that the person has a habit of this sort, and ask merely what degree of opinion that the toadstool is unwholesome it would be best for him to entertain when he sees it ; i.e. granting that he is going to think always in the same way about all yellow toadstools, we can ask what degree of confidence it would be best for him to have that they are unwholesome. And the answer is that it will in general be best for his degree of belief that a yellow toadstool is unwholesome to be equal to the proportion of yellow toadstools which are in fact unwholesome. (This follows from the meaning of degree of belief.) This conclusion is necessarily vague in regard to the spatio-temporal range of toadstools which it includes, but hardly vaguer than the question which it answers. (Cf. density at a point of gas composed of molecules.)

Let us put it in another way : whenever I make an inference, I do so according to some rule or habit. An inference is not completely given when we are given the premiss and conclusion ; we require also to be given the relation between them in virtue of which the inference is made. The mind works by general laws ; therefore if it infers q from p, this will generally be because q is an instance of a function ϕx and p the corresponding instance of a function ψx such that the mind would always infer ϕx from ψx. When therefore we criticize not opinions but the processes by which they are formed, the rule of the inference determines for us a range to which the frequency theory can be applied. The rule of the inference may be narrow, as when seeing lightning I expect thunder, or wide, as when considering 99 instances of a generalization which I have observed to be true I conclude that the 100th is true also. In the first case the habit which determines the process is ' After lightning expect thunder ' ; the degree of expectation which it would be best for this habit to produce is equal to the proportion of cases of lightning which are actually followed by thunder. In the second case the habit is the more general one of inferring from 99 observed instances of a certain sort of generalization that the 100th instance is true also ; the degree of belief it would be best for this habit to produce is equal to the proportion of all cases of 99 instances of a generalization being true, in which the 100th is true also.

Thus given a single opinion, we can only praise or blame it on the ground of truth or falsity : given a habit of a certain form, we can praise or blame it accordingly as the degree of belief it produces is near or far from the actual proportion in which the habit leads to truth. We can then praise or blame opinions derivatively from our praise or blame of the habits that produce them.

This account can be applied not only to habits of inference but also to habits of observation and memory ; when we have a certain feeling in connection with an image we think the image represents something which actually happened to us, but we may not be sure about it ; the degree of direct confidence in our memory varies. If we ask what is the best degree of confidence to place in a certain specific memory feeling, the answer must depend on how often when that feeling occurs the event whose image it attaches to has actually taken place.

Among the habits of the human mind a position of peculiar importance is occupied by induction. Since the time of Hume a great deal has been written about the justification for inductive inference. Hume showed that it could not be reduced to deductive inference or justified by formal logic. So far as it goes his demonstration seems to me final ; and the suggestion of Mr Keynes that it can be got round by regarding induction as a form of probable inference cannot in my view be maintained. But to suppose that the situation which results from this is a scandal to philosophy is, I think, a mistake.

We are all convinced by inductive arguments, and our conviction is reasonable because the world is so constituted that inductive arguments lead on the whole to true opinions. We are not, therefore, able to help trusting induction, nor if we could help it do we see any reason why we should, because we believe it to be a reliable process. It is true that if any one has not the habit of induction, we cannot prove to him that he is wrong ; but there is nothing peculiar in that. If a man doubts his memory or his perception we cannot prove to him that they are trustworthy ; to ask for such a thing to be proved is to cry for the moon, and the same is true of induction. It is one of the ultimate sources of knowledge just as memory is : no one regards it as a scandal to philosophy that there is no proof that the world did not begin two minutes ago and that all our memories are not illusory.

We all agree that a man who did not make inductions would be unreasonable: the question is only what this means. In my view it does not mean that the man would in any way sin against formal logic or formal probability; but that he had not got a very useful habit, without which he would be very much worse off, in the sense of being much less likely [1] to have true opinions.

This is a kind of pragmatism : we judge mental habits by whether they work, i.e. whether the opinions they lead

---

[1] ' Likely ' here simply means that I am not sure of this, but only have a certain degree of belief in it.

to are for the most part true, or more often true than those which alternative habits would lead to.

Induction is such a useful habit, and so to adopt it is reasonable. All that philosophy can do is to analyse it, determine the degree of its utility, and find on what characteristics of nature this depends. An indispensable means for investigating these problems is induction itself, without which we should be helpless. In this circle lies nothing vicious. It is only through memory that we can determine the degree of accuracy of memory ; for if we make experiments to determine this effect, they will be useless unless we remember them.

Let us consider in the light of the preceding discussion what sort of subject is inductive or human logic—the logic of truth. Its business is to consider methods of thought, and discover what degree of confidence should be placed in them, i.e. in what proportion of cases they lead to truth. In this investigation it can only be distinguished from the natural sciences by the greater generality of its problems. It has to consider the relative validity of different types of scientific procedure, such as the search for a causal law by Mill's Methods, and the modern mathematical methods like the *a priori* arguments used in discovering the Theory of Relativity. The proper plan of such a subject is to be found in Mill[1]; I do not mean the details of his Methods or even his use of the Law of Causality. But his way of treating the subject as a body of inductions about inductions, the Law of Causality governing lesser laws and being itself proved by induction by simple enumeration. The different scientific methods that can be used are in the last resort judged by induction by simple enumeration ; we choose the simplest law that fits the facts, but unless we found that laws so obtained also fitted facts other than those they were made to fit, we should discard this procedure for some other.

[1] Cf. also the account of ' general rules ' in the Chapter ' Of Unphilosophical Probability ' in Hume's *Treatise*.

C. PROBABILITY AND PARTIAL BELIEF

The defect of my paper on probability was that it took partial belief as a psychological phenomenon to be defined and measured by a psychologist. But this sort of psychology goes a very little way and would be quite unacceptable in a developed science. In fact the notion of a belief of degree $\frac{2}{3}$ is useless to an outside observer, except when it is used by the thinker himself who says ' Well, I believe it to an extent $\frac{2}{3}$ ', i.e. (this at least is the most natural interpretation) ' I have the same degree of belief in it as in $p\text{v}q$ when I think p, q, r equally likely and know that exactly one of them is true.' Now what is the point of this numerical comparison ? how is the number used ? In a great many cases it is used simply as a basis for getting further numbers of the same sort issuing finally in one so near 0 or 1 that it is taken to be 0 or 1 and the partial belief to be full belief. But sometimes the number is used itself in making a practical decision. How ? I want to say in accordance with the law of mathematical expectation; but I cannot do this, for we could only use that rule if we had measured goods and bads. But perhaps in some sort of way we approximate to it, as we are supposed in economics to maximize an unmeasured utility. The question also arises why just this law of mathematical expectation. The answer to this is that if we use probability to measure utility, as explained in my paper, then consistency requires just this law. Of course if utility were measured in any other way, e.g. in money, we should not use mathematical expectation.

If there is no meaning in equal differences of utility, then money is as good a way as any of measuring them. A meaning may, however, be given by our probability method, or by means of time : i.e. $x-y = y-z$ if x for 1 day and z for 1 day $= y$ for 2 days. But the periods must be long or associated with different lives or people to prevent mutual influence. Do these two methods come to the same thing? Could we prove it by Bernoulli? Obviously not; Bernoulli only evaluates chances. A man might regard 1 good and 1 bad as equal to 2 neutral; but regard 2 bad as simply awful, not worth taking any chance of. (But it could be made up! No, there would be a chance of its not being.) I think this shows my method of measuring to be the sounder; it alone goes for *wholes*.

All this is just an idea; what sense is there really in it? We can, I think, say this :—

A *theory* is a set of propositions which contains (p and q) whenever it contains p and q, and if it contains any p contains all its logical consequences. The *interest* of such sets comes from the possibility of our adopting one of them as all we believe.

A *probability-theory* is a set of numbers associated with pairs of propositions obeying the calculus of probabilities. The *interest* of such a set comes from the possibility of acting on it consistently.

Of course, the mathematician is only concerned with the form of probability; it is quite true that he only deals in certainties.

REASONABLE DEGREE OF BELIEF (1928)

When we pass beyond reasonable = my, or = scientific, to define it precisely is quite impossible. Following Peirce we predicate it of a habit not of an individual judgment. Roughly, reasonable degree of belief = proportion of cases in which habit leads to truth. But in trying to be more exact we encounter the following difficulties :—

(1) We cannot always take the actual habit : this may be correctly derived from some previous accidentally misleading experience. We then look to wider habit of forming such a habit.

(2) We cannot take proportion of *actual* cases ; e.g. in a card game very rarely played, so that of the particular combination in question there are very few actual instances.

(3) We sometimes really assume a *theory* of the world with laws and chances, and mean not the proportion of actual cases but what is chance on our theory.

(4) But it might be argued that this complication was not necessary on account of (1) by which we only consider very general habits of which there are so many instances that, if chance on our theory differed from the actual proportion, our theory would have to be wrong.

(5) Also in an ultimate case like induction, there could be no *chance* for it : it is not the sort of thing that has a chance.

Fortunately there is no point in fixing on a precise sense of ' reasonable ' ; this could only be required for one of two reasons : either because the reasonable was the subject-matter of a science (which is not the case) ; or because it helped us to be reasonable to know what reasonableness is (which it does not, though some false notions might hinder us). To make clear that it is not needed for either of these purposes we must consider (1) the content of logic

and   (2) the utility of logic.

THE CONTENT OF LOGIC

(1) Preliminary philosophico-psychological investigation into nature of thought, truth and reasonableness.

(2) Formulae for formal inference = mathematics.

(3) Hints for avoiding confusion (belongs to medical psychology).

(4) Outline of most general propositions known or used as habits of inference from an abstract point of view ; either crudely inductive, as ' Mathematical method has solved all these other problems, therefore . . .', or else systematic, when it is called metaphysics. All this might anyhow be called metaphysics ; but it is regarded as logic when adduced as bearing on an unsolved problem, not simply as information interesting for its own sake.

The only one of these which is a distinct science is evidently (2).

THE UTILITY OF LOGIC

That of (1) above and of (3) are evident : the interesting ones are (2) and (4). (2) = mathematics is indispensable for manipulating and systematizing our knowledge. Besides this (2) and (4) help us in some way in coming to conclusions in judgment.

Logic as Self-Control (Cf. Peirce)

Self-control in general means either

(1) not acting on the temporarily uppermost desire, but stopping to think it out ; i.e. pay regard to all desires and see which is really stronger ; its value is to eliminate inconsistency in action ;

or (2) forming as a result of a decision habits of acting not in response to temporary desire or stimulus but in a definite way adjusted to permanent desire.

The difference is that in (1) we stop to think it out but in (2) we've thought it out before and only stop to do what we had previously decided to do.

So also logic enables us

(1) Not to form a judgment on the evidence immediately before us, but to stop and think of all else that we know in any way relevant. It enables us not to be inconsistent, and also to pay regard to very general facts, e.g. all crows I've seen are black, so this one will be—No ; colour is in such and such other species a variable quality. Also e.g. not merely to argue from $\phi a \cdot \phi b \ldots$ to $(x) \cdot \phi x$ probable, but to consider the bearing of $a, b \ldots$ are the class I've seen (and visible ones are specially likely or unlikely to be ϕ). This difference between *biassed* and *random* selection. [1]

(2) To form certain fixed habits of procedure or interpretation only revised at intervals when we think things out. In this it is the same as any general judgment ; we should only regard the process as ' logic ' when it is very general, not e.g. to expect a woman to be unfaithful, but e.g. to disregard correlation coefficients with a probable error greater than themselves.

With regard to forming a judgment or a partial judgment

[1] *Vide infra* ' Chance '.

(which is a decision to have a belief of such a degree, i.e. to act in a certain way) we must note :—

(*a*) What we ask is '*p* ? ' not ' Would it be true to think *p* ? ' nor ' Would it be reasonable to think *p* ? ' (But these might be useful first steps.)

but (*b*) ' Would it be true to think *p* ? ' can never be settled without settling *p* to which it is equivalent.

(*c*) ' Would it be reasonable to think *p* ? ' means simply ' Is *p* what usually happens in such a case ? ' and is as vague as ' usually '. To put this question may help us, but it will often seem no easier to answer than *p* itself.

(*d*) Nor can the precise sense in which ' reasonable ' or ' usually ' can usefully be taken be laid down, nor weight assigned on any principle to different considerations of such a sort. E.g. the death-rate for men of 60 is $\frac{1}{10}$, but all the 20 red-haired 60-year-old men I've known have lived till 70. What should I expect of a new red-haired man of 60 ? I can but put the evidence before me, and let it act on my mind. There is a conflict of two ' usually's ' which must work itself out in my mind ; one is not the really reasonable, the other the really unreasonable.

(*e*) When, however, the evidence is very complicated, statistics are introduced to simplify it. They are to be chosen in such a way as to influence me as nearly as possible in the same way as would the whole facts they represent if I could apprehend them clearly. But this cannot altogether be reduced to a formula ; the rest of my knowledge may affect the matter ; thus *p* may be equivalent in influence to *q*, but not *ph* to *qh*.

(*f*) There are exceptional cases in which ' It would be reasonable to think *p* ' absolutely settles the matter. Thus if we are told that one of these people's names begins with A and that there are 8 of them, it is reasonable to believe to degree $\frac{1}{8}$th that any particular one's name begins with A, and this is what we should all do (unless we felt there was something else relevant).

(*g*) Nevertheless, to introduce the idea of ' reasonable ' is really a mistake ; it is better to say ' usually ', which makes clear the vagueness of the range : what is reasonable depends on what is taken as relevant ; *if we take enough as relevant*, whether it is reasonable to think *p* becomes at least as difficult a question as *p*. If we take everything as relevant, they are the same.

(*h*) What ought we to take as relevant ? Those sorts of things which it is useful to take as relevant ; if we could rely on being reasonable in regard to what we do take as relevant, this would mean everything. Otherwise it is impossible to say ; but the question is one asked by a spectator not by the thinker himself : if the thinker feels a thing relevant he can't dismiss it ; and if he feels it irrelevant he can't use it.

(*i*) Only then if we in fact feel very little to be relevant, do or can we answer the question by an appeal to what is reasonable, this being then equivalent to what we know and consider relevant.

(*j*) What are or are not taken as relevant are not only propositions but formal facts, e.g. $a = a$: we may react differently to ϕa than to any other ϕx not because of anything we know about a but e.g. for emotional reasons.

STATISTICS (1928)

The science of statistics is concerned with abbreviating facts about numerous individuals which are interpreted as a random selection from an infinite ' population '. If the qualities concerned are discrete, this means simply that we consider the proportions of the observed individuals which have the qualities, and ascribe these proportions to the hypothetical population. If the qualities are continuous, we take the population to be of a convenient simple form containing various parameters which are then chosen to give the highest probability to the instances observed. In either case the probable error is calculated for such a sample from such a population. (For all this see Fisher.) [1]

The significance of this procedure is that we record in a convenient simple form

(1) The approximate proportions having the given qualities in different degrees,

(2) The number of instances which we have observed (the weight of our induction) (probable error).

For the use of the figures to give a degree of belief with regard to a new instance no rule can be given.

The introduction of an infinite population is a stupid fiction, which cannot be defended except by some reference to proceeding to a limit, which destroys its sense. The procedure of calculating parameters by maximum likelihood and probable error can be defined as a process in pure mathematics ; its significance is in suggesting a theory or set

---

[1] R. A. Fisher," Theory of statistical estimation," *Proc. Camb. Phil. Soc.*, 22, pp. 700–725 (1925), and *Statistical Methods for Research Workers*.

of chances. Proportion of infinite population should be replaced by chance.

Of course the purpose is not always simple induction but causal analysis : we find the chances are not what we expect, therefore the die is biassed or people are more careful nowadays etc.

CHANCE (1928)

(1) There are no such things as objective chances in the sense in which some people imagine there are, e.g. N. Campbell, Nisbet.[1]

There is, for instance, no established fact of the form ' In n consecutive throws the number of heads lies between $\frac{n}{2} \pm \varepsilon(n)$ '. On the contrary we have good reason to believe that any such law would be broken if we took enough instances of it.

Nor is there any fact established empirically about infinite series of throws ; this formulation is only adopted to avoid contradiction by experience ; and what no experience can contradict, none can confirm, let alone establish.

(N. Campbell makes a simple mistake about this.)

A *crude* frequency theory is ruled out because it justifies the ' maturity of odds ' argument, e.g. in regard to sex of offspring.

(2) Hence chances must be defined by degrees of belief ; but they do not correspond to anyone's actual degrees of belief ; the chances of 1,000 heads, and of 999 heads followed by a tail, are equal, but everyone expects the former more than the latter.

(3) Chances are degrees of belief within a certain system of beliefs and degrees of belief ; not those of any actual person, but in a simplified system to which those of actual people, especially the speaker, in part approximate.

(4) This system of beliefs consists, firstly, of natural laws,

[1] R. H. Nisbet, "The Foundations of Probability," *Mind*, 1926.

which are in it believed for certain, although, of course, people are not really quite certain of them.

(5) Besides these the system contains various things of this sort : when knowing ψx and nothing else relevant, always expect ϕx with degree of belief p (what is or is not relevant is also specified in the system) ; which is also written the chance of ϕ given ψ is p (if $p = 1$ it is the same as a law). These chances together with the laws form a deductive system according to the rules of probability, and the actual beliefs of a user of the system should approximate to those deduced from a combination of the system and the particular knowledge of fact possessed by the user, this last being (inexactly) taken as certain.

(6) The chances in such a system must not be confounded with frequencies ; the chance of ϕx given ψx might be different even from the *known* frequency of ψ's which are ϕ's. E.g. the chance of a coin falling heads yesterday is $\frac{1}{2}$ since 'yesterday' is irrelevant, but the proportion that actually fell heads yesterday might be 1.

(7) It is, however, obvious that we are not armed with systems giving us a degree of belief in every possible proposition for any basis of factual knowledge. Our systems only cover part of the field ; and where we have no system we say we do not know the chances.

(8) The phenomena for which we have systematic chances are games of chance, births, deaths, and all sorts of correlation coefficients.

(9) What we mean by objective chance is not merely our having in our system a chance $\dfrac{\phi(x)}{\psi(x)}$, but our having no hope of modifying our system into a pair of laws $\alpha x . \psi x . \supset_x . \phi x :$ $\beta x . \psi x . \supset_x . \sim \phi x$, etc., where $\alpha x, \beta x$ are disjunctions of readily observable properties (previous in time to ϕx). This

105

occurs, as Poincaré points out,[1] when small causes produce large effects.

Chances are in another sense objective, in that everyone agrees about them, as opposed e.g. to odds on horses.

(10) What we mean by an event not being a coincidence, or not being due to chance, is that if we came to know it, it would make us no longer regard our system as satisfactory, although on our system the event may be no more improbable than any alternative. Thus 1,000 heads running would not be due to chance ; i.e. if we observed it we should change our system of chances for that penny. If it is called h, the chances in our system with h as hypothesis are markedly different from our actual degrees of belief in things given h.

By saying a thing is not due to chance, we only mean that our system of chances must be changed, not that it must become a system of laws. Thus for a biassed coin to come down heads is not due to chance even though it doesn't always do so ; e.g. chance may $= \frac{2}{3}$ say, not $\frac{1}{2}$.

If we say ' Our meeting was not due to chance ', i.e. *designed*, design is simply a factor modifying the chances ; it might also be e.g. that we walk in the same road.

(11) This is why N. Campbell thinks coincidences cannot be allowed to occur ; i.e. coincidences . $\supset$. system wrong, $\therefore$ system . $\supset$. no coincidences. Apparently formally conclusive ; but this is a mistake because the system is not a proposition which is true or false, but an imperfect approximation to a state of mind where imperfections can in certain circumstances become particularly glaring.

(12) By things being *ultimately* due to chance, we mean that there is no law (here generalization of no more than manageable complexity), known or unknown, which determines the future from the past. If we suppose further that they have ultimate

[1] See *Science et Hypothèse* and *Science et Méthode*.

chances, this means a sort of best possible system in which they have these chances.

(13) In choosing a system we have to compromise between two principles : subject always to the proviso that the system must not contradict any facts we know, we choose (other things being equal) the simplest system, and (other things being equal) we choose the system which gives the highest chance to the facts we have observed. This last is Fisher's ' Principle of Maximum Likelihood ', and gives the only method of verifying a system of chances.

(14) Probability in Physics means chance as here explained, with possibly some added complexity because we are concerned with a ' theory ' in Campbell's sense, not merely an ordinary system which is a generalization of Campbell's ' law. ' What chance in a theory is can hardly be explained until we know more about the nature of theories.[1]

(15) Statistical science must be briefly dealt with from our point of view ; it has three parts :—

(a) Collection and arrangement of selections from multitudinous data.

(b) Induction = forming a system of chances from the data by means of the Principle of Maximum Likelihood.

(c) Causal analysis ; e.g. this die falls so often this way up, therefore its centre of gravity must be displaced towards the opposite face.

(16) The only difficulty presented is in connection with (c) causal analysis, in which we seem to take a statement of chances as a fact, and to argue ' Its falling so often six is not due to chance ' ∴ ' chance $> \frac{1}{6}$ ' ∴ ' c.g. displaced '. Reasoning which seems incompatible with our solution of the paradox that chance $= \frac{1}{6}$ is inconsistent with this coincidence, which was that ' chance $= \frac{1}{6}$ ', ' chance $> \frac{1}{6}$ ', were not propositions

[1] [See Chapter 6].

and so could not serve as premisses or conclusions of arguments.

(17) The difficulty is removed by the reflection that the system we are ultimately using not only gives us degree of belief or chance of x falling six given x is tossed $= \frac{1}{6}$, but also that that of x falling six given x is tossed and biassed $> \frac{1}{6}$. Consequently by transposition x is biassed / x falls six. x is tossed $> x$ is biassed / x is tossed. If $a/bh > a/h$, then $b/ah > b/h$, and this is how we are arguing. The chance of a x falling six is p seems to be treated as a genuine proposition, but what is really meant is an *unexpressed condition*, which on our system when added to the hypothesis makes the chance p.

(18) We can state it this way : statistical causal analysis presupposes a fundamental system within which it moves and which it leaves unchanged ; this neither is nor appears to be treated like a proposition. What appears to be so treated is a narrower system derived or derivable from the fundamental system by the addition of an empirical premiss, and what is really treated as a proposition and modified or rejected is not the narrower system but the empirical premiss on which it is based.

Of course this empirical premiss may be unknown or very vaguely known ; e.g. I conclude from the fact that more boys are born than girls to some superiority in the number, mobility or capacity for fertilization of male-bearing spermatazoa or one of a thousand other possible causes, because by the Principle of Indifference, which is part of my fundamental system, the observed inequality would be so unlikely if there were no such difference. But there seems no fundamental difference between this case and the biassed coin.

(19) Note on Poincaré's problem ' Why are chance events subject to law ? ' The fundamental answer to this is that they are not, taking the whole field of chance events no generalizations about them are possible (consider e.g. infectious diseases,

dactyls in hexameters, deaths from horse kicks, births of great men).

Poincaré says it is paradoxical that the actuary can from ignorance derive so easily such useful conclusions whereas if he knew the laws of health he would have to go through endless calculations. In fact it is not from ignorance that he works, but from experience of frequencies.

(20) Note on ' random '.

Keynes [1] gives a substantially correct account of this. But

(a) It is essential to bring in the notion of a description. What we want is not a is a random member of $\hat{x}(Sx)$ for the purpose of ϕx, but the description $(\imath x)(\psi x)$ is a random description when $x = (\imath x)(\psi x)$ is irrelevant to $\phi x/Sx \cdot h$.

(b) It is essential to extend the term to cover not merely a selection of one term but of many; thus, $\psi \hat{x}$ gives a random selection of n S's with regard to $\phi \hat{x}$ means $a = \hat{x}(\psi x)$ is irrelevant to probabilities of the form : Proportion of a which is $\phi = \lambda/a\epsilon n \cdot a \subset \hat{x}(Sx) \cdot h$.

The idea of random selection is useful in induction, where the value of the argument ' A proportion λ of ψS's are ϕ's ' $\therefore$ ' A proportion λ of S's are ϕ's ' depends on whether ψ is a random selector. If $\lambda = 1$ of course the value of the argument is strengthened if ψ is biassed against ϕ, weakened if ψ is biassed in favour of it.

---

[1] *Treatise on Probability*, p. 291.

5

KNOWLEDGE (1929)

I have always said that a belief was knowledge if it was (i) true, (ii) certain, (iii) obtained by a reliable process. But the word ' process ' is very unsatisfactory ; we can call inference a process, but even then unreliable seems to refer only to a fallacious method not to a false premiss as it is supposed to do. Can we say that a memory is obtained by a reliable process ? I think perhaps we can if we mean the causal process connecting what happens with my remembering it. We might then say, a belief obtained by a reliable process must be caused by what are not beliefs in a way or with accompaniments that can be more or less relied on to give true beliefs, and if in this train of causation occur other intermediary beliefs these must all be true ones.

E.g. ' Is telepathy knowledge ? ' may mean : (*a*) Taking it there is such a process, can it be relied on to create true beliefs in the telepathee (within some limits, e.g. when what is believed is about the telepathee's thoughts) ? or (*b*) Supposing we are agnostic, does the feeling of being telepathed to guarantee truth ? Ditto for female intuition, impressions of character, etc. Perhaps we should say not (iii) obtained by a reliable process, but (iii) formed in a reliable way.

We say ' I know ', however, whenever we are certain, without reflecting on reliability. But if we did reflect then we should remain certain if, and only if, we thought our way reliable. (Supposing us to know it ; if not, taking it merely as described it would be the same, e.g. God put it into my mind : a supposedly reliable process.) For to think the way reliable is simply to formulate in a variable hypothetical the habit of following the way.

One more thing. Russell says in his *Problems of Philosophy* that there is no doubt that we are sometimes mistaken, so that all our knowledge is infected with some degree of doubt. Moore used to deny this, saying of course it was self-contradictory, which is mere pedantry and ignoration of the kind of knowledge meant.

But substantially the point is this: we cannot without self-contradiction say p and q and r and . . . and one of p, q, r . . . is false. (N.B.—We know what we know, otherwise there would not be a contradiction). But we can be nearly certain that one is false and yet nearly certain of each; but p, q, r are then infected with doubt. But Moore is right in saying that not necessarily all are so infected; but if we exempt some, we shall probably become fairly clear that one of the exempted is probably wrong, and so on.

6

THEORIES (1929)

Let us try to describe a theory simply as a language for discussing the facts the theory is said to explain. This need not commit us on the philosophical question of whether a theory is only a language, but rather if we knew what sort of language it would be if it were one at all, we might be further towards discovering if it is one. We must try to make our account as general as possible, but we cannot be sure that we have in fact reached the most general type of theory, since the possible complication is infinite.

First, let us consider the facts to be explained. These occur in a universe of discourse which we will call the *primary system*, this system being composed of all the terms [1] and propositions (true or false) in the universe in question. We must suppose the primary system in some way given to us so that we have a notation capable of expressing every proposition in it. Of what sort must this notation be?

It might in the first case consist of names of different types any two or more of which conjoined together gave an atomic proposition; for instance, the names $a, b \ldots z$, ' red ', ' before '. But I think the systems we try to explain are rarely of this kind; if for instance we are concerned with a series of experiences, we do not try to explain their time order (which we could not explain by anything simpler) or

---

[1] The ' universe ' of the primary system might contain ' blue or red ' but not ' blue ' or ' red '; i.e. we might be out to explain when a thing was ' blue or red ' as opposed to ' green or yellow ', but not which it was, blue or red. ' Blue-or-red ' would then be a term: ' blue ', ' red ' nonsense for our present purpose.

even, assuming *an* order, whether it is *a* or *b* that comes first ; we take for granted that they are in order and that *a* comes before *b*, etc., and try to explain which is red, which blue, etc. *a* is essentially one before *b*, and ' *a* ', ' *b* ', etc., are not really names but descriptions except in the case of the present. We take it for granted that these descriptions describe uniquely, and instead of ' *a* was red ' we have e.g. ' The 3rd one ago was red '. The symbols we want are not names but numbers : the 0th (i.e. the present), 1st, –1th, etc., in general the nth, and we can use red (n) to mean the nth is red counting forward or backward from a particular place. If the series terminates at say 100, we could write $N(101)$, and generally $N(m)$ if $m > 100$, meaning ' There is no mth ' ; or else simply regard e.g. red (m) as nonsense if $m > 100$, whereas if we wrote $N(m)$ we should say red (m) was false. I am not sure this is necessary, but it seems to me always so in practice ; i.e. the terms of our primary system have a structure, and any structure can be represented by numbers (or pairs or other combinations of numbers).

It may be possible to go further than this, for of the terms in our primary system not merely some but even all may be best symbolized by numbers. For instance, colours have a structure, in which any given colour may be assigned a place by three numbers, and so on. Even smells may be so treated : the presence of the smell being denoted by 1, the absence by 0 (or all total smell qualities may be given numbers). Of course, we cannot make a proposition out of numbers without some link. Moment 3 has colour 1 and smell 2 must be written $\chi(3) = 1$ and $\phi(3) = 2$, χ and ϕ corresponding to the general forms of colour and smell, and possibly being functions with a limited number of values, so that e.g. $\phi(3) = 55$ might be nonsense, since there was no 55th smell.

Whether or no this is possible, it is not so advantageous where we have relatively few terms (e.g. a few smells) to deal with. Where we have a multitude as e.g. with times, we cannot name them, and our theory will not explain a primary system in which they have names, for it will take no account of their individuality but only of their position. In general nothing is gained and clarity may be lost by using numbers when the order, etc., of the numbers corresponds to nothing in the nature of the terms.

If all terms were represented by numbers, the propositions of the primary system would all take the form of assertions about the values taken by certain one–valued numerical functions. These would not be mathematical functions in the ordinary sense ; for that such a function had such-and-such a value would always be a matter of fact, not a matter of mathematics.

We have spoken as if the numbers involved were always integers, and if the finitists are right this must indeed be so in the ultimate primary system, though the integers may, of course, take the form of rationals. This means we may be concerned with pairs (m, n) with $(\lambda m, \lambda n)$ always identical to (m, n). If, however, our primary system is already a secondary system from some other theory, real numbers may well occur.

So much for the primary system ; now for the theoretical construction.

We will begin by taking a typical form of theory, and consider later whether or not this form is the most general. Suppose the atomic propositions of our primary system are such as $A(n), B(m, n)$ . . . where m, n, etc., take positive or negative integral values subject to any restrictions, e.g. that in $B(m, n)$ m may only take the values 1, 2.

Then we introduce new propositional functions $\alpha(n)$, $\beta(n)$, $\gamma(m, n)$, etc., and by propositions of the *secondary system* we shall mean any truth-functions of the values of α, β, γ, etc. We shall also lay down propositions about these values, e.g. $(n). \overline{\alpha(n). \beta(n)}$ which we shall call *axioms*, and whatever propositions of the secondary system can be deduced from the axioms we shall call *theorems*.

Besides this we shall make a *dictionary* which takes the form of a series of definitions of the functions of the primary system $A, B, C. \ldots$ in terms of those of the secondary system α, β, γ, e.g. $A(n) = \alpha(n) \cdot \mathbf{v} \cdot \gamma(O, n^2)$. By taking these ' definitions ' as equivalences and adding them to the axioms we may be able to deduce propositions in the primary system which we shall call *laws* if they are general propositions, *consequences* if they are singular. The totality of laws and consequences will be the eliminant when $\alpha, \beta, \gamma \ . \ .$, etc., are eliminated from the dictionary and axioms, and it is this totality of laws and consequences which our theory asserts to be true.

We may make this clearer by an example [1] ; let us interpret numbers n, n_1, n_2, etc.. as instants of time and suppose the primary system to contain the following functions :—

$A(n) =$ I see blue at n.

$B(n) =$ I see red at n.

$[\bar{A}(n) \cdot \bar{B}(n) =$ I see nothing at n].

$C(n) =$ Between n–1 and n I feel my eyes open.

$D(n) =$ Between n–1 and n I feel my eyes shut.

$E(n) =$ I move forward a step at n.

$F(n) =$ I move backward a step at n.

and that we construct a theory in the following way :

[1] [The example *seems* futile, therefore try to invent a better ; but it in fact brings out several good points, which it would be difficult otherwise to bring out. It may however niiss some points which we will consider later. A defect in all Nicod's examples is that they do not give an external world in which anything *happens*.—F. P. R.]

First m will be understood to take only the values **1, 2, 3,**

and $f(m)$ is defined by $\begin{cases} f(1) = 2 \\ f(2) = 3 \\ f(3) = 1 \end{cases}$

Then we introduce

$a(n, m)$ = At time n I am at place m.

$\beta(n, m)$ = At time n place m is blue.

$\gamma(n)$ = At time n my eyes are open.

And the axioms

$(n, m, m'):$ $\quad a(n, m) \cdot a(n, m') \cdot \supset \cdot m = m'.$

$(n).$ $\quad (\exists m). \quad a(n, m).$

$(n).$ $\quad \beta(n, 1).$

$(n):$ $\quad \beta(n, 2) . \equiv . \bar{\beta}(n + 1, 2).$

And the dictionary

$A(n) = (\exists m) \cdot a(n, m) \cdot \beta(n, m) \cdot \gamma(n).$

$B(n) = (\exists m) \cdot a(n, m) \cdot \bar{\beta}(n, m) \cdot \gamma(n).$

$C(n) = \bar{\gamma}(n - 1) \cdot \gamma(n).$

$D(n) = \gamma(n - 1) \cdot \bar{\gamma}(n).$

$E(n) = (\exists m) \cdot a(n - 1, m) \cdot a\{n, f(m)\}.$

$F(n) = (\exists m) \cdot a\{n - 1, f(m)\} \cdot a(n, m).$

This theory can be said to represent me as moving among 3 places, ' forwards ' being in the sense $ABCA$, ' backwards ' $ACBA$. Place A is always blue, place B alternately blue and red, place C blue or red according to a law I have not discovered. If my eyes are open I see the colour of the place

I am in, if they are shut I see no colour. The laws resulting from the theory can be expressed as follows :

(1) $(n) . \{\bar{A}(n) \vee \bar{B}(n)\} : \{\bar{C}(n) \vee \bar{D}(n)\} . \{\bar{E}(n) \vee \bar{F}(n)\}$

(2) $(n_1, n_2) \{n_1 > n_2 . C(n_1) . C(n_2) . \supset . (\exists n_3) . n_1 > n_3 > n_2 . D(n_3)\}$

(2^1) (2) with the C's and D's interchanged

Let us define 0 (n_1, n_2) to mean
$$\begin{matrix} 1 \\ 2 \end{matrix}$$

$$Nc' \ \hat{\nu} \{n_1 < \nu \leqslant n_2 . E(\nu)\}$$

$$-Nc' \ \hat{\nu} \{n_1 < \nu \leqslant n_2 . F(\nu)\} \equiv 0 \ (\mathrm{mod} \ 3)$$
$$\begin{matrix} 1 \\ 2 \end{matrix}$$

(3) $[(\exists n_1) . C(n_1) . n_1 \leqslant n . n \geqslant \nu > n_1 . \supset_\nu . \dot{D}(\nu)] \supset_n :$ $A(n) \vee B(n)$

(4) $[(\exists n_1) . D(n_1) . n_1 \leqslant n . n \geqslant \nu \geqslant n_1 . \supset_\nu . \dot{C}(\nu)] \supset_n :$ $\bar{A}(n) . \bar{B}(n).$

(5) $(n) :. (\exists m) : m = 0, 1, \text{ or } 2 : m(\nu, n) \supset_\nu \bar{B}(\nu)$

$: (m-1) \ (\nu_1, n) . (m-1) \ (\nu_2, n) . \nu_1 \not\equiv \nu_2 \ (\mathrm{mod} \ 2)$

$. \supset_{\nu_1, \nu_2} . \bar{A}(\nu_1) \vee \bar{A}(\nu_2) . \bar{B}(\nu_1) \vee \bar{B}(\nu_2).$

[Where $0 - 1 = 2$ for this purpose.]

These can then be compared with the axioms and dictionary, and there is no doubt that to the normal mind the axioms and dictionary give the laws in a more manageable form.

Let us now put it all into mathematics by writing

$$A(n) \qquad \text{as } \phi(n) = 1$$

$$B(n) \qquad \text{as } \phi(n) = -1$$

$$\bar{A}(n) . \bar{B}(n) \text{ as } \phi(n) = 0$$
$$C(n) \qquad \text{as } \chi(n) = 1$$
$$D(n) \qquad \text{as } \chi(n) = -1$$
$$\bar{C}(n) . \bar{D}(n) \text{ as } \chi(n) = 0$$
$$E(n) \qquad \text{as } \psi(n) = 1$$
$$F(n) \qquad \text{as } \psi(n) = -1$$
$$\bar{E}(n) \ \bar{F}(n) \text{ as } \psi(n) = 0.$$

Instead of $a(n, m)$ have $a(n)$ a function taking values $1, 2, 3$

$\beta(n, m)$	,,	$\beta(n, m)$	,,	,,	$1, -1$
$\gamma(n)$		$\gamma(n)$			$1, 0$

Our axioms are just

(1) $(n) . a(n) = 1 \vee 2 \vee 3$

(2) $(n) . \beta(n, 1) = 1$

(3) $(n) . \beta(n, 2) \neq \beta(n + 1, 2)$

(4) $(n, m) . \beta(n, m) = 1 \vee -1$

(5) $(n) . \gamma(n) = 0 \vee 1$

Of these (1) (4) (5) hardly count since they merely say what values the functions are capable of taking.

Our definitions become.

(i) $\phi(n) = \gamma(n) \times \beta\{n, a(n)\}$

(ii) $\chi(n) = \gamma(n) - \gamma(n - 1)$

(iii) $\psi(n) = $ Remainder mod 3 of $a(n) - a(n - 1)$

Our laws are of course that ϕ, χ, ψ must be such that a, β, γ can be found to satisfy 1–5, i–iii. Going through the old laws we have instead of

(1) $\phi(n) = -1 \vee 0 \vee 1, \chi(n) = -1 \vee 0 \vee 1, \psi(n) = -1 \vee 0 \vee 1$

[understood].

(2) $(n, m) \cdot \left| \sum\limits_{r=n}^{m} \chi(\nu) \right| \leqslant 1.$

(3) $(\exists m) \cdot \sum\limits_{r=m}^{n} \chi(r) = 1 : \supset_n : \phi(n) \neq 0.$

(4) $(\exists m) \cdot \sum\limits_{r=m}^{n} \chi(r) = -1 : \supset_n \cdot \phi(n) = 0.$

(5) $(n) :. (\exists m) : \sum\limits_{r=n}^{n'} \psi(r) \equiv m \ (\text{mod } 3) \cdot \supset_{n'} \cdot \phi(n') \neq -1$

$: \sum\limits_{r=n}^{n'} \psi(r) \equiv \sum\limits_{r=n}^{n''} \psi(r) \equiv m - 1 \ (\text{mod } 3). \ n' \equiv n'' + 1 \ (\text{mod } 2)$

$. \supset_{n', n''} \cdot \phi(n') \phi(n'') = 0 \ \text{v} - 1.$

So far we have only shown the genesis of *laws ; consequences* arise when we add to the axioms a proposition involving e.g. a particular value of n, from which we can deduce propositions in the primary system not of the form (n) . . . These we call the *consequences*.

If we take it in its mathematical form we can explain the idea of a theory as follows : Instead of saying simply what we know about the values of the functions with which we are concerned, we say that they can be constructed in a definite way given by the dictionary out of functions satisfying certain conditions given by the axioms.

Such then is an example of a theory ; before we go on to discuss systematically the different features of the example and whether they occur in any theory, let us take some questions that might be asked about theories and see how they would be answered in the present case.

1. Can we say anything in the language of this theory that we could not say without it ?

Obviously not ; for we can easily eliminate the functions of the second system and so say in the primary system all that the theory gives us.

119

2. Can we reproduce the structure of our theory by means of explicit definitions within the primary system ?

[This question is important because Russell, Whitehead, Nicod and Carnap all seem to suppose that we can and must do this.[1]]

Here there are some distinctions to make. We might, for instance, argue as follows. Supposing the laws and consequences to be true, the facts of the primary system must be such as to allow functions to be defined with all the properties of those of the secondary system, and these give the solution of our problem. But the trouble is that the laws and consequences can be made true by a number of different sets of facts, corresponding to each of which we might have different definitions. So that our problem of finding a single set of definitions which will make the dictionary and axioms true whenever the laws and consequences are true, is still unsolved. We can, however, at once solve it formally, by disjoining the sets of definitions previously obtained; i.e. if the different sets of facts satisfying the laws and consequences are P_1, P_2, P_3, and the corresponding definitions of $a(n, m)$ are

$$a(n, m) = L_1 \{A, B, C \ldots, n, m\}$$

$$L_2 \{A, B, C, \ldots, n, m\} \text{ etc.}$$

we make the definition

$$a(n, m) = P_1 \supset L_1 \{A, B, C \ldots n, m\}.$$

$$P_2 \supset L_2 \{A, B, C \ldots n, m\}.$$

etc.

Such a definition is formally valid and evidently fulfils our requirements.

[1] Jean Nicod, *La Géométrie dans le Monde Sensible* (1924), translated in his *Problems of Geometry and Induction* (1930) : Rudolf Carnap, *Der Logische Aufbau der Welt* (1928).

What can be objected to it is complexity and arbitrariness, since L_1, L_2 . . . can probably be chosen each in many ways.

Also it explicitly assumes that our primary system is finite and contains a definite number of assignable atomic propositions.

Let us therefore see what other ways there are of proceeding.

We might at first sight suppose that the key lay simply in the dictionary; this gives definitions of A, B, C . . . in terms of a, β, γ . . . Can we not invert it to get definitions of a, β, γ . . . in terms of A, B, C . . . ? Or, in the mathematical form, can we not solve the equations for a, β, γ . . . in terms of ϕ, χ, ψ . . ., at any rate if we add to the dictionary, as we legitimately can, those laws and axioms which merely state what values the functions are capable of taking ?

When, however, we look at these equations (i), (ii), (iii) what we find is this : If we neglect the limitations on the values of the functions they possess an integral solution provided $\gamma(n)$ can be found from (ii) so as always to be a factor of $\phi(n)$, i.e. in general always to be ± 1 or 0 and never to vanish unless $\phi(n)$ vanishes. This is, of course, only true in virtue of the conditions laid on ϕ and χ by the laws ; assuming these laws and the limitation on values, we get the solution

$$a(n) \equiv \sum_{o}^{n} \psi(n) + C_1 \pmod 3$$

$$\gamma(n) = \sum_{o}^{u} \chi(n) + C_2$$

for a and γ.

And for $\beta(n, m)$ no definite solution but e.g. the trivial one $\beta(n, m) = \phi(n)$ (assuming $\gamma(n) = 1$ or 0).

Here C_2 must be chosen so as to make $\gamma(n)$ always 1 or 0 ; and the value necessary for this purpose depends on the facts of the primary system and cannot be deduced simply from the laws. It must in fact be one or nought :

(a) If there is a least positive or zero n for which $\chi(n) \neq 0$, according as $\chi(n)$ for that n is -1 or $+1$.

(b) If there is a least negative n for which $\chi(n) \neq 0$, according as $\chi(n)$ for that n is $+1$ or -1.

(c) If for no n $\chi(n) \neq 0$ it does not matter whether C_2 is $+1$ or -1.

We thus have a disjunctive definition of C_2 and so of $\gamma(n)$. Again although any value of C_1 will satisfy the limitations on the value of $a(n)$, probably only one such will satisfy the *axioms*, and this value will again have to be disjunctively defined. And, thirdly, $\beta(n, m)$ is not at all fixed by the equations, and it will be a complicated matter in which we shall again have to distinguish cases, to say which of the many possible solutions for $\beta(n, m)$ will satisfy the axioms.

We conclude, therefore, that there is neither in this case nor in general any simple way of inverting the dictionary so as to get either a unique or an obviously preeminent solution which will also satisfy the axioms, the reason for this lying partly in difficulties of detail in the solution of the equations, partly in the fact that the secondary system has a higher multiplicity, i.e. more degrees of freedom, than the primary. In our case the primary system contains three one valued functions, the secondary virtually five [$\beta(n, 1)$, $\beta(n, 2)$, $\beta(n, 3)$, $a(n)$, $\gamma(n)$] each taking 2 or 3 values, and such an increase of multiplicity is, I think, a *universal* characteristic of useful theories.

Since, therefore, the dictionary alone does not suffice, the next hopeful method is to use both dictionary and axioms in a way which is referred to in many popular discussions of theories when it is said that the meaning of a proposition about the external world is what we should ordinarily regard as the *criterion* or *test* of its truth. This suggests that we should define propositions in the secondary system by their criteria in the primary.

In following this method we have first to distinguish the *sufficient* criterion of a proposition from its *necessary* criterion. If p is a proposition of the secondary system, we shall mean by its sufficient criterion, $\sigma(p)$, the disjunction of all propositions q of the primary system such that p is a logical consequence of q together with the dictionary and axioms, and such that $\sim q$ is not a consequence of the dictionary and axioms.[1] On the other hand, by the necessary criterion of p, $\tau(p)$ we shall mean the conjunction of all those propositions of the primary system which follow from p together with the dictionary and axioms.

We can elucidate the connection of $\sigma(p)$ and $\tau(p)$ as follows. Consider all truth-possibilities of atomic propositions in the primary system which are compatible with the dictionary and axioms. Denote such a truth-possibility by r, the dictionary and axioms by a. Then $\sigma(p)$ is the disjunction of every r such that

$$r \, \bar{p} \, a \text{ is a contradiction,}$$

$\tau(p)$ the disjunction of every r such that

$$r \, p \, a \text{ is not a contradiction.}$$

If we denote by L the totality of laws and consequences, i.e. the disjunction of every r here in question, then we have evidently

$$\sigma(p) : \equiv : L . \sim \tau(\sim p), \tag{i}$$

---

[1] The laws and consequences need not be added, since they follow from the dictionary and axioms. It might be thought, however, that we should take them *instead* of the axioms, but it is easy to see that this would merely increase the divergence between sufficient and necessary criteria and in general the difficulties of the method. The last clause could be put as that $\sim q$ must not follow from or be a law or consequence.

123

$$\tau\,(p) : \equiv : L \, . \sim \sigma(\sim p), \qquad\qquad \text{(ii)}$$

$$\sigma(p) \vee \tau\,(\sim p) \, . \equiv . \, L. \qquad\qquad \text{(iii)}$$

We have also

$$\sigma(p_1 \, . \, p_2) : \equiv : \sigma(p_1) \, . \, \sigma(p_2), \qquad\qquad \text{(iv)}$$

for $p_1 \, . \, p_2$ follows from q when and only when p_1 and p_2 both follow.

Whence, or similarly, we get the dual

$$\tau\,(p_1 \vee p_2) \, . \equiv . \, \tau\,(p_1) \vee \tau\,(p_2). \qquad\qquad \text{(v)}$$

We also have

$$\sigma(p) \supset \tau\,(p), \qquad\qquad \text{(vi)}$$

(Consider the r's above.)

$$\sigma(p) \vee \sigma(\sim p) \, . \supset . \, L \, . \supset . \, \tau\,(p) \vee \tau\,(\sim p), \qquad \text{(vii)}$$
$$\text{(from iii)}$$

and from (vi), (ii), (iii).

$$\sigma(p) \, . \supset . \sim \sigma(\sim p) \, . \, L, \qquad\qquad \text{(viii)}$$

$$L \, . \sim \tau\,(\sim p) \, . \supset . \, \tau\,(p). \qquad\qquad \text{(ix)}$$

Lastly we have

$$\sigma(p_1) \vee \sigma(p_2) \, . \supset . \, \sigma(p_1 \vee p_2). \qquad\qquad \text{(x)}$$

Since if q follows either from p_1 or from p_2 it follows from $p_1 \vee p_2$; and the dual

$$\tau(p_1 \, . \, p_2) \, . \supset . \, \tau\,(p_1) \, . \, \tau\,(p_2). \qquad\qquad \text{(xi)}$$

On the other hand, and this is a very important point, the converses of (vi)–(xi) are not in general true. Let us illustrate this by taking (x) and considering this ' r ' :

$$B(0) \, . \, \bar{A}(0) : n \neq 0 \, . \supset_n \, . \, \bar{A}(n) \, . \, \bar{B}(n).$$

124

$$C(n) \ . \ \equiv_n . \ n = 0 : D(n) \ . \ \equiv_n . \ n = 1.$$

$$(n) \ . \ \bar{E}n \ . \ \bar{F}n,$$

i.e. that the man's eyes are only open once when he sees blue. From this we can deduce $a(0, 2) \vee a(0, 3)$

$\therefore$ This $r \supset \sigma\{a(0, 2) \vee a(0, 3)\}$.

But we cannot deduce from it $a(0, 2)$ or $a(0, 3)$, since it is equally compatible with either. Hence neither $\sigma\{a(0, 2)\}$ nor $\sigma\{a(0, 3)\}$ is true. Hence we do not have

$$\sigma \ \{a(0, 2) \vee a(0, 3)\} \supset \sigma \ \{a(0, 2)\} \vee \sigma \ \{a(0, 3)\}.$$

It follows from this that we cannot give definitions such that, if p is any proposition of the secondary system, p will in virtue of the definitions mean $\sigma(p)$ [or alternatively $\tau (p)$], for if p_1 is defined to mean $\sigma(p_1)$, p_2 to mean $\sigma(p_2)$, $p_1 \vee p_2$ will mean $\sigma(p_1) \vee \sigma(p_2)$, which is not, in general, the same as $\sigma(p_1 \vee p_2)$. We can therefore only use σ to define some of the propositions of the secondary systems, what we might call *atomic* secondary propositions, from which the meanings of the others would follow.

For instance, taking our functions a, β, γ we could proceed as follows :

$\gamma(n)$ is defined as $A(n) \vee B(n)$, where there is no difficulty as $A(n) \vee B(n) \equiv \sigma\{\gamma(n)\} \equiv \tau \{\gamma(n)\}$.

$\beta(n, m)$ could be defined to mean $\sigma\{\beta(n, m)\}$, i.e. we should say place m was ' blue ' at time n, only if there were proof that it was. Otherwise we should say it was not 'blue' ('red' in common parlance).

$\bar{\beta}(n, m)$ would then mean $\bar{\sigma}\{\beta(n, m)\}$ not $\sigma\{\bar{\beta}(n, m)\}$.

Alternatively we could use τ, and define

$$\beta(n, m) \text{ to be } \tau \{\beta(n, m)\},$$

$$\text{and } \bar{\beta}(n, m) \text{ would be } \bar{\tau} \{\beta(n, m)\}$$

In this case we should say m was 'blue' whenever there was no proof that it was not; this could, however, have been achieved by means of σ if we had defined $\beta(n, m)$ to be $\sim \beta'(n, m)$, and $\beta'(n, m)$ to be $\sigma\{\beta'(n, m)\}$, i.e. applied σ to $\bar{\beta}$ instead of β.

In general it is clear that τ always gives what could be got from applying σ to the contradictory, and we may confine our attention to σ.

It makes, however, a real difference whether we define β or $\bar{\beta}$ by means of σ, especially in connection with place 3. For we have no law as to the values of $\beta(n, 3)$, nor any way of deducing one except when $a(n, 3)$ is true and $A(n)$ or $B(n)$ is true.

If we define $\beta(n, 3)$ to be $\sigma\{\beta(n, 3)\}$, we shall say that 3 is never blue except when we observe it to be; if we define $\bar{\beta}(n, 3)$ to be $\sigma\{\bar{\beta}(n, 3)\}$ we shall say it is always blue except when we observe it not to be.

Coming now to $a(n, m)$ we could define

$$a(n, 1) = \sigma\{a(n, 1)\},$$

$$a(n, 2) = \sigma\{a(n, 1) \vee a(n, 2)\} \cdot \bar{\sigma}\{a(n, 1)\},$$

$$a(n, 3) = \bar{\sigma}\{a(n, 1) \vee a(n, 2)\};$$

and we should for any n have one and only one of $a(n, 1)$, $a(n, 2)$, $a(n, 3)$ true: whereas if we simply put

$$a(n, m) = \sigma\{a(n, m)\},$$

this would not follow, since

$$\sigma\{a(n, 1)\}, \ \sigma\{a(n, 2)\}, \ \sigma\{a(n, 3)\}$$

could quite well all be false.

$$[\text{E.g. if } (n) \cdot \bar{A}(n) \cdot \bar{B}(n)]$$

Of course in all these definitions we must suppose $\sigma\{a(n, m)\}$ etc., replaced by what on calculation we find them to be. As they stand the definitions look circular, but are not when interpreted in this way.

For instance $\sigma\{a(n, 1)\}$ is L, i.e. laws (1)–(5) together with

$$(\exists n_1, n_2) \cdot 2(n_1, n) \cdot 2(n_2, n) \cdot n_1 \not\equiv n_2 \,(\text{mod } 2) \cdot Bn_1 \cdot Bn_2 \cdot$$

v. $(\exists n_1, n_2, n_3) \cdot 2(n_1, n) \cdot 2(n_2, n) \cdot 2(n_3, n) \cdot n_1 \not\equiv n_2 \,(\text{mod } 2).$
$$An_1 \cdot An_2 \cdot Bn_3 \cdot$$

v. $(\exists n_1, n_2) \cdot 1(n_1, n) \cdot 2(n_2, n) \cdot Bn_1 \cdot Bn_2.$

Such then seem to be the definitions to which we are led by the popular phrase that the meaning of a statement in the second system is given by its criterion in the first. Are they such as we require ?

What we want is that, using these definitions, the axioms and dictionary should be true whenever the theory is applicable, i.e. whenever the laws and consequences are true ; i.e. that interpreted by means of these definitions, the axioms and dictionary should follow from the laws and consequences.

It is easy to see that they do not so follow. Take for instance the last axiom on p. 216 :

$$(n) : \beta(n, 2) \cdot \equiv \cdot \bar{\beta}(n + 1,\ 2),$$

which means according to our definitions

$$(n) : \sigma\{\beta(n, 2)\} \cdot \equiv \cdot \bar{\sigma}\{\beta(n + 1,\ 2)\},$$

which is plainly false, since if, as is perfectly possible, the man has never opened his eyes at place 2, both $\sigma\{\beta\,(n, 2)\}$ and $\sigma\{\beta(n + 1,\ 2)\}$ will be false.

[The definition by τ is no better, since $\tau\{\beta\,(n, 2)\}$ and $\tau\,(\beta\,(n + 1,\ 2))$ would both be true.]

This line of argument is, however, exposed to an objection of the following sort: If we adopt these definitions it is true that the axioms will not follow from the laws and consequences, but it is not really necessary that they should. For the laws and consequences cannot represent the whole empirical (i.e. primary system) basis of the theory. It is, for instance, compatible with the laws and consequences that the man should never have had his eyes open at place 2; but how could he then have ever formulated this theory with the peculiar law of alternation which he ascribes to place 2 ? What we want in order to construct our theory by means of explicit definitions is not that the axioms should follow from the laws and consequences alone, but from them together with certain existential propositions of the primary system representing experiences the man must have had in order to be able with any show of reason to formulate the theory.

Reasonable though this objection is in the present case, it can be seen by taking a slightly more complicated theory to provide us with no general solution of the difficulty; that is to say, such propositions as could in this way be added to the laws and consequences would not always provide a sufficient basis for the axioms. For instance, suppose the theory provided for a whole system of places identified by the movement sequences necessary to get from one to another, and it was found and embodied in the theory that the colour of each place followed a complicated cycle, the same for each place, but that the places differed from one another as to the phase of this cycle according to no ascertainable law. Clearly such a theory could be reasonably formed by a man who had not had his eyes open at each place, and had no grounds for thinking that he ever would open his eyes at all the places or even visit them at all. Suppose then m is a place he never goes to, and that $\beta(n, m)$ is a function of the second system, signifying that m is blue at n; then unless he knows the phase of m, we can never have $\sigma\{\beta(n, m)\}$, but if e.g. the cycle gives a blue colour once in six, we must have from an axiom $\beta(0, m) \vee \beta(1, m) \vee \ldots \vee \beta(6, m)$. We have, therefore, just the same difficulty as before.

If, therefore, our theory is to be constructed by explicit definitions, these cannot be simple definitions by means of σ (or τ), but must be more complicated. For instance, in regard to place 2 in our original example we can define

$$\beta(0, 2) \text{ as } \sigma\{\beta(0, 2)\},$$

$$\beta(n, 2) \text{ as } \sigma\{\beta(0, 2)\} \text{ if } n \text{ is even,}$$

$$\sim \sigma\{\beta(0, 2)\} \text{ if } n \text{ is odd.}$$

I.e. if we do not know which phase it is, we assume it to be a certain one, including that ' assumption ' in our definition. E.g. by saying the phase is blue-even, red-odd, we mean that we have reason to think it is; by saying the phase is blue-odd, red-even, we mean not that we have reason to think it is but merely that we have no reason to think the contrary.

But in general the definitions will have to be very complicated ; we shall have, in order to verify that they are complete, to go through all the cases that satisfy the laws and consequences (together with any other propositions of the primary system we think right to assume) and see that in each case the definitions satisfy the axioms, so that in the end we shall come to something very like the general disjunctive definitions with which we started this discussion (p. 220). At best we shall have disjunctions with fewer terms and more coherence and unity in their construction ; how much will depend on the particular case.

We could see straight off that (in a finite scheme) such definitions were always possible, and by means of σ and τ we have reached no real simplification.

3. We have seen that we *can* always reproduce the structure of our theory by means of explicit definitions. Our next question is ' Is this *necessary* for the legitimate use of the theory ? '

To this the answer seems clear that it cannot be necessary, or a theory would be no use at all. Rather than give all these definitions it would be simpler to leave the facts, laws and consequences in the language of the primary system. Also the arbitrariness of the definitions makes it impossible for them to be adequate to the theory as something in process of growth. For instance, our theory does not give any law for the colour of place 3 ; we should, therefore, in embodying our theory in explicit definition, define place 3 to be red unless it was observed to be blue (or else *vice versa*). Further observation might now lead us to add to our theory a new axiom about the colour of place 3 giving say a cycle which it followed ; this would appear simply as an addition to the axioms, the other axioms and the dictionary being unaltered.

But if our theory had been constructed by explicit definitions, this new axiom would not be true unless we changed the definitions, for it would depend on quite a different assignment of colours to place 3 at times when it was unobserved from our old one (which always made it red at such times), or indeed from *any* old one, except exactly that prescribed by our new axiom, which we should never have hit on to use in our definitions unless we knew the new axiom already. That is to say, if we proceed by explicit definition we cannot add to our theory without changing the definitions, and so the meaning of the whole.

[But though the use of explicit definitions cannot be necessary, it is, I think, instructive to consider (as we have done) how such definitions could be constructed, and upon what the possibility of giving them simply depends. Indeed I think this is essential to a complete understanding of the subject.]

4. Taking it then that explicit definitions are not necessary, how are we to explain the functioning of our theory without them ?

Clearly in such a theory judgment is involved, and the judgments in question could be given by the laws and consequences, the theory being simply a language in which they are clothed, and which we can use without working out the laws and consequences.

The best way to write our theory seems to be this $(\exists\alpha, \beta, \gamma)$: dictionary . axioms.

The dictionary being in the form of equivalences.

Here it is evident that α, β, γ are to be taken purely extensionally. Their extensions may be filled with intensions or not, but this is irrelevant to what can be deduced in the primary system.

Any additions to the theory, whether in the form of new axioms or particular assertions like $\alpha(0, 3)$, are to be made within the scope of the original α, β, γ. They are not, therefore, strictly propositions by themselves just as the different sentences in a story beginning ' Once upon a time ' have not complete meanings and so are not propositions by themselves.

This makes both a theoretical and a practical difference :

(a) When we ask for the meaning of e.g. $\alpha(0, 3)$ it can only be given when we know to what stock of ' propositions ' of the *first and second* systems $\alpha(0, 3)$ is to be added. Then the meaning is the difference in the first system between $(\exists\alpha, \beta, \gamma)$: stock . $\alpha(0, 3)$, and $(\exists\alpha, \beta, \gamma)$. stock. (We include propositions of the primary system in our stock although these do not contain α, β, γ.)

This account makes $\alpha(0, 3)$ mean something like what we called above $\tau\{\alpha(0, 3)\}$, but it is really the difference between $\tau\{\alpha(0, 3) + \text{stock}\}$ and τ (stock).

(b) In practice, if we ask ourselves the question " Is $\alpha(0, 3)$ true ? ", we have to adopt an attitude rather different from that which we should adopt to a genuine proposition.

For we do not add $\alpha(0, 3)$ to our stock whenever we think we could truthfully do so, i.e. whenever we suppose $(\exists \alpha, \beta, \gamma)$: stock . $\alpha(0, 3)$ to be true. $(\exists \alpha, \beta, \gamma)$: stock . $\bar{a}(0, 3)$ might also be true. We have to think what else we might be going to add to our stock, or hoping to add, and consider whether $\alpha(0, 3)$ would be certain to suit any further additions better than $\bar{a}(0, 3)$. E.g. in our little theory either $\beta(n, 3)$ or $\bar{\beta}(n, 3)$ could always be added to any stock which includes $\bar{a}(n, 3)$. $\vee$. $\bar{A}(n)$. $\bar{B}(n)$. But we do not add either, because we hope from the observed instances to find a law and then to fill in the unobserved ones according to that law, not at random beforehand.

So far, however, as *reasoning* is concerned, that the values of these functions are not complete propositions makes no difference, provided we interpret all logical combination as taking place within the scope of a single prefix $(\exists \alpha, \beta, \gamma)$; e.g.

$$\overline{\beta(n, 3) . \bar{\beta}(n, 3)} \text{ must be } (\exists \beta) : \overline{\beta(n, 3)} . \overline{\bar{\beta}(n, 3)},$$

$$\text{not } (\exists \beta) \, \beta(n, 3) . (\exists \beta) \, \bar{\beta}(n, 3).$$

For we can reason about the characters in a story just as well as if they were really identified, provided we don't take part of what we say as about one story, part about another.

We can say, therefore, that the incompleteness of the ' propositions ' of the secondary system affects our *disputes* but not our *reasoning*.

5. This mention of ' disputes ' leads us to the important question of the relations between theories. What do we mean by speaking of equivalent or contradictory theories ? or by saying that one theory is contained in another, etc. ?

In a theory we must distinguish two elements :

(1) What it asserts : its meaning or content.

(2) Its symbolic form.

Two theories are called *equivalent* if they have the same

content, *contradictory* if they have contradictory contents, *compatible* if their contents are compatible, and theory A is said to be *contained* in theory B if A's content is contained in B's content.

If two theories are equivalent, there may be more or less resemblance between their symbolic forms. This kind of resemblance is difficult if not impossible to define precisely. It might be thought possible to define a definite degree of resemblance by the possibility of defining the functions of B in terms of those of A, or conversely ; but this is of no value without some restriction on the complexity of the definitions. If we allow definitions of any degree of complexity, then, at least in the finite case, this relation becomes simply equivalence. For each set of functions *can* be defined in terms of the primary system and therefore of those of the other secondary system *via* the dictionary.

Two theories may be compatible without being equivalent, i.e. a set of facts might be found which agreed with both, and another set too which agreed with one but not with the other. The adherents of two such theories could quite well dispute, although neither affirmed anything the other denied. For a dispute it is not necessary that one disputant should assert p, the other $\bar{p}$. It is enough that one should assert something which the other refrains from asserting. E.g. one says ' If it rains, Cambridge will win ', the other ' Even if it rains, they will lose '. Now, taken as material implications (as we must on this view of science), these are not incompatible, since if it does not rain both are true. Yet each can show grounds for his own belief and absence of grounds for his rival's.

People sometimes ask whether a ' proposition ' of the secondary system has any meaning. We can interpret this as the question whether a theory in which this proposition was denied would be equivalent to one in which it was affirmed.

This depends of course on what else the theory is supposed to contain ; for instance, in our example $\beta(n, 3)$ is meaningless coupled with $\bar{a}(n, 3) \vee \bar{\gamma}(n)$. But not so coupled it is not meaningless, since it would then exclude my seeing red under certain circumstances, whereas $\bar{\beta}(n, 3)$ would exclude my seeing blue under these circumstances. It is possible that these circumstances should arise, and therefore that the theories are not equivalent. In realistic language we say it could be observed, or rather might be observed (since 'could' implies a dependence on our will, which is frequently the case but *irrelevant*), but not that it will be observed.

Even coupled with $\bar{a}(n, 3) \vee \bar{\gamma}(n)$, $\beta(n, 3)$ might receive a meaning later if we added to our theory some law about the colour of 3. [Though then again $\beta(n, 3)$ would probably be a consequence of or a contradiction to the rest : we should then, I think, say it had meaning since e.g. $\beta(n, 3)$ would give a theory, $\bar{\beta}(n, 3)$ a contradiction.]

It is highly relevant to this question of whether propositions have meaning, not merely what general axioms we include in our theory, but also what particular propositions. Has it meaning to say that the back of the moon has a surface of green cheese ? If our theory allows as a possibility that we might go there or find out in any other way, then it has meaning. If not, not ; i.e. our theory of the *moon* is very relevant, not merely our theory of things in general.

6. We could ask : in what sort of theories does every 'proposition' of the secondary system have meaning in this sense ?

I cannot answer this properly, but only very vaguely and uncertainly, nor do I think it is very important. If the theory is to correspond to an actual state of knowledge it must contain the translations through the dictionary of many particular propositions of the primary system. These will, almost certainly, prevent many 'propositions' of the secondary system from having any *direct* meaning. E.g. if it is stated in the theory that at time n I am at place 1, then for place 2 to be blue at that time n can have no direct meaning, nor for any very distant place at time $n + 1$. If then such 'propositions' are to have meaning at all, it must either be because they or their contradictories are included in the theory itself (they then mean 'nothing' or 'contradiction') or in virtue of causal axioms connecting them with other possible primary facts, where 'possible' means not declared in the theory to be false.

This causation is, of course, in the second system, and must be laid down in the theory.

Besides causal axioms in the strict sense governing succession in time, there may be others governing arrangement in space requiring, for instance, continuity and simplicity. But these can only be laid down if we are sure that they will not come into conflict with future experience combined with the causal axioms. In a field in which our theory ensures this we can add such axioms of continuity. To assign to nature the simplest course except when experience proves the contrary is a good maxim of theory making, but it cannot be put *into* the theory in the form 'Natura non facit saltum' except when we see her do so.

Take, for instance, the problem " Is there a planet of the size and shape of a tea-pot ? " This question has meaning so long as we do not know that an experiment could not decide the matter. Once we know this it loses meaning, unless we restore it by new axioms, e.g. an axiom as to the orbits possible to planets.

But someone will say " Is it not a clear question with the *onus probandi* by definition on one side ? " Clearly it means " Will experience reveal to us such a tea-pot ? " I think not ; for there are three cases :

(1) Experience will show there is such a tea-pot.

(2) Experience will show there is not such a tea-pot.

(3) Experience will not show anything.

And we can quite well distinguish (2) from (3) though the objector confounds them.

This tea-pot is not in principle different from a tea-pot in the kitchen cupboard.

CAUSAL QUALITIES (1929)

In dealing with the motion of bodies we introduce the notion of mass, a quality which we do not observe but which we use to account for motion. We can only ' define ' it hypothetically, which is not really intelligible when you think it out. E.g. ' It had a mass 3 = If we had fired at it a given body (mass 1) at 3 times its velocity which coalesced with it the resulting body would have been at rest ' is an unfulfilled conditional intelligible only as a consequence of a law, namely a law of mechanics stated in terms of mass. The truth is that we deal with our primary system as part of a fictitious secondary system. Here we have a fictitious quality, and we can also have fictitious individuals. This is all made clear in my account of theories.

Singular propositions in the secondary system we believe with such and such degrees of probability just as in the primary system. Fictitiousness is simply ignored; we speculate about a body's weight just as much as about its position, without for a moment supposing that it has not one exact weight. The only difference is that we are not ultimately interested in fictitious propositions, but use them merely as intermediaries: we do not care about them for their own sake. General propositions in the secondary system we treat just like variable hypotheticals, and so with chances.

A theory is a way of saying the singular primary propositions and the variable hypotheticals that follow from it. If two theories agree in these they are equivalent, and there is a more or less complicated translation of one into the other. Otherwise they differ like two disagreeing variable hypotheticals.

No proposition of the secondary system can be understood apart from the whole theory to which it belongs. If a man says ' Zeus hurls thunderbolts ', that is not nonsense because Zeus does not appear in my theory, and is not definable in terms of my theory. I have to consider it as part of a theory and attend to its consequences, e.g. that sacrifices will bring the thunderbolts to an end.

It is possible to have a ' realism ' about terms in the theory similar to that about causal laws, and this is equally foolish. ' There is such a quality as mass ' is nonsense unless it means merely to affirm the consequences of a mechanical theory. This must be set out fully sometime as part of an account of existential judgments. I think perhaps it is true that the theory of general and existential judgments is the clue to everything.

[What can be asked about mass, is the possibility of defining it in some way. E.g. ' Arsenic ' is not an indefinable now, but was at the beginning of chemistry. N.B.—Hypothetical definition is not definition ; e.g. ' If I were dissolving it, it would . . . ', but I'm not.]

An interesting problem arises as to what would happen if another man's thinking lay in my secondary system. [Or even my own thinking ? Some analogy to alleged circularity in theory of causation.] This would be the case if he were acquainted with mass or electric charge, but of course no one is. But I feel there may be more in it when we get to a sensational level. For instance, a blind man is going to be operated on, and thinks he is going to be able to see : then colour is to him (we can plausibly suppose) at present merely a theoretical idea, i.e. a term of his secondary system, with which he thinks he will be acquainted ; i.e. part of his future thinking lies in his present secondary system.

Of course, causal, fictitious, or ' occult ' qualities may cease to be so as science progresses. E.g. heat, the fictitious cause of certain phenomena of expansion (and sensations, but these could be disregarded and heat considered simply so far as it comes into mechanics), is discovered to consist in the motion of small particles.

So perhaps with bacteria and Mendelian characters or genes.

This means, of course, that in a later theory these parametric functions are replaced by functions of the given system.

It is quite false to say with Norman Campbell that ' really ' is the sign of a theoretical idea. Any change in a theory by which some simple term is replaced by a complex one can be expressed by saying it ' really ' is so-and-so. Especially when a fictitious idea is replaced by primary ones as in the above examples. Campbell thinks that e.g. atomic theory of gases explains primary properties, e.g. temperature, by fictitious ones, e.g. bombardment. But the use of ' really ' is only natural on the exactly contrary view.

7

LAW AND CAUSALITY

A. UNIVERSALS OF LAW AND OF FACT (1928)

1 The difference according to Johnson [1] is that universals of law apply over a wider range than do universals of fact, i.e. over a wider range than everything, which is impossible (range of x in $(x).\phi x \supset \psi x$ is everything).

2 The difference according to many is that when all A are B is a universal of fact it is short for this A is B, that A is B, . . . ; this is not true ; the universal may in the first instance be discovered in this sense, but as soon as it is told to someone else it ceases to have this sense, because the hearer does not know how many, or what, As there are, but merely that all that there are are B. But this does not mean that to the hearer the universal is one of law.

3 The difference according to Braithwaite [2] is that universals of law are believed on grounds which are not demonstrative. This will not do because

(a) some universals of law are not believed at all

(b) some universals of fact are believed on non-demonstrative grounds

(c) some universals of law are believed on grounds which in his sense are demonstrative.

Any one of these contentions is enough to upset his definition. Let us take them in turn.

4 (a) We many of us think many characteristics of

---

[1] W. E. Johnson, *Logic, Part III* (1924), Chapter 1.
[2] R. B. Braithwaite, " The Idea of Necessary Connexion ", *Mind* 36 (1927), pp. 467–77 ; 37 (1928), pp. 62–72.

offspring are caused by (unknown) characteristics of the chromosomes of the uniting cells; but on Braithwaite's view to think this is to think that we know what characteristics of the chromosomes they are; it is not enough to say

$$(\exists\phi): \phi(\text{chromosomes}) \supset_{\text{always}} \psi(\text{offspring}) ;$$

if we say the universal is causal we mean

$$(\exists\phi): \phi(\text{chromosomes}) \supset_{\text{always}} \psi(\text{offspring}) \text{ is believed,}$$

which is patently false until ϕ has been discovered. It might be replied that what we want is not ' is believed ' but either ' will be believed ', ' would be believed ', or ' could be believed '.

5 Of these amended versions ' will ' clearly will not do; the causes of hereditary characteristics are not altered, if a new barbarian invasion checks the progress of science; ' would ' would be circular as it means that certain circumstances would cause it to be believed; ' could ' be believed would either mean this too or else something radically different to be considered later.

6 (b) What is clearly only a universal of fact, e.g. ' everyone there was asleep ', may easily not be believed on demonstrative grounds: e.g. it may be believed on testimony; or because I said something which anyone who was awake would probably have answered.

7 (c) This point is not so clear as the others, owing to an ambiguity as to what ' universal of law ' is supposed to include; if it means a universal whose subject term does not mention any particular portion of space-time, it would be better to make this clearly part of the definition. Otherwise take ' Whenever this balloon was filled with hydrogen and let go, it rose '; this, or something like it only more complicated, is surely a universal of law and yet might be believed as a result of observing all its instances.

8 In order to get nearer a correct solution let us classify universals a little more precisely; as we have the following

classes

(1) the ultimate laws of nature

(2) derivative laws of nature, i.e. general propositions deducible from the ultimate laws

(3) what are called laws in a loose sense ; i.e. general propositions deducible from the ultimate laws together with various facts of existence assumed to be known by everyone, e.g. bodies fall

(4) universals of fact ; but these cannot be sharply distinguished from (3) ; on a determinist view all of them could be deducible from the ultimate laws together with enough facts of existence.

9 This table of classes might perhaps suggest the following solution ; the fundamental distinction is between (1) and (2) on the one hand, and (3) and (4) on the other, and it is that universals in classes (1) and (2) mention no particular portion of space-time whereas those in (3) and (4) do (hence the need for facts of existence to deduce them). Between (1) and (2), and between (3) and (4), the distinction is a vague one, in the first case of artificial arrangement, in the second of amount of fact required for their deduction.

10 This solution would not, however, do ; because there are universals belonging to (3) and (4), which mention no particular portion of space-time but still do not follow from the ultimate laws ; thus all Conservative prime ministers of England between 1903 and 1928 have names beginning with B ; and so probably all Conservative prime ministers of a country with 40,000,000–50,000,000 inhabitants, whose capital is called ' London ' and has 7,000,000 inhabitants . . . at a time when that country has between 2–27 years previously lost a queen who has ruled for 64 years . . . have their names beginning with B. If we put in enough detail we shall (unless the world repeats itself endlessly with just a few details

different each time) get a true generalization which mentions no particular portion of space-time but this would not be a law of nature.

11 What is it then that is true of universals of classes (1) and (2) and not of those classes (3) and (4) ? We have seen that it is not their spatio-temporal indifference, not that they are believed ; nor we may remark is it any combination of these characters, for the fact that they are believed or might be believed is quite irrelevant ; anything whatever can be believed on authority or testimony. Also the difference would still persist if we knew everything.

12 This last point gives us the clue ; even if we knew everything, we should still want to systematize our knowledge as a deductive system, and the general axioms in that system would be the fundamental laws of nature. The choice of axioms is bound to some extent to be arbitrary, but what is less likely to be arbitrary if any simplicity is to be preserved is a body of fundamental generalizations, some to be taken as axioms and others deduced. Some other true generalizations will then only be able to be deduced from these by the help of particular facts of existence. These fundamental generalizations will then be our universals of classes (1) and (2), the axioms forming class (1).

13 As it is, we do not know everything ; but what we do know we tend to organize as a deductive system and call its axioms laws, and we consider how that system would go if we knew a little more and call the further axioms or deductions there would then be, laws (we think there would be ones of a certain kind but don't know exactly what). We also think how all truth could be organized as a deductive system and call its axioms ultimate laws.

14 The property of a universal that it *would* be an axiom in a deductive system covering everything is not really hypothetical ; the concealed if is only a *spurious* one ; what

is asserted is simply something about the whole world, namely that the true general propositions are of such forms that they form a system of the required sort with the given proposition in the required place ; it is the facts that form the system in virtue of internal relations, not people's beliefs in them in virtue of spatio-temporal ones. Of course the system is required to be as simple as possible ; but this is another vague formal property, not a causal one, or if causal shorn of its causality ; see § 16.

15 It will be objected that when we use the notion of a law as in a statement of causal implication, we do not say anything about a grand deductive system. The answer is that we do do this so soon as we pass beyond the mere material or formal implication. But that the important part of statements of causal implication is always just the material or formal implication which has no reference to system. It is only the philosopher or systematizer or emotionalist who is interested in the rest. All the practical man wants to know is that all people who take arsenic die, not that this is a causal implication, for a universal of fact is *within its scope* just as good a guide to conduct as a universal of law.

16 A danger always to be thought of, is that belief being a causal fact we must not involve it in the analysis of cause. The above theory avoids that ; see § 14. An alternative way of avoiding it is to say that the belief, if any, that occurs in the analysis of cause is belief shorn of its causality, i.e. with the causal implications reduced to material ones.

17 The laws involved in *causal implications* are classes (1), (2) above. Not class (3) ; in the cases in which we should naturally appeal to a universal of class (3), we can by extending our r make $pr \supset q$ an instance of one of class (2) instead ; and it is the possibility of doing this within the implied limitations on r which in effect distinguishes class (3) from class (4).

B. GENERAL PROPOSITIONS AND CAUSALITY (1929)

Let us consider the meaning of general propositions in a clearly defined given world. (In particular in the common sense material world.) This includes the ordinary problem of causality.

As everyone except us [1] has always said these propositions are of two kinds. First *conjunctions*: e.g. 'Everyone in Cambridge voted'; the variable here is, of course, not people in Cambridge, but a limited region of space varying according to the definiteness of the speaker's idea of 'Cambridge', which is 'this town' or 'the town in England called Cambridge' or whatever it may be.

Old-fashioned logicians were right in saying that these are conjunctions, wrong in their analysis of what conjunctions they are. But right again in radically distinguishing them from the other kind which we may call *variable hypotheticals*: e.g. Arsenic is poisonous: All men are mortal.

Why are these not conjunctions?

Let us put it this way first: What have they in common with conjunctions, and in what do they differ from them? Roughly we can say that when we look at them subjectively they differ altogether, but when we look at them objectively, i.e. at the conditions of their truth and falsity, they appear to be the same.

$(x) \cdot \phi x$ differs from a conjunction because

(*a*) It cannot be written out as one.

(*b*) Its constitution as a conjunction is never used; we never use it in class-thinking except in its application to a finite class, i.e. we use only the applicative rule.

[1] [I.e. Ramsey and Braithwaite: see A above].

145

(c) [This is the same as (b) in another way.] It always goes beyond what we know or want ; cf. Mill on ' All men are mortal ' and ' The Duke of Wellington is mortal '. It expresses an inference we are at any time prepared to make, not a belief of the primary sort.

A belief of the primary sort is a map of neighbouring space by which we steer. It remains such a map however much we complicate it or fill in details. But if we professedly extend it to infinity, it is no longer a map ; we cannot take it in or steer by it. Our journey is over before we need its remoter parts.

(d) The relevant degree of certainty is the certainty of the particular case, or of a finite set of particular cases ; not of an infinite number which we never use, and of which we couldn't be certain at all.

(x) . ϕx resembles a conjunction

(a) In that it contains all lesser, i.e. here all finite, conjunctions, and appears as a sort of infinite product.

(b) When we ask what would make it true, we inevitably answer that it is true if and only if every x has ϕ ; i.e. when we regard it as a proposition capable of the two cases truth and falsity, we are forced to make it a conjunction, and to have a theory of conjunctions which we cannot express for lack of symbolic power.

[But what we can't say we can't say, and we can't whistle it either.]

If then it is not a conjunction, it is not a proposition at all ; and then the question arises in what way can it be right or wrong.

Now in the case of a proposition right and wrong, i.e. true or false, occur doubly. They occur to the man who makes the proposition whenever he makes a truth-function of it, i.e. argues disjunctively about the cases of its truth and falsity.

146

Now this we never do with these variable hypotheticals except in mathematics in which it is now recognized as fallacious. We may seem to do so whenever we discuss the different theories obtainable by combining different proposed laws of nature. But here, if P is such a law, we do not consider the alternatives P, i.e. $(x) \cdot \phi x$, and $\bar{P}$, i.e. $\overline{(x) \cdot \phi x}$, but we consider either having P or not having P (where not having it as a law in no way implies the law's falsity, i.e. $(\exists x) \cdot \overline{\phi x}$) or else having $P = (x) \cdot \overline{\phi x}$ or having $Q = (x) \cdot \overline{\phi x}$.

The other way in which right and wrong occur in connection with propositions is to an onlooker who says that the man's belief in the proposition is right or wrong. This, of course, turns simply on what the onlooker thinks himself and results from identity or difference between his view and what he takes to be that of the man he is criticising. If A thinks p and thinks also that B thinks p, he says B thinks truly; if he thinks p and thinks that B thinks $\bar{p}$, he says B thinks falsely. But criticism may not always be of this simple type; it is also possible when B thinks p, and A thinks neither p nor $\bar{p}$, but regards the question as unsettled. He may deem B a fool for thinking p, without himself thinking $\bar{p}$. This happens almost always with hypotheticals. If B says ' If I eat this mince pie I shall have a stomach-ache ', and A says ' No, you won't ', he is not really contradicting B's proposition—at least if this is taken as a material implication. Nor is he contradicting a supposed assertion of B's that the evidence proves that so-and-so. B may make no such assertion, in fact cannot always reasonably even if he is in the right. For he may be in the right without having *proof* on his side.

In fact agreement and disagreement is possible in regard to any aspect of a man's view and need not take the simple form of 'p', '$\bar{p}$'.

Many sentences express cognitive attitudes without being propositions; and the difference between saying yes or no

147

to them is not the difference between saying yes or no to a proposition. This is even true of the ordinary hypothetical [as can be seen from the above example, it asserts something for the case when its protasis is true : we apply the Law of Excluded Middle not to the whole thing but to the consequence only] ; and much more of the variable hypothetical.

In order therefore to understand the variable hypothetical and its rightness or wrongness we must consider the different possible attitudes to it ; if we know what these are and involve we can proceed easily to explain the meaning of saying that such an attitude is right or wrong, for this is simply having such an attitude oneself and thinking that one's neighbour has the same or a different one.

What then are the possible attitudes to the question—Are all men mortal ?

(1) To believe it with more or less conviction.

(2) Not to have considered it.

(3) Not to believe it because it is unproven.

(4) *Not* to believe it because convinced that a certain type of man, who *might* exist, would be immortal.

(5) To disbelieve it as convinced that a particular man is immortal.

We have to analyse these attitudes ; obviously in the first instance the analysis must be in terms of beliefs in singular propositions, and such an analysis will suffice for our present purpose.

To believe that all men are mortal—what is it ? Partly to say so, partly to believe in regard to any x that turns up that if he is a man he is mortal. The general belief consists in

(*a*) A general enunciation,

(*b*) A habit of singular belief.

These are, of course, connected, the habit resulting from

the enunciation according to a psychological law which makes the meaning of ' all '.

We thus explain

(1) In terms of the notion of a ' *habit* ' ;

(2) Offers no problem ;

(3) May seem to give a problem if we ask—What is it that the thinker considers ? But there is really no problem : it is not considering whether a thing is so or not, nor again considering whether or not to do something, but a kind of intermediary. The idea of the general statement rises, the evidence is considered and it falls again.

In (4) and (5) it falls more decisively for the reasons given : namely, in (4) we have another general statement which combined with the proposed one would give a conclusion we are disinclined for (itself a third general statement, namely ' All men are not of that type ') ; and in (5) we have a singular statement flatly contradicting the one proposed.

Variable hypotheticals or causal laws form the system with which the speaker meets the future ; they are not, therefore, subjective in the sense that if you and I enunciate different ones we are each saying something about ourselves which pass by one another like ' I went to Grantchester ', ' I didn't.' For if we meet the future with different systems we disagree even if the actual future agrees with both so long as it *might* (logically) agree with one but not with the other, i.e. so long as we don't believe the same things. (Cf. If A is certain, B doubtful, they can still dispute.)

Variable hypotheticals are not judgments but rules for judging ' If I meet a ϕ, I shall regard it as a ψ '. This cannot be *negated* but it can be *disagreed* with by one who does not adopt it.

These attitudes seem therefore to involve no puzzling idea except that of habit ; clearly any proposition about a habit is general, and hence the criticism of a man's general judgments is itself a general judgment. But since all belief involves habit, so does the criticism of any judgment whatever, and I do not see anything objectionable in this. There is a feeling of circularity about it, but I think it is illusory. Anyway we shall recur to it below.

This account of causal laws has a certain resemblance to Braithwaite's,[1] and we must compare them closely to see whether it escapes the objections to which his is liable. He said that a universal of law was one believed on grounds not demonstrative, and I said[2] that that would not do for three separate reasons :—

(a) Some universals of law are not believed at all, e.g. unknown causal laws.

(b) Some universals of fact are believed on grounds not demonstrative.

(c) Some (derivative and localized) universals of law are believed on demonstrative grounds.

I, therefore, put up a different theory by which causal laws were consequences of those propositions which we should take as axioms if we knew everything and organized it as simply as possible in a deductive system.

What is said above means, of course, a complete rejection of this view (for it is impossible to know everything and organize it in a deductive system) and a return to something nearer Braithwaite's. A causal generalization is not, as I then thought, one which is simple, but one we trust (cf. the ages at death of poets' cooks). We may trust it because it is simple, but that is another matter. When I say this I must not be misunderstood ; variable hypotheticals are not distinguished from conjunctions by the fact that we believe

[1] R. B. Braithwaite, " The Idea of Necessary Connexion," *Mind*, 1927 and 1928.
[2] [In A above].

them, they are much more radically different. But the evidence of a variable hypothetical being (often at least) a conjunction, such a conjunction is distinguished from others in that we trust it to guide us in a new instance, i.e. derive from it a variable hypothetical.

This explains how Braithwaite came to say that laws were those which were believed ; but, put as he puts it, it is of course wrong, being open to the objections made above. Braithwaite's problem was to explain the meaning of ' P is a law of nature '. Our solution is that to say this, is to assert P after the manner of a variable hypothetical. [Or of course we may extend law of nature to any conjunction following from one in the above sense.] But this solution is incomplete because it does not at all explain what we mean when we speak of an unknown law of nature, or one described but not stated, e.g. the law that characteristics of people depend in some way on chromosomes (but no one knows how), or, he has discovered a law governing the extension of springs (but I don't know what law), where in the second instance I say he believes a variable hypothetical, and further imply that it is true, but since I do not know what it is I cannot myself adopt his attitude towards it.

Thus in each of these cases we seem to be treating the unknown law as a true proposition in the way our theory says is impossible.

The same difficulty also occurs in the finitist theory of mathematics, when we speak of an unknown true mathematical proposition. In this clearer field the solution should be easier and then extensible to the other.

An unknown truth in the theory of numbers cannot be interpreted as an (unknown) proposition true of all numbers, but as one proved or provable. Provable in turn means provable in any number of steps, and on finitist principles the number must in some way be limited, e.g. to the humanly

151

possible. ' So-and-so has discovered a new theorem ' means therefore that he has constructed a proof of a certain limited size.

When we turn to an unknown causal law, what is there to correspond to the process of proof on which the above solution turns ? Clearly only the process of collecting evidence for the causal law, and to say that there is such a law, though we don't know it, must mean that there are such singular facts in some limited sphere (a disjunction) as would lead us, did we know them, to assert a variable hypothetical. But this is not enough, for there must not merely be facts leading to the generalization, but this when made must not mislead us. (Or we could not call it a true causal law.) It must therefore be also asserted to hold within a certain limited region taken to be the scope of our possible experience.

There was nothing corresponding to this in the mathematical case, for a mathematical generalization must if proved hold in any particular case, but an empirical generalization cannot be proved ; and for there to be evidence leading to it and for it to hold in other cases also are separate facts.

To this account there are two possible objections on the score of circularity. We are trying to explain the meaning of asserting the existence of an unknown causal law, and our explanation may be said to be in terms of the assertion of such laws, and that in two different ways. We say it means that there are facts which *would lead* us to assert a *variable hypothetical* ; and here it may be urged that this means that they would lead us in virtue of one possibly unknown causal law to form a habit which would be constituted by another unknown causal law.

To this we answer, first, that the causal law in virtue of which the facts would lead us to the generalization must not be any unknown law, e.g. one by which knowledge of the facts would first drive us mad and so to the mad generalization, but the known laws expressing our methods of inductive reasoning; and, secondly, that the unknown variable hypothetical must here be taken to mean an unknown statement (whose syntax will of course be known but not its terms or their meanings), which would, of course, lead to a habit in virtue of a known psychological law.

What we have said is, I think, a sufficient outline of the answers to the relevant problems of analysis, but it is apt to leave us muddled and unsatisfied as to what seems the main question—a question not of psychological analysis but of metaphysics which is ' Is causation a reality or a fiction; and, if a fiction, is it useful or misleading, arbitary or indispensable ? '

We can begin by asking whether these variable hypotheticals play an essential part in our thought; we might, for instance, think that they could simply be eliminated and replaced by the primary propositions which serve as evidence for them. This is, I think, the view of Mill, who argued that instead of saying 'All men die, therefore the Duke of Wellington will', we could say ' Such-and-such men have died,[1] therefore the Duke will '. This view can be supported by observing that the ultimate purpose of thought is to guide our action, and that on any occasion our action depends only on beliefs or degrees of belief in singular propositions. And since it would be possible to organize our singular beliefs without using variable intermediaries, we are tempted to conclude that they are purely superfluous.

But this would, I think, be wrong; apart from their value in simplifying our thought, they form an essential part of our mind. That we think explicitly in general terms is at the root

---

[1] We may be inclined to say that the evidence is not merely that A, B, C have died, but that A, B, C have died, and none so far as we know not died; i.e. ' all we know about have died '. But the extra is not part of the evidence, but a description of it, saying ' and this is all the evidence '.

of all praise and blame and much discussion. We cannot blame a man except by considering what would have happened if he had acted otherwise, and this kind of unfulfilled conditional cannot be interpreted as a material implication, but depends essentially on variable hypotheticals. Let us consider this more closely.

When we deliberate about a possible action, we ask ourselves what will happen if we do this or that. If we give a definite answer of the form ' If I do p, q will result ,' this can properly be regarded as a material implication or disjunction ' Either not-p or q.' But it differs, of course, from any ordinary disjunction in that one of its members is not something of which we are trying to discover the truth, but something within our power to make true or false.[1] If we go on to ' And if q, then r ', we get more material implications of a more ordinary kind.

Besides definite answers ' If p, q will result ', we often get ones ' If p, q might result ' or ' q would probably result '. Here the degree of probability is clearly not a degree of belief in ' Not-p or q ', but a degree of belief in q given p, which it is evidently possible to have without a definite degree of belief in p, p not being an intellectual problem. And our conduct is largely determined by these degrees of hypothetical belief.

Now suppose a man is in such a situation. For instance, suppose that he has a cake and decides not to eat it, because he thinks it will upset him, and suppose that we consider his conduct and decide that he is mistaken. Now the belief on which the man acts is that if he eats the cake he will be ill, taken according to our above account as a material implication. We cannot contradict this proposition either before or after the event, for it is true provided the man doesn't eat the

---

[1] It is possible to take one's future voluntary action as an intellectual problem : ' Shall I be able to keep it up ? ' But only by dissociating one's future self.

cake, and before the event we have no reason to think he will eat it, and after the event we know he hasn't. Since he thinks nothing false, why do we dispute with him or condemn him ?

Before the event we do differ from him in a quite clear way : it is not that he believes p, we $\bar{p}$; but he has a different degree of belief in q given p from ours ; and we can obviously try to convert him to our view.[1] But after the event we both know that he did not eat the cake and that he was not ill ; the difference between us is that he thinks that if he had eaten it he would have been ill, whereas we think he would not. But this is *prima facie* not a difference of degrees of belief in any proposition, for we both agree as to all the facts.

The meaning of these assertions about unfulfilled conditions, and the fact that whether the conditions are fulfilled or not makes no difference to the difference between us, the common basis, as we may say, of the dispute lies in the fact that we think in general terms. We each of us have variable hypo-theticals (or, in the case of uncertainty, chances) which we apply to any such problem ; and the difference between us is a difference in regard to these. We have degrees of expectation, vague or clear, as to the outcome of any state of affairs when-ever or wherever it may occur. Where there is apt to be ambiguity is in the definition of the state of affairs ; for instance, in considering what would have happened if a man had acted differently, we are apt to introduce any fact we know, whether he did or could know it, e.g. the actual position of all the cards at bridge as opposed to their probabilities of position from his point of view. But what is clear is that

[1] If two people are arguing ' If p will q ? ' and are both in doubt as to p, they are adding p hypothetically to their stock of knowledge and arguing on that basis about q ; so that in a sense ' If p, q ' and ' If p, $\bar{q}$ ' are contradictories. We can say they are fixing their degrees of belief in q given p. If p turns out false, these degrees of belief are rendered *void*. If either party believes $\bar{p}$ for certain, the question ceases to mean anything to him except as a question about what follows from certain laws or hypotheses.

our expectations are general ; when the sort is clearly defined
we expect with the same probabilities in any case of the sort.
If not, and we expected differently in every real case, expectation in an imaginary case could have no meaning.

All this applies, of course, equally well to the consequences
of any hypothetical event and not only to human actions.
I have chosen to expound it with reference to the latter
because I think they are of quite peculiar importance in
explaining the special position possessed by causal laws, which
are an important but not the only type of variable hypotheticals. In order to deal with this question let us begin
with hypotheticals in general.

' If p, then q ' can in no sense be true unless the material
implication $p \supset q$ is true ; but it generally means that $p \supset q$ is
not only true but deducible or discoverable in some particular
way not explicitly stated.[1] This is always evident when
' If p then q ' or ' Because p, q ' (*because* is merely a variant on
if, when p is known to be true) is thought worth stating
even when it is already known either that p is false or that
q is true. In general we can say with Mill that ' If p then
q ' means that q is inferrible from p, that is, of course, from p
together with certain facts and laws not stated but in some
way indicated by the context. This means that $p \supset q$ follows
from these facts and laws, which if true is in no way a hypothetical fact ; so that, in spite of the sound of *inferrible*, Mill's

---

[1] ' If p, then q' may also mean $pr \supset q$ where r is not a fact or law, or
not only composed of facts or laws, but also composed of propositions
in a secondary system. E.g., from a solipsistic standpoint, ' If I open
my eyes I shall see red.' The hypotheticals in Mill's theory of the
external world are of this nature, and cannot be used to define the
external world. All that could be used are *laws* from which, combined
with my past experience, it might follow that if I open my eyes I shall
see red. But this could not cover *conjectures* as to the external world,
unless we think sufficient knowledge of law would enable us to make all
such conjectures certain. I do conjecture something ; this can only
be hypothetical if the hypothesis can refer to a secondary system.

Mill's view must be replaced by saying that the external world is a
secondary system, and that any proposition about it commits one to
no more judgments than a denial of all courses of experience inconsistent with it.

explanation is not circular as Bradley thought. Of course that $p \supset q$ follows from the facts is not a proposition of logic but a description of the facts : ' They are such as to involve $p \supset q$.' Corresponding to the kind of laws or facts intended we get various subtle syntactical variations. For instance, ' If he was there, he must have voted for it (for it was passed unanimously), but if he had been there, he would have voted against it (such being his nature).' [In this, law = variable hypothetical.]

One class of cases is particularly important, namely those in which, as we say, our ' if ' gives us not only a *ratio cognoscendi* but also a *ratio essendi*. In this case which is e.g. the normal one when we say ' If p had happened, q would have happened ', $p \supset q$ must follow from a hypothetical $(x) . \phi x \supset \psi x$ and facts $r, pr \supset q$ being an instance of $\phi x \supset \psi x$ and q describing events not earlier than any of those described in pr. A variable hypothetical of this sort we call a *causal law*.

We have now to explain the peculiar importance and objectivity ascribed to causal laws ; how, for instance, the deduction of effect from cause is conceived as so radically different from that of cause from effect. (No one would say that the cause existed because of the effect.) It is, it seems, a fundamental fact that the future is due to the present, or, more mildly, is affected by the present, but the past is not. What does this mean ? It is not clear and, if we try to make it clear, it turns into nonsense or a definition : ' We speak of *ratio essendi* when the protasis is earlier than the apodasis Df.' We feel that this is wrong ; we think there is some difference between before and after at which we are getting ; but what can it be ? There are differences between the laws deriving effect from cause and those deriving cause from effect ; but can they really be what we mean ? No ; for they are found *a posteriori*, but what we mean is *a priori*. [The Second Law of Thermodynamics is *a posteriori* ; what is peculiar is that it

157

seems to result merely from absence of law (i.e. chance), but there might be a law of shuffling.]

What then do we believe about the future that we do not believe about the past ; the past, we think, is settled ; if this means more than that it is past, it might mean that it is settled *for us*, that nothing now could change our opinion of it, that any present event is irrelevant to the probability for us of any past event. But that is plainly untrue. What is true is this, that any possible present volition of ours is (for us) irrelevant to any past event. To another (or to ourselves in the future) it can serve as a sign of the past, but to us now what we do affects only the probability of the future.

This seems to me the root of the matter ; that I cannot affect the past, is a way of saying something quite clearly true about my degrees of belief. Again from the situation when we are deliberating seems to me to arise the general difference of cause and effect. We are then engaged not on disinterested knowledge or classification (to which this difference is utterly foreign), but on tracing the different consequences of our possible actions, which we naturally do in sequence forward in time, proceeding from cause to effect not from effect to cause. We can produce A or A' which produces B or B' which etc. . . . ; the probabilities of A, B are mutually dependent, but *we* come to A first from our present volition.

Other people we say can affect only the future and not the past for two reasons; first, by analogy with ourselves we know they can affect the future and not the past from their own point of view ; and secondly, if we subsume their action under the general category of cause and effect, it can only be a cause of what is later than it. This means ultimately that by affecting it we can only affect indirectly (in our calculation) events later than it. In a sense my present action is an ultimate and the only ultimate contingency.

[Of course it is our own past we know we cannot affect; our own future we know we can. The branching out of influence with at most the velocity of light is known by experience.]

It is clear that the notion and use of causal laws presupposes no ' law of causation ' to the effect that every event has a cause. We have some variable hypotheticals of the form ' If ϕx, then ψx ' with ψ later than ϕ, called causal laws: others of the form ' If ϕx, then probability a for ψx '; this is called a chance. We suppose chance to be ultimate if we see no hope of replacing it by law if we knew enough facts. There is no reason to suppose it is not ultimate. A law is a chance unity; of course, as is shown in my essay on chance, the chances do not give actual degrees of belief but a simpler system to which the actual ones approximate. So too we do not believe the laws for certain.

On the view that we have been explaining, causal necessity is not a fact; when we assert a causal law we are asserting not a fact, not an infinite conjunction, nor a connection of universals, but a variable hypothetical which is not strictly a proposition at all, but a formula from which we derive propositions.

The most obvious criticism of this view is that it is circular, for it seeks to explain away causality by means of a notion, namely that of a variable hypothetical, which itself involves causality. For the existence of a variable hypothetical depends on our using it as such, i.e. according to a causal law of our own nature proceeding from it to particular beliefs. We must try to make the answer to this criticism really clear, for it is certainly unsound.

One minor point may be made first: variable hypotheticals involve causality no more and no less than ordinary beliefs; for it belongs to the essence of any belief that we deduce from it, and act on it in a certain way, and this notion involves causality just as much as does the variable hypothetical. The causal law connected with the latter is more complicated, but not essentially different. E.g. there is no hierarchy of types of causal laws, but merely growing homogeneous complication like (x) . ., $(x)(y)$ . . ., $(x)(y)(z)$ . . .

But now for the main point. The world, or rather that part of it with which we are acquainted, exhibits as we must all agree a good deal of regularity of succession. I contend that over and above that it exhibits no feature called causal necessity, but that we make sentences called causal laws from which (i.e. having made which) we proceed to actions and propositions connected with them in a certain way, and say that a fact asserted in a proposition which is an instance of causal law is a case of causal necessity. This is a regular feature of our conduct, a part of the general regularity of things ; as always there is nothing in this beyond the regularity to be called causality, but we can again make a variable hypothetical about this conduct of ours and speak of it as an instance of causality.

But may there not be something which might be called real connections of universals ? I cannot deny it, for I can understand nothing by such a phrase ; what we call causal laws I find to be nothing of the sort.

So too there may be an infinite totality, but what seem to be propositions about it are again variable hypotheticals and ' infinite collection ' is really nonsense.

Variable hypotheticals have formal analogies to other propositions which make us take them sometimes as facts about universals, sometimes as infinite conjunctions. The analogies are misleading, difficult though they are to escape, and emotionally satisfactory as they prove to different types of mind. Both these forms of ' realism ' must be rejected by the realistic spirit.

The sort of thing that makes one want to take a realistic

view of causality is this. Suppose the human race for no reason always supposed strawberries would give them stomach-ache and so never ate them; then all their beliefs, strictly so-called, e.g. that if I eat strawberries I shall have a pain, would be true ; but would there not really be something wrong ? Is it not a fact that if they had eaten them they wouldn't have had a pain ?

No, it is not a fact ; it is a consequence of my rule. What is a fact is that I have eaten them and not had a pain. If we regarded the unfulfilled conditional as a fact we should have to suppose that any such statement as ' If he had shuffled the cards, he would have dealt himself the ace ' has a clear sense true or false, which is absurd. We only regard it as sense if it, or its contradictory, can be deduced from our system. Otherwise we say ' You can't say what would have happened ', which sounds like a confession of ignorance, and is so indeed, because it means we can't foretell what *will* happen in a similar case, but not because ' what would have happened ' is a reality of which we are ignorant.

But their system, you say, fitted all the facts known to them ; if two systems both fit the facts, is not the choice capricious ? We do, however, believe that the system is uniquely determined and that long enough investigation will lead us all to it. This is Peirce's notion of truth as what everyone will believe in the end ; it does not apply to the truthful statement of matters of fact, but to the ' true scientific system '.

What was wrong with our friends the strawberry abstainers was that they did not experiment. Why should one experiment ? To increase the weight of one's probabilities : if q is relevant to p, it is good to find out q before acting in a way involving p. But if q is known it is not worth while ; they knew, so they thought, what the issue of the experiment would be and so naturally couldn't bother to do it.

161

The difficulty comes fundamentally from taking every sentence to be a proposition ; when it is seen by considering the position of coincidences that chances are not propositions then it should be clear that laws are not either, quite apart from other reasons.

NOTES

(1) All theories, chances and laws are constructed with a view to supplementation by discovery of further facts ; these facts are always taken as known for certain. What is to be done when we are not certain of them is left quite vague, just as is the allowance to be made for uncertainty about the theory itself.

(2) Chance and law are used in the same way in a theoretical system as in a primary system ; cause, too, if the theoretical system is temporal. Of course the theoretical system is all like a variable hypothetical in being there just to be deduced from ; and a law in the theoretical system is at two removes of deduction.

(3) If the consequences of a law or theory are not clear, i.e. if there is no test whether something can or cannot be deduced from it, then it must be taken *formally* ; it is a habit not of believing ψ whenever we see ϕ, but of believing the meaning of any symbol deduced from these marks.

(4) Something should be said of the relation of this theory to Hume's. Hume said, as we do, that there was nothing but regularity, but he seemed to contradict himself by speaking of determination in the mind and a feeling of determination as giving the idea of necessity. We are accused of the same circularity unjustly : he got into a mess by taking an ' idea ' of necessity and looking for an ' impression '. It is not clear to me that there is such an idea and such an impression, but there may be. When we are necessitated as a result of experience to think in a particular way, we probably do have a different feeling from when we freshly make up our mind. But we must not say we feel ourselves being necessitated, for in the mind there is only regularity : the necessity is as always a figure of speech. I think

he understood this very well, and gave his readers credit for more intelligence than they display in their literal interpretations.

(5) As opposed to a purely *descriptive* theory of science, mine may be called a *forecasting* theory. To regard a law as a summary of certain facts seems to me inadequate; it is also an attitude of expectation for the future. The difference is clearest in regard to chances; the facts summarized do not preclude an equal chance for a coincidence which would be summarized by and, indeed, lead to a quite different theory.

8

THE FOUNDATIONS OF
MATHEMATICS (1925)

PREFACE

The object of this paper is to give a satisfactory account of the Foundations of Mathematics in accordance with the general method of Frege, Whitehead and Russell. Following these authorities, I hold that mathematics is part of logic, and so belongs to what may be called the logical school as opposed to the formalist and intuitionist schools. I have therefore taken *Principia Mathematica* as a basis for discussion and amendment ; and believe myself to have discovered how, by using the work of Mr Ludwig Wittgenstein, it can be rendered free from the serious objections which have caused its rejection by the majority of German authorities, who have deserted altogether its line of approach.

CONTENTS

I. INTRODUCTION

In this chapter we shall be concerned with the general nature of pure mathematics,[1] and how it is distinguished from

[1] In future by ' mathematics ' will always be meant ' pure mathematics '.

other sciences. Here there are really two distinct categories of things of which an account must be given—the ideas or concepts of mathematics, and the propositions of mathematics. This distinction is neither artificial nor unnecessary, for the great majority of writers on the subject have concentrated their attention on the explanation of one or other of these categories, and erroneously supposed that a satisfactory explanation of the other would immediately follow.

Thus the formalist school, of whom the most eminent representative is now Hilbert, have concentrated on the propositions of mathematics, such as ' $2 + 2 = 4$ '. They have pronounced these to be meaningless formulae to be manipulated according to certain arbitrary rules, and they hold that mathematical knowledge consists in knowing what formulae can be derived from what others consistently with the rules. Such being the propositions of mathematics, their account of its concepts, for example the number 2, immediately follows. ' 2 ' is a meaningless mark occurring in these meaningless formulae. But, whatever may be thought of this as an account of mathematical propositions, it is obviously hopeless as a theory of mathematical concepts ; for these occur not only in mathematical propositions, but also in those of everyday life. Thus ' 2 ' occurs not merely in ' $2 + 2 = 4$ ', but also in ' It is 2 miles to the station ', which is not a meaningless formula, but a significant proposition, in which ' 2 ' cannot conceivably be a meaningless mark. Nor can there be any doubt that ' 2 ' is used in the same sense in the two cases, for we can use ' $2 + 2 = 4$ ' to infer from ' It is two miles to the station and two miles on to the Gogs ' that ' It is four miles to the Gogs via the station ', so that these ordinary meanings of two and four are clearly involved in ' $2 + 2 = 4$ '. So the hopelessly inadequate formalist theory is, to some extent, the result of considering only the propositions of mathematics and neglecting the analysis of its concepts, on which additional light can be thrown by their occurrence outside mathematics in the propositions of everyday life.

Apart from formalism, there are two main general attitudes to the foundation of mathematics : that of the intuitionists or finitists, like Brouwer and Weyl in his recent papers, and that of the logicians—Frege, Whitehead, and Russell. The theories of the intuitionists admittedly involve giving up many of the most fruitful methods of modern analysis, for no reason, as it seems to me, except that the methods fail to conform to their private prejudices. They do not, therefore, profess to give any foundation for mathematics as we know it, but only for a narrower body of truth which has not yet been clearly defined. There remain the logicians whose work culminated in *Principia Mathematica*. The theories there put forward are generally rejected for reasons of detail, especially the apparently insuperable difficulties connected with the Axiom of Reducibility. But these defects in detail seem to me to be results of an important defect in principle, first pointed out by Mr Wittgenstein.

The logical school has concentrated on the analysis of mathematical concepts, which it has shown to be definable in terms of a very small number of fundamental logical concepts; and, having given this account of the concepts of mathematics, they have immediately deduced an account of mathematical propositions—namely, that they were those true propositions in which only mathematical or logical concepts occurred. Thus Russell, in *The Principles of Mathematics*, defines pure mathematics as ' the class of all propositions of the form " p implies q " where p and q are propositions containing one or more variables, the same in the two propositions, and neither p nor q contains any constants except logical constants '.[1] This reduction of mathematics to symbolic logic was rightly described by Mr Russell as one of the greatest discoveries of our

[1] Russell, *The Principles of Mathematics* (1903), p. 3

age [1] ; but it was not the end of the matter, as he seemed to suppose, because he was still far from an adequate conception of the nature of symbolic logic, to which mathematics had been reduced. I am not referring to his naive theory that logical constants were names for real objects (which he has since abandoned), but to his belief that any proposition which could be stated by using logical terms [2] alone must be a proposition of logic or mathematics.[3] I think the question is made clearer by describing the class of propositions in question as the completely general propositions, emphasizing the fact that they are not about particular things or relations, but about some or all things and relations. It is really obvious that not all such propositions are propositions of mathematics or symbolic logic. Take for example ' Any two things differ in at least thirty ways ' ; this is a completely general proposition, it could be expressed as an implication involving only logical constants and variables, and it may well be true. But as a mathematical or logical truth no one could regard it ; it is utterly different from such a proposition as ' Any two things together with any other two things make four things,' which is a logical and not merely an empirical truth. According to our philosophy we may differ in calling the one a contingent, the other a necessary proposition, or the one a genuine proposition, the other a mere tautology ; but we must all agree that there is some essential difference between the two, and that a definition of mathematical propositions must include not merely their complete generality but some further property as well. This is pointed out, with a reference to Wittgenstein, in Russell's *Introduction to Mathematical Philosophy* [4] ; but there is no trace of it in *Principia Mathematica,* nor does Mr Russell

---

[1] Loc. cit., p. 5.
[2] i.e. variables and logical constants.
[3] I neglect here, as elsewhere, the arbitrary and trivial proviso that the proposition must be of the form ' p implies q '.
[4] p. 205.

seem to have understood its tremendous importance, for example, in the consideration of primitive propositions. In the passage referred to in the *Introduction to Mathematical Philosophy*, Mr Russell distinguishes between propositions which can be enunciated in logical terms from those which logic can assert to be true, and gives as the additional characteristic of the latter that they are ' tautological' in a sense which he cannot define. It is obvious that a definition of this characteristic is essential for a clear foundation of our subject, since the idea to be defined is one of the essential sides of mathematical propositions—their content and their form. Their content must be completely generalized and their form tautological.

The formalists neglected the content altogether and made mathematics meaningless, the logicians neglected the form and made mathematics consist of any true generalizations ; only by taking account of both sides and regarding it as composed of tautologous generalizations can we obtain an adequate theory.

We have now to explain a definition of tautology which has been given by Mr Wittgenstein in his *Tractatus Logico-Philosophicus* and forms one of the most important of his contributions to the subject. In doing this we cannot avoid some explanation of his theory of propositions in general.

We must begin with the notion of an *atomic proposition*[1]; this is one which could not be analysed in terms of other propositions and could consist of names alone without logical constants. For instance, by joining ' ϕ ', the name of a quality, to 'a ', the name of an individual, and writing ' ϕa ', we have an atomic proposition asserting that the individual has the quality. Thus, if we neglect the fact that ' Socrates ' and ' wise ' are incomplete symbols and regard them as names,

---

[1] Wittgenstein calls these ' elementary propositions '; I have called them ' atomic ' in order to follow Mr Russell in using ' elementary ' with a different meaning.

' Socrates is wise ' is an atomic proposition ; but ' All men are wise ', ' Socrates is not wise ', are not atomic.

Suppose now we have, say, n atomic propositions p, q, r, ... With regard to their truth or falsity there are 2^n mutually exclusive ultimate possibilities, which we could arrange in a table like this (T signifies truth, and F falsity, and we have taken $n = 2$ for brevity).

p	q
T	T
F	T
T	F
F	F

These 2^n possibilities we will call the truth-possibilities of the n atomic propositions. We may wish to pick out any sub-set of them, and assert that it is a possibility out of this sub-set which is, in fact, realized—that is, to express our agreement with some of the possibilities and our disagreement with the remainder. We can do this by setting marks T and F against the possibilities with which we agree and disagree respectively. In this way we obtain a proposition.

Thus

' p	q	'
T	T	F
F	T	T
T	F	T
F	F	T

is the proposition ' Not both p and q are true ', or 'p is incompatible with q ', for we have allowed all the possibilities except the first, which we have disallowed.

Similarly

'
p	q	
T	T	T
F	T	T
T	F	F
F	F	T
'

is the proposition ' If p, then q '.

A proposition which expresses agreement and disagreement with the truth-possibilities of p, q, . . . (which need not be atomic) is called a truth-function of the arguments p, q, . . . Or, more accurately, P is said to be the same truth-function of p, q, . . . as R is of r, s, . . . if P expresses agreement with the truth-possibilities of p, q, . . . corresponding by the substitution of p for r, q for s, . . . to the truth-possibilities of r, s, . . . with which R expresses agreement. Thus 'p and q ' is the same truth-function of p, q as 'r and s ' is of r, s, in each case the only possibility allowed being that both the arguments are true. Mr Wittgenstein has perceived that, if we accept this account of truth-functions as expressing agreement and disagreement with truth-possiblities, there is no reason why the arguments to a truth-function should not be infinite in number.[1] As no previous writer has considered truth-functions as capable of more than a finite number of

[1] Thus the logical sum of a set of propositions is the proposition that one at least of the set is true, and it is immaterial whether the set is finite or infinite. On the other hand, an infinite algebraic sum is not really a sum at all, but a *limit*, and so cannot be treated as a sum except subject to certain restrictions.

arguments, this is a most important innovation. Of course if the arguments are infinite in number they cannot all be enumerated and written down separately; but there is no need for us to enumerate them if we can determine them in any other way, as we can by using propositional functions.

A propositional function is an expression of the form '$f\hat{x}$', which is such that it expresses a proposition when any symbol (of a certain appropriate logical type depending on f) is substituted for '$\hat{x}$'. Thus '$\hat{x}$ is a man' is a propositional function. We can use propositional functions to collect together the range of propositions which are all the values of the function for all possible values of x. Thus '$\hat{x}$ is a man' collects together all the propositions 'a is a man', 'b is a man', etc. Having now by means of a propositional function defined a set of propositions, we can, by using an appropriate notation, assert the logical sum or product of this set. Thus, by writing '$(x) . fx$' we assert the logical product of all propositions of the form 'fx'; by writing '$(\exists x). fx$' we assert their logical sum. Thus '$(x) . x$ is a man' would mean 'Everything is a man'; '$(\exists x). x$ is a man', 'There is something which is a man'. In the first case we allow only the possibility that all the propositions of the form 'x is a man' are true; in the second we exclude only the possibility that all the propositions of the form 'x is a man' are false.

Thus general propositions containing 'all' and 'some' are found to be truth-functions, for which the arguments are not enumerated but given in another way. But we must guard here against a possible mistake. Take such a proposition as 'All men are mortal'; this is not as might at first sight be supposed the logical product of the propositions 'x is mortal' for such values of x as are men. Such an interpretation can easily be shown to be erroneous (see, for example, *Principia Mathematica*, I, 1st ed., p. 47, 2nd ed., p. 45). 'All men are mortal' must be interpreted as meaning '$(x) .$ if x is a man, x is mortal ', i.e. it is the logical product of all the values of the function ' if x is a man, x is mortal '.

Mr Wittgenstein maintains that all propositions are, in the sense defined, truth-functions of elementary propositions. This is hard to prove, but is on its own merits extremely plausible ; it says that, when we assert anything, we are saying that it is one out of a certain group of ultimate possibilities which is realized, not one out of the remaining possibilities. Also it applies to all the propositions which could be expressed in the symbolism of *Principia Mathematica* ; since these are built up from atomic propositions by using firstly conjunctions like ' if ', ' and ', ' or ', and secondly various kinds of generality (apparent variables). And both these methods of construction have been shown to create truth-functions.[1]

From this account we see when two propositional symbols are to be regarded as instances of the same proposition— namely, when they express agreement and disagreement with the same sets of truth-possibilities of atomic propositions.

Thus in the symbolism of *Principia Mathematica*

$$`p \supset q : \sim p \, . \, \supset \, . \, q`, \, `q \vee : p \, . \, \sim p`$$

are both more complicated ways of writing ' q '.

Given any set if n atomic propositions as arguments, there are 2^n corresponding truth-possibilities, and therefore 2^{2^n} sub-classes of their truth-possibilities, and so 2^{2^n} truth-functions of n arguments, one expressing agreement with each sub-class and disagreement with the remainder. But among these 2^{2^n} there are two extreme cases of great importance : one in which we express agreement with all the truth-possibilities, the other in which we express agreement with none of them. A proposition of the first kind is called a *tautology*, of the second a *contradiction*. Tautologies and contradictions are

---

[1] The form ' A believes p ' will perhaps be suggested as doubtful. This is clearly not a truth-function of ' p ', but may nevertheless be one of other atomic propositions.

not real propositions, but degenerate cases. We may, perhaps, make this clear most easily by taking the simplest case, when there is only one argument.

The tautology is '

p	
T	T
F	T

', i.e. ' p or not-p '.

This really asserts nothing whatever; it leaves you no wiser than it found you. You know nothing about the weather, if you know that it is either raining or not raining.[1]

The contradiction is '

p	
T	F
F	F

',

i.e. ' p is neither true nor false '.

This is clearly self-contradictory and does not represent a possible state of affairs whose existence could be asserted.

Tautologies and contradictions can be of all degrees of complexity; to give other examples ' $(x).\phi x : \supset : \phi a$ ' is a tautology, ' $\sim.(\exists x).\phi x : \phi a$ ' a contradiction. Clearly by negating a contradiction we get a tautology, and by negating a tautology a contradiction. It is important to see that tautologies are not simply true propositions, though for many purposes they can be treated as true propositions. A genuine proposition asserts something about reality, and it is true if reality is as it is asserted to be. But a tautology is a symbol constructed so as to say nothing whatever about reality, but to express total ignorance by agreeing with every possibility.

[1] Wittgenstein, *Tractatus Logico-Philosophicus*, 4·461.

The assimilation of tautologies and contradictions with true and false propositions respectively results from the fact that tautologies and contradictions can be taken as arguments to truth-functions just like ordinary propositions, and for determining the truth or falsity of the truth-function, tautologies and contradictions among its arguments must be counted as true and false respectively. Thus, if 't' be a tautology, 'c' a contradiction, 't and p', 'If t, then p', 'c or p' are the same as 'p', and 't or p', 'if c, then p' are tautologies.

We have here, thanks to Mr Wittgenstein, to whom the whole of this analysis is due, a clearly defined sense of tautology; but is this, it may be asked, the sense in which we found tautology to be an essential characteristic of the propositions of mathematics and symbolic logic? The question must be decided by comparison. Are the propositions of symbolic logic and mathematics tautologies in Mr Wittgenstein's sense?

Let us begin by considering not the propositions of mathematics but those of *Principia Mathematica*.[1] These are obtained by the process of deduction from certain primitive propositions, which fall into two groups——those expressed in symbols and those expressed in words. Those expressed in words are nearly all nonsense by the Theory of Types, and should be replaced by symbolic conventions. The real primitive propositions, those expressed in symbols, are, with one exception, tautologies in Wittgenstein's sense. So, as the process of deduction is such that from tautologies only tautologies follow, were it not for one blemish the whole structure would consist of tautologies. The blemish is of course the Axiom of Reducibility, which is, as will be shown below,[2] a genuine proposition, whose truth or falsity is a

---

[1] This distinction is made only because *Principia Mathematica* may be a wrong interpretation of mathematics; in the main I think it is a right one.

[2] See Section V.

matter of brute fact, not of logic. It is, therefore, not a tautology in any sense, and its introduction into mathematics is inexcusable. But suppose it could be dispensed with, and *Principia Mathematica* were modified accordingly, this would consist entirely of tautologies in Wittgenstein's sense. And therefore, if *Principia Mathematica* is on the right lines as a foundation and interpretation of mathematics, it is Wittgenstein's sense of tautology in which mathematics is tautologous.

But the adequacy of *Principia Mathematica* is a matter of detail ; and, since we have seen it contains a very serious flaw, we can no longer be sure that mathematics is the kind of thing Whitehead and Russell suppose it to be, or therefore that it consists of tautologies in Wittgenstein's sense. One thing is, however, clear : that mathematics does not consist of genuine propositions or assertions of fact which could be based on inductive evidence, as it was proposed to base the Axiom of Reducibility, but is in some sense necessary or tautologous. In actual life, as Wittgenstein says, " it is never a mathematical proposition which we need, but we use mathematical propositions *only* in order to infer from propositions which do not belong to mathematics to others which equally do not belong to mathematics ".[1] Thus we use ' $2 \times 2 = 4$ ' to infer from ' I have two pennies in each of my two pockets ' to ' I have four pennies altogether in my pockets '. ' $2 \times 2 = 4$ ' is not itself a genuine proposition in favour of which inductive evidence can be required, but a tautology which can be seen to be tautologous by anyone who can fully grasp its meaning. When we proceed further in mathematics the propositions become so complicated that we cannot see immediately that they are tautologous, and have to assure ourselves of this by deducing them from more obvious tautologies. The primitive propositions on which we fall back in the end must be such that no evidence could be required

[1] Wittgenstein, op. cit., 6·211.

for them, since they are patent tautologies like ' If p, then p '. But the tautologies of which mathematics consist may perhaps turn out not to be of Wittgenstein's kind, but of some other. Their essential use is to facilitate logical inference ; this is achieved in the most obvious way by constructing tautologies in Wittgenstein's sense, for if ' If p, then q ' is a tautology, we can logically infer ' q ' from ' p ', and, conversely, if ' q ' follows logically from ' p ', ' If p, then q ' is a tautology.[1]   But it is possible that there are other kinds of formulae which could be used to facilitate inference ; for instance, what we may call identities such as ' $a = b$ ', signifying that ' a ', ' b ' may be substituted for one another in any proposition without altering it. I do not mean without altering its truth or falsity, but without altering what proposition it is. ' $2 + 2 = 4$ ' might well be an identity in this sense, since ' I have $2 + 2$ hats ' and ' I have 4 hats ' are the same proposition, as they agree and disagree with the same sets of ultimate truth-possibilities.

Our next problem is to decide whether mathematics consists of tautologies (in the precise sense defined by Wittgenstein, to which we shall in future confine the word ' tautology ') or of formulae of some other sort. It is fairly clear that geometry, in which we regard such terms as ' point ', ' line ' as meaning any things satisfying certain axioms, so that the only constant terms are truth-functions like ' or ', ' some ', consists of tautologies. And the same would be true of analysis if we regarded numbers as any things satisfying Peano's axioms. Such a view would however be certainly inadequate, because since the numbers from 100 on satisfy Peano's axioms, it would give us no means of distinguishing ' This equation has three roots ' from ' This equation has a hundred and three roots '. So numbers must be defined not as variables but as

---

[1] This may perhaps be made clearer by remarking that if ' q ' follows logically from ' p ', ' $p . \sim q$ ' must be self-contradictory, therefore ' $\sim (p . \sim q)$ ' tautologous or ' $p \supset q$ ' tautologous.

constants, and the nature of the propositions of analysis becomes doubtful.

I believe that they are tautologies, but the proof of this depends on giving a detailed analysis of them, and the disproof of any other theory would depend on finding an insuperable difficulty in the details of its construction. In this chapter I propose to discuss the question in a general way, which must inevitably be rather vague and unsatisfactory. I shall first try to explain the great difficulties which a theory of mathematics as tautologies must overcome, and then I shall try to explain why the alternative sort of theory suggested by these difficulties seem hopelessly impracticable. Then in the following chapters I shall return to the theory that mathematics consists of tautologies, discuss and partially reject the method for overcoming the difficulties given in *Principia Mathematica*, and construct an alternative and, to my mind, satisfactory solution.

Our first business is, then, the difficulties of the tautology theory. They spring from a fundamental characteristic of modern analysis which we have now to emphasize. This characteristic may be called *extensionality*, and the difficulties may be explained as those which confront us if we try to reduce a calculus of extensions to a calculus of truth-functions. Here, of course, we are using ' extension ' in its logical sense, in which the extension of a predicate is a class, that of a relation a class of ordered couples ; so that in calling mathematics extensional we mean that it deals not with predicates but with classes, not with relations in the ordinary sense but with possible correlations, or " relations in extension " as Mr Russell calls them. Let us take as examples of this point three fundamental mathematical concepts——the idea of a real number, the idea of a function (of a real variable), and the idea of similarity of classes (in Cantor's sense).

Real numbers are defined as segments of rationals ; any

segment of rationals is a real number, and there are $2^{\aleph_0}$ of them. It is not necessary that the segment should be defined by any property or predicate of its members in any ordinary sense of predicate. A real number is therefore an extension, and it may even be an extension with no corresponding intension. In the same way a function of a real variable is a relation in extension, which need not be given by any real relation or formula.

The point is perhaps most striking in Cantor's definition of similarity. Two classes are said to be similar (*i.e.* have the same cardinal number) when there is a one-one relation whose domain is the one class and converse domain the other. Here it is essential that the one-one relation need only be a relation in extension ; it is obvious that two classes could be similar, i.e. capable of being correlated, without there being any relation actually correlating them.

There is a verbal point which requires mention here ; I do not use the word ' class ' to imply a principle of classification, as the word naturally suggests, but by a ' class ' I mean any set of things of the same logical type. Such a set, it seems to me, may or may not be definable either by enumeration or as the extension of a predicate. If it is not so definable we cannot mention it by itself, but only deal with it by implication in propositions about all classes or some classes. The same is true of relations in extension, by which I do not merely mean the extensions of actual relations, but any set of ordered couples. That this is the notion occurring in mathematics seems to me absolutely clear from the last of the above examples, Cantor's definition of similarity, where obviously there is no need for the one-one relation in extension to be either finite or the extension of an actual relation.

Mathematics is therefore essentially extensional, and may be called a calculus of extensions, since its propositions assert relations between extensions. This, as we have said, is hard to reduce to a calculus of truth-functions, to which it must be reduced if mathematics is to consist of tautologies; for tautologies are truth-functions of a certain special sort, namely those agreeing with all the truth-possibilities of their arguments. We can perhaps most easily explain the difficulty by an example.

Let us take an extensional assertion of the simplest possible sort : the assertion that one class includes another. So long as the classes are defined as the classes of things having certain predicates ϕ and ψ, there is no difficulty. That the class of ψ's includes the class of ϕ's means simply that everything which is a ϕ is a ψ, which, as we have seen above is a truth-function. But we have seen that mathematics has (at least apparently) to deal also with classes which are not given by defining predicates. (Such classes occur not merely when mentioned separately, but also in any statement about ' all classes ', ' all real numbers '.) Let us take two such classes as simple as possible—the class (a, b, c) and the class (a, b). Then that the class (a, b, c) includes the class (a, b) is, in a broad sense, tautological and apart from its triviality would be a mathematical proposition ; but it does not seem to be a tautology in Wittgenstein's sense, that is a certain sort of truth-function of elementary propositions. The obvious way of trying to make it a truth-function is to introduce identity and write ' (a, b) is contained in (a, b, c)' as ' $(x) : . x = a.$ $\mathbf{v}. x = b : \supset : x = a . \mathbf{v} . x = b . \mathbf{v} . x = c$'. This certainly looks like a tautological truth-function, whose ultimate arguments are values of ' $x = a$ ', ' $x = b$ ', ' $x = c$ ', that is propositions like ' $a = a$ ', ' $b = a$ ', ' $d = a$ '. But these are not real propositions at all ; in ' $a = b$ ' either ' a ', ' b ' are names of the same thing, in which case the proposition says nothing, or of different things, in which case it is absurd. In neither case is it the assertion of a fact ; it only appears to be a real assertion by confusion with the case when ' a ' or ' b ' is not a name but a description.[1] When 'a', 'b' are both names, the only significance which can be placed on '$a = b$' is that it indicates that we use 'a', 'b' as names of the same thing or, more generally, as equivalent symbols.

The preceding and other considerations led Wittgenstein to the view that mathematics does not consist of tautologies, but of what he called 'equations', for which I should prefer to substitute 'identities'. That is, formulae of the form '$a = b$' where 'a', 'b' are equivalent symbols. There is a certain plausibility in such an account of, for instance, '$2 + 2 = 4$.' Since 'I have $2 + 2$ hats', 'I have 4 hats' are the same proposition,[2] '$2 + 2$' and '4' are equivalent symbols. As it stands this is obviously a ridiculously narrow view of mathematics, and confines it to simple arithmetic; but it is interesting to see whether a theory of mathematics could not be constructed with identities for its foundation. I have spent a lot of time developing such a theory, and found that it was faced with what seemed to me insuperable difficulties. It would be out of place here to give a detailed survey of this blind alley, but I shall try to indicate in a general way the obstructions which block its end.

First of all we have to consider of what kind mathematical propositions will on such a theory be. We suppose the most primitive type to be the identity '$a = b$', which only becomes a real proposition if it is taken to be about not the things meant by 'a', 'b', but these symbols themselves; mathematics then consists of propositions built up out of identities by a process analogous to that by which ordinary propositions are constructed out of atomic ones; that is to say, mathematical propositions are (on this theory), in some sense, truth-functions of identities. Perhaps this is an overstatement,

---

[1] For a fuller discussion of identity see the next chapter.
[2] In the sense explained above. They clearly are not the same sentence, but they are the same truth-function of atomic propositions and so assert the same fact.

and the theory might not assert all mathematical propositions to be of this form ; but it is clearly one of the important forms that would be supposed to occur. Thus

$$' x^2 - 3x + 2 = 0 : \supset_x : x = 2 . \vee . x = 1 \, '$$

would be said to be of this form, and would correspond to a verbal proposition which was a truth-function of the verbal propositions corresponding to the arguments ' $x = 2$ ', etc. Thus the above proposition would amount to ' If " $x^2 - 3x + 2$ " means 0, " x " means 2 or 1 '. Mathematics would then be, in part at least, the activity of constructing formulae which corresponded in this way to verbal propositions. Such a theory would be difficult and perhaps impossible to develop in detail, but there are, I think, other and simpler reasons for dismissing it. These arise as soon as we cease to treat mathematics as an isolated structure, and consider the mathematical elements in non-mathematical propositions. For simplicity let us confine ourselves to cardinal numbers, and suppose ourselves to know the analysis of the proposition that the class of ϕ's is n in number $[\hat{x}(\phi x)\epsilon n]$. Here ϕ may be any ordinary predicate defining a class, e.g. the class of ϕ's may be the class of Englishmen. Now take such a proposition as ' The square of the number of ϕ's is greater by two than the cube of the number of ψ's '. This proposition we cannot, I think, help analysing in this sort of way :

$$(\exists m, n) . \hat{x} \, (\phi x) \, \epsilon m . \hat{x} \, (\psi x) \, \epsilon n . m^2 = n^3 + 2.$$

It is an empirical not a mathematical proposition, and is about the ϕ's and ψ's, not about symbols ; yet there occurs in it the mathematical pseudo-proposition $m^2 = n^3 + 2$, of which, according to the theory under discussion, we can only make sense by taking it to be about symbols, thereby making the whole proposition to be partly about symbols. Moreover, being an empirical proposition, it is a truth-function of elementary propositions expressing agreement with those possibilities which give numbers of ϕ's and ψ's satisfying $m^2 = n^3 + 2$. Thus ' $m^2 = n^3 + 2$ ' is not, as it seems to be, one of the truth-arguments in the proposition above, but rather part of the truth-function like ' $\sim$ ' or ' $\vee$ ' or ' $\exists$, m. n,' which determine which truth-function of elementary propositions it is that we are asserting. Such a use of $m^2 = n^3 + 2$ the identity theory of mathematics is quite inadequate to explain.

On the other hand, the tautology theory would do everything which is required ; according to it $m^2 = n^3 + 2$ would be a tautology for the values of m and n which satisfy it, and a contradiction for all others. So

$$\hat{x} \ (\phi x) \ \epsilon m \ . \ \hat{x} \ (\psi x) \ \epsilon n \ . \ m^2 = n^3 + 2$$

would for the first set of values of m, n be equivalent to

$$\hat{x} \ (\phi x) \ \epsilon m \ . \ \hat{x} \ (\psi x) \ \epsilon n$$

simply, ' $m^2 = n^3 + 2$ ' being tautologous, and therefore superfluous ; and for all other values it would be self-contradictory. So that

$$' \ (\exists m, n) : \hat{x} \ (\phi x) \ \epsilon m . \hat{x} \ (\psi x) \ \epsilon n . m^2 = n^3 + 2 \ '$$

would be the logical sum of the propositions

$$' \ \hat{x} \ (\phi x) \ \epsilon m . \hat{x} \ (\psi x) \ \epsilon n \ '$$

for all m, n satisfying $m^2 = n^3 + 2$, and of contradictions for all other m, n ; and is therefore the proposition we require, since in a logical sum the contradictions are superfluous. So this difficulty, which seems fatal to the identity theory, is escaped altogether by the tautology theory, which we are therefore encouraged to pursue and see if we cannot find a way of overcoming the difficulties which we found would confront us in attempting to reduce an extensional calculus to a calculus of truth-functions. Such a solution is attempted in *Principia Mathematica*, and will be discussed in the next chapter ; but before we proceed to this we must say something about the well-known contradictions of the theory of aggregates which our theory will also have to escape.

It is not sufficiently remarked, and the fact is entirely neglected in *Principia Mathematica*, that these contradictions fall into two fundamentally distinct groups, which we will call A and B. The best known ones are divided as follows :—

A. (1) The class of all classes which are not members of themselves.

(2) The relation between two relations when one does not have itself to the other.

(3) Burali Forti's contradiction of the greatest ordinal.

B. (4) ' I am lying.'

(5) The least integer not nameable in fewer than nineteen syllables.

(6) The least indefinable ordinal.

(7) Richard's Contradiction.

(8) Weyl's contradiction about ' heterologisch '.[1]

The principle according to which I have divided them is of fundamental importance. Group A consists of contradictions which, were no provision made against them, would occur in a logical or mathematical system itself. They involve only logical or mathematical terms such as class and number, and show that there must be something wrong with our logic or mathematics. But the contradictions of Group B are not purely logical, and cannot be stated in logical terms alone ; for they all contain some reference to thought, language, or symbolism, which are not formal but empirical terms. So

[1] For the first seven of these see *Principia Mathematica*, I (1910), p. 63. For the eighth see Weyl, *Das Kontinuum*, p. 2.

they may be due not to faulty logic or mathematics, but to faulty ideas concerning thought and language. If so, they would not be relevant to mathematics or to logic, if by ' logic ' we mean a symbolic system, though of course they would be relevant to logic in the sense of the analysis of thought.[1]

This view of the second group of contradictions is not original. For instance, Peano decided that " Exemplo de Richard non pertine ad Mathematica, sed ad linguistica ",[2] and therefore dismissed it. But such an attitude is not completely satisfactory. We have contradictions involving both mathematical and linguistic ideas ; the mathematician dismisses them by saying that the fault must lie in the linguistic elements, but the linguistician may equally well dismiss them for the opposite reason, and the contradictions will never be solved. The only solution which has ever been given,[3] that in *Principia Mathematica*, definitely attributed the contradictions to bad logic, and it is up to opponents of this view to show clearly the fault in what Peano called linguistics, but what I should prefer to call epistemology, to which these contradictions are due.

II. PRINCIPIA MATHEMATICA

In the last chapter I tried to explain the difficulties which faced the theory that the propositions of mathematics are tautologies ; in this we have to discuss the attempted solution of these difficulties given in *Principia Mathematica*. I shall try to show that this solution has three important defects, and the remainder of this essay will be devoted to expounding a modified theory from which these defects have been removed.

[1] These two meanings of ' logic ' are frequently confused. It really should be clear that those who say mathematics is logic are not meaning by ' logic ' at all the same thing as those who define logic as the analysis and criticism of thought.

[2] *Rivista di Mat.*, 8 (1906), p. 157.

[3] Other so-called solutions are merely inadequate excuses for not giving a solution.

The theory of *Principia Mathematica* is that every class or aggregate (I use the words as synonyms) is defined by a propositional function—that is, consists of the values of x for which ' ϕx ' is true, where ' ϕx ' is a symbol which expresses a proposition if any symbol of appropriate type be substituted for ' x '. This amounts to saying that every class has a defining property. Let us take the class consisting of a and b ; why, it may be asked, must there be a function $\phi\hat{x}$ such that ' ϕa ', ' ϕb ' are true, but all other ' ϕx's false ? This is answered by giving as such a function ' $x = a . \vee . x = b$ '. Let us for the present neglect the difficulties connected with identity, and accept this answer ; it shows us that any finite class is defined by a propositional function constructed by means of identity ; but as regards infinite classes it leaves us exactly where we were before, that is, without any reason to suppose that they are all defined by propositional functions, for it is impossible to write down an infinite series of identities. To this it will be answered that a class can only be given to us either by enumeration of its members, in which case it must be finite, or by giving a propositional function which defines it. So that we cannot be in any way concerned with infinite classes or aggregates, if such there be, which are not defined by propositional functions.[1] But this argument contains a common mistake, for it supposes that, because we cannot consider a thing individually, we can have no concern with it at all. Thus, although an infinite indefinable class cannot be mentioned by itself, it is nevertheless involved in any statement beginning ' All classes ' or ' There is a class such that ', and if indefinable classes are excluded the meaning of all such statements will be fundamentally altered.

Whether there are indefinable classes or not is an empirical question ; both possibilities are perfectly conceivable. But even if, in fact, all classes are definable, we cannot in our logic

[1] For short I shall call such classes ' indefinable classes '.

identify classes with definable classes without destroying the apriority and necessity which is the essence of logic. But in case any one still thinks that by classes we mean definable classes, and by ' There is a class ' ' There is a definable class ', let him consider the following illustration. This illustration does not concern exactly this problem, but the corresponding problem for two variables—the existence of relations in extension not definable by propositional functions of two variables. But this question is clearly so analogous to the other that the answers to both must be the same.

Consider the proposition ' $\hat{x}(\phi x)\mathrm{sm}\hat{x}(\psi x)$ ' (i.e. the class defined by $\phi\hat{x}$ has the same cardinal as that defined by $\psi\hat{x}$) ; this is defined to mean that there is a one-one relation in extension whose domain is $\hat{x}(\phi x)$ and whose converse domain is $\hat{x}(\psi x)$. Now if by relation in extension we mean definable relation in extension, this means that two classes have the same cardinal only when there is a real relation or function $f(x, y)$ correlating them term by term. Whereas clearly what was meant by Cantor, who first gave this definition, was merely that the two classes were such that they could be correlated, not that there must be a propositional function which actually correlated them.[1] Thus the classes of male and female angels may be infinite and equal in number, so that it would be possible to pair off completely the male with the female, without there being any real relation such as marriage correlating them. The possibility of indefinable classes and relations in extension is an essential part of the extensional attitude of modern mathematics which we emphasized in Chapter I, and that it is neglected in *Principia Mathematica* is the first of the three great defects in that work. The mistake is made not by having a primitive proposition asserting that all classes are definable, but by giving a definition of class which applies only to definable classes, so that all

[1] Cf. W. E. Johnson, *Logic Part II* (1922), p. 159.

mathematical propositions about some or all classes are misinterpreted. This misinterpretation is not merely objectionable on its own account in a general way, but is especially pernicious in connection with the Multiplicative Axiom, which is a tautology when properly interpreted, but when misinterpreted after the fashion of *Principia Mathematica* becomes a significant empirical proposition, which there is no reason to suppose true. This will be shown in Chapter V.

The second defect in *Principia Mathematica* represents a failure to overcome not, like the first, the difficulties raised by the extensionality of mathematics, but those raised by the contradictions discussed at the end of Chapter I. These contradictions it was proposed to remove by what is called the Theory of Types, which consists really of two distinct parts directed respectively against the two groups of contradictions. These two parts were unified by being both deduced in a rather sloppy way from the ' vicious-circle principle ', but it seems to me essential to consider them separately.

The contradictions of Group A are removed by pointing out that a propositional function cannot significantly take itself as argument, and by dividing functions and classes into a hierarchy of types according to their possible arguments. Thus the assertion that a class is a member of itself is neither true nor false, but meaningless. This part of the Theory of Types seems to me unquestionably correct, and I shall not discuss it further.

The first part of the theory, then, distinguishes types of propositional functions by their arguments ; thus there are functions of individuals, functions of functions of individuals, functions of functions of functions of individuals, and so on. The second part designed to meet the second group of contradictions requires further distinctions between the different functions which take the same arguments, for instance between the different functions of individuals. The following explanation of these distinctions is based on the Introduction to the Second Edition of *Principia Mathematica*.

We start with atomic propositions, which have been explained in Chapter I. Out of these by means of the *stroke* ($p/q =$ not both p and q are true) we can construct any truth-function of a finite number of atomic propositions as arguments. The assemblage of propositions so obtained are called elementary propositions. By substituting a variable for the name of an individual in one or more of its occurrences in an elementary proposition we obtain an elementary function of individuals. An *elementary function* of individuals, '$\phi\hat{x}$', is therefore one whose values are elementary propositions, that is, truth-functions of a finite number of atomic propositions. Such functions were called, in the First Edition of *Principia Mathematica, predicative functions*. We shall speak of them by their new name, and in the next chapter use ' predicative function ' in a new and original sense, for which it seems more appropriate. In general, an elementary function or *matrix* of one or more variables, whether these are individuals or not, is one whose values are elementary propositions. Matrices are denoted by a mark of exclamation after the functional symbol. Thus ' $F ! (\hat{\phi} ! \hat{z}, \hat{\psi} ! \hat{z}, \hat{x}, \hat{y})$ ' is a matrix having two individuals and two elementary functions of individuals as arguments.

From an elementary function '$\phi ! \hat{x}$' we obtain, as in Chapter I, the propositions ' $(x).\phi ! x$ ' and ' $(\exists x).\phi ! x$ ' which respectively assert the truth of all and of at least one of the values of ' $\phi ! x$ '. Similarly from an elementary function of two individuals $\phi ! (\hat{x}, \hat{y})$ we obtain functions of one individual such as $(y).\phi ! (\hat{x}, y), (\exists y).\phi ! (\hat{x}, y)$. The values of these functions are propositions such as $(y).\phi ! (a, y)$ which are not elementary propositions ; hence the functions themselves are not elementary functions. Such functions, whose values result from generalizing a matrix all of whose values are individuals, are called first-order functions, and written $\phi_1\hat{z}$.

Suppose a is a constant. Then ' $\phi \,!\, a$ ' will denote for the various values of ϕ all the various elementary propositions of which a is a constituent. We can thus form the propositions $(\phi).\phi \,!\, a$, $(\exists\phi).\,\phi \,!\, a$ asserting respectively the truth of all, and of at least one of the above assemblage of propositions. More generally we can assert by writing $(\phi).F \,!\, (\phi \,!\, \hat{z})$, $(\exists\phi).F \,!\, (\phi \,!\, \hat{z})$ the truth of all and of at least one of the values of $F \,!\, (\phi \,!\, \hat{z})$. Such propositions are clearly not elementary, so that such a function as $(\phi).F \,!\, (\phi \,!\, \hat{z}, x)$ is not an elementary function of x. Such a function involving the totality of elementary functions is said to be of the second order and written $\phi_2 x$. By adopting the new variable ϕ_2 " we shall obtain other new functions

$$(\phi_2).f \,!\, (\phi_2 \,\hat{z}, x), \quad (\exists\phi_2).f \,!\, (\phi_2\hat{z}, x),$$

which are again not among values for $\hat{\phi}_2 x$ (where ϕ_2 is the argument), because the totality of values of $\phi_2\hat{z}$, which is now involved, is different from the totality of values of $\phi \,!\, \hat{z}$, which was formerly involved. However much we may enlarge the meaning of ϕ, a function of x in which ϕ occurs as apparent variable has a correspondingly enlarged meaning, so that, however ϕ may be defined, $(\phi).f \,!\, (\phi\hat{z}, x)$ and $(\exists\phi).f \,!\, (\phi\hat{z}, x)$ can never be values for ϕx. To attempt to make them so is like attempting to catch one's own shadow. It is impossible to obtain one variable which embraces among its values all possible functions of individuals." [1]

For the way in which this distinction of functions into orders of which no totality is possible is used to escape the contradictions of Group B, which are shown to result from the ambiguities of language which disregard this distinction,

[1] *Principia Mathematica*, I, 2nd ed., (1925), p. xxxiv.

reference may be made to *Principia Mathematica*.[1] Here it may be sufficient to apply the method to a contradiction not given in that work which is particularly free from irrelevant elements : I mean Weyl's contradiction concerning ' heterologisch ',[2] which must now be explained. Some adjectives have meanings which are predicates of the adjective word itself ; thus the word ' short ' is short, but the word ' long ' is not long. Let us call adjectives whose meanings are predicates of them, like ' short ', autological; others heterological. Now is ' heterological ' heterological ? If it is, its meaning is not a predicate of it; that is, it is not heterological. But if it is not heterological, its meaning is a predicate of it, and therefore it is heterological. So we have a complete contradiction.

According to the principles of *Principia Mathematica* this contradiction would be solved in the following way. An adjective word is the symbol for a propositional function, *e.g.* ' ϕ ' for $\phi\hat{x}$. Let R be the relation of meaning between ' ϕ ' and $\phi\hat{x}$. Then ' w is heterological' is ' $(\exists\phi) . wR(\phi\hat{x}) . \sim \phi w$ '. In this, as we have seen, the apparent variable ϕ must have a definite range of values (*e.g.* the range of elementary functions), of which $Fx = :.(\exists\phi) : xR(\phi\hat{x}) . \sim \phi x$ cannot itself be a member. So that ' heterological ' or ' F ' is not itself an adjective in the sense in which ' ϕ ' is. We do not have $(\exists\phi) .$ ' F ' $R(\phi\hat{x})$ because the meaning of ' F ' is not a function included in the range of ' ϕ '. So that when heterological and autological are unambiguously defined, ' heterological ' is not an adjective in the sense in question, and is neither heterological nor autological, and there is no contradiction.

Thus this theory of a hierarchy of orders of functions of individuals escapes the contradictions ; but it lands us in an almost equally serious difficulty, for it invalidates many

---

[1] *Principia Mathematica*, I, 1st ed., (1910), p. 117.
[2] Weyl, *Das Kontinuum*, p. 2.

important mathematical arguments which appear to contain exactly the same fallacy as the contradictions. In the First Edition of *Principia Mathematica* it was proposed to justify these arguments by a special axiom, the Axiom of Reducibility, which asserted that to every non-elementary function there is an equivalent elementary function.[1] This axiom there is no reason to suppose true ; and if it were true, this would be a happy accident and not a logical necessity, for it is not a tautology. This will be shown positively in Chapter V ; but for the present it should be sufficient that it does not seem to be a tautology and that there is no reason to suppose that it is one. Such an axiom has no place in mathematics, and anything which cannot be proved without using it cannot be regarded as proved at all.

It is perhaps worth while, parenthetically, to notice a point which is sometimes missed. Why, it may be asked, does not the Axiom of Reducibility reproduce the contradictions which the distinction between elementary and other functions avoided ? For it asserts that to any non-elementary there is an equivalent elementary function, and so may appear to lose again whatever was gained by making the distinction. This is not, however, the case, owing to the peculiar nature of the contradictions in question; for, as pointed out above, this second set of contradictions are not purely mathematical, but all involve the ideas of thought or meaning, in connection with which equivalent functions (in the sense of equivalent explained above) are not interchangeable ; for instance, one can be meant by a certain word or symbol, but not the other, and one can be definable, and not the other.[2] On the

[1] Two functions are called equivalent when the same arguments render them both true or both false. (German *umfangsgleich*).

[2] Dr L. Chwistek appears to have overlooked this point that, if a function is definable, the equivalent elementary function need not also be definable in terms of given symbols. In his paper " Über die Antinomien der Prinzipien der Mathematik " in *Math. Zeitschrift*, 14, (1922), pp. 236–243, he denotes by S a many-one relation between the natural numbers and the classes defined by functions definable in

other hand, any purely mathematical contradiction which arose from confusing elementary and non-elementary functions would be reinstated by the Axiom of Reducibility, owing to the extensional nature of mathematics, in which equivalent functions are interchangeable. But no such contradiction has been shown to arise, so that the Axiom of Reducibility does not seem to be self-contradictory. These considerations bring out clearly the peculiarity of this second group of contradictions, and make it even more probable that they have a psychological or epistemological and not a purely logical or mathematical solution ; so that there is something wrong with the account of the matter given in *Principia*.

The principal mathematical methods which appear to require the Axiom of Reducibility are mathematical induction and Dedekindian section, the essential foundations of arithmetic and analysis respectively. Mr Russell has succeeded in dispensing with the axiom in the first case,[1] but holds out no hope of a similar success in the second. Dedekindian section is thus left as an essentially unsound method, as has often been emphasized by Weyl,[2] and ordinary analysis crumbles into dust. That these are its consequences is the second defect in the theory of *Principia Mathematica*, and, to my mind, an absolutely conclusive proof that there is something wrong. For as I can neither accept the Axiom of Reducibility nor reject ordinary analysis, I cannot believe in a theory which presents me with no third possibility.

The third serious defect in *Principia Mathematica* is the

---

terms of certain symbols. $\phi\hat{z}$ being a non-elementary function of this kind, he concludes that there must be an n such that $nS\hat{z}(\phi z)$. This is, however, a fallacy, since $nS\hat{z}(\phi z)$ means by definition

$$(\exists\psi):\psi\,!\,x\equiv_x\phi x\,.\,nS\,(\psi\,!\,\hat{z})$$

and since $\psi!\hat{z}$ is not necessarily definable in terms of the given symbols, there is no reason for there being any such n.

[1] See *Principia Mathematica*, I, 2nd ed., (1925), Appendix B.

[2] See H. Weyl, *Das Kontinuum*, and " Über die neue Grundlagen-krise der Mathematik ", *Math. Zeitschrift*, 10 (1921), pp. 39–79.

treatment of identity. It should be explained that what is meant is numerical identity, identity in the sense of counting as one, not as two. Of this the following definition is given :

$$' x = y . =: (\phi) : \phi \, ! \, x . \supset . \phi \, ! \, y : \text{Df.} \, '\,^1$$

That is, two things are identical if they have all their elementary properties in common.

In *Principia* this definition is asserted to depend on the Axiom of Reducibility, because, apart from this axiom, two things might have all their elementary properties in common, but still disagree in respect of functions of higher order, in which case they could not be regarded as numerically identical.[2] Although, as we shall see, the definition is to be rejected on other grounds, I do not think it depends in this way on the Axiom of Reducibility. For though rejecting the Axiom of Reducibility destroys the obvious general proof that two things agreeing in respect of all elementary functions agree also in respect of all other functions, I think that this would still follow and could probably be proved in any particular case. For example, take typical functions of the second order

$$(\phi) . f \, ! \, (\phi \, ! \, \hat{z}, x), \quad (\exists \, \phi) . f \, ! \, (\phi \, ! \, \hat{z}, x).$$

Then, if we have $\quad (\phi) : \phi \, ! \, x . \equiv . \phi \, ! \, y \quad (x = y),$

it follows that $\quad (\phi) : f \, ! \, (\phi \, ! \, \hat{z}, x) . \equiv . f \, ! \, (\phi \, ! \, \hat{z}, y),$

because $f \, ! \, (\phi \, ! \, \hat{z}, x)$ is an elementary function of x. Whence

$$(\phi) . f \, ! \, (\phi \, ! \, \hat{z}, x) : \equiv : (\phi) . f \, ! \, (\phi \, ! \, \hat{z}, y)$$

and $\quad (\exists \, \phi) . f \, ! \, (\phi \, ! \, \hat{z}, x) : \equiv : (\exists \, \phi) . f \, ! \, (\phi \, ! \, \hat{z}, y).$

Hence rejecting the Axiom of Reducibility does not immediately lead to rejecting the definition of identity.

The real objection to this definition of identity is the same

---

[1] 13.01. [2] *Principia Mathematica*, I, 1st ed. (1910), 177.

as that urged above against defining classes as definable classes : that it is a misinterpretation in that it does not define the meaning with which the symbol for identity is actually used. This can be easily seen in the following way : the definition makes it self-contradictory for two things to have all their elementary properties in common. Yet this is really perfectly possible, even if, in fact, it never happens. Take two things, a and b. Then there is nothing self-contradictory in a having any self-consistent set of elementary properties, nor in b having this set, nor therefore, obviously, in both a and b having them, nor therefore in a and b having all their elementary properties in common. Hence, since this is logically possible, it is essential to have a symbolism which allows us to consider this possibility and does not exclude it by definition.

It is futile to raise the objection that it is not possible to distinguish two things which have all their properties in common, since to give them different names would imply that they had the different properties of having those names. For although this is perfectly true—that is to say, I cannot, for the reason given, know of any two particular indistinguishable things—yet I can perfectly well consider the possibility, or even know that there are two indistinguishable things without knowing which they are. To take an analogous situation : since there are more people on the earth than hairs on any one person's head, I know that there must be at least two people with the same number of hairs, but I do not know which two people they are.

These arguments are reinforced by Wittgenstein's discovery that the sign of identity is not a necessary constituent of logical notation, but can be replaced by the convention that different signs must have different meanings. This will be found in *Tractatus Logico-Philosophicus*, p. 139 ; the convention is slightly ambiguous, but it can be made definite, and is then workable, although generally inconvenient. But even if of no other value, it provides an effective proof that identity can be replaced by a symbolic convention, and is therefore no genuine propositional function, but merely a logical device.

We conclude, therefore, that the treatment of identity in *Principia Mathematica* is a misinterpretation of mathematics, and just as the mistaken definition of classes is particularly unfortunate in connection with the Multiplicative Axiom, so the mistaken definition of identity is especially misleading with regard to the Axiom of Infinity ; for the two propositions ' There are an infinite number of things ' and ' There are an infinite number of things differing from one another with regard to elementary functions ' are, as we shall see in Chapter V, extremely different.

III. PREDICATIVE FUNCTIONS

In this chapter we shall consider the second of the three objections which we made in the last chapter to the theory of the foundations of mathematics given in *Principia Mathematica*. This objection, which is perhaps the most serious of the three, was directed against the Theory of Types, which seemed to involve either the acceptance of the illegitimate Axiom of Reducibility or the rejection of such a fundamental type of mathematical argument as Dedekind section. We saw that this difficulty came from the second of the two parts into which the theory was divided, namely, that part which concerned the different ranges of functions of given arguments, e.g. individuals ; and we have to consider whether this part of the Theory of Types cannot be amended so as to get out of the difficulty. We shall see

THE FOUNDATIONS OF MATHEMATICS

that this can be done in a simple and straightforward way, which is a natural consequence of the logical theories of Mr Wittgenstein.

We shall start afresh from part of his theory of propositions, of which something was said in the first chapter. We saw there that he explains propositions in general by reference to atomic propositions, every proposition expressing agreement and disagreement with truth-possibilities of atomic propositions. We saw also that we could construct many different symbols all expressing agreement and disagreement with the same sets of possibilities. For instance,

$$ `p \supset q` \quad `\sim p . \vee . q,` \quad `\sim : p . \sim q,` \quad `\sim q . \supset . \sim p` $$

are such a set, all agreeing with the three possibilities

$$ `p . q,` \quad `\sim p . q,` \quad `\sim p . \sim q,` $$

but disagreeing with $`p . \sim q`$. Two symbols of this kind, which express agreement and disagreement with the same sets of possibilities, are said to be instances of the same proposition. They are instances of it just as all the ' the ' 's on a page are instances of the word ' the '. But whereas the ' the ' 's are instances of the same word on account of their physical similarity, different symbols are instances of the same proposition because they have the same sense, that is, express agreement with the same sets of possibilities. When we speak of propositions we shall generally mean the types of which the individual symbols are instances, and we shall include types of which there may be no instances. This is inevitable, since it cannot be any concern of ours whether anyone has actually symbolized or asserted a proposition, and we have to consider all propositions in the sense of all possible assertions whether or not they have been asserted.

Any proposition expresses agreement and disagreement with complementary sets of truth-possibilities of atomic propositions; conversely, given any set of these truth-possibilities, it would be logically possible to assert agreement with them and disagreement with all others, and the set of truth-possibilities therefore determines a proposition. This proposition may in practice be extremely difficult to express through the poverty of our language, for we lack both names for many objects and methods of making assertions involving an infinite number of atomic propositions, except in relatively simple cases, such as ' $(x).\phi x$ ', which involves the (probably) infinite set of (in certain cases) atomic propositions, ' ϕa,' ' ϕb,' etc. Nevertheless, we have to consider propositions which our language is inadequate to express. In ' $(x).\phi x$ ' we assert the truth of all possible propositions which would be of the form ' ϕx ' whether or not we have names for all the values of x. General propositions must obviously be understood as applying to everything, not merely to everything for which we have a name.

We come now to a most important point in connection with the Theory of Types. We explained in the last chapter what was meant by an elementary proposition, namely, one constructed explicitly as a truth-function of atomic propositions. We have now to see that, on the theory of Wittgenstein, elementary is not an adjective of the proposition-type at all, but only of its instances. For an elementary and a non-elementary propositional symbol could be instances of the same proposition. Thus suppose a list was made of all individuals as ' a ', ' b,' ..., ' z.' Then, if $\phi \hat{x}$ were an elementary function, ' $\phi a.\phi b ... \phi z$ ' would be an elementary proposition, but ' $(x).\phi x$ ' non-elementary; but these would express agreement and disagreement with the same possibilities and therefore be the same proposition. Or to take an example which could really occur, ' ϕa ' and ' $\phi a : (\exists x).\phi x$ ', which are the same proposition, since $(\exists x).\phi x$ adds nothing to ϕa. But the first is elementary, the second non-elementary.

Hence some instances of a proposition can be elementary, and others non-elementary ; so that elementary is not really a characteristic of the proposition, but of its mode of expression. ' Elementary proposition ' is like ' spoken word ' ; just as the same word can be both spoken and written, so the same proposition can be both elementarily and non-elementarily expressed.

After these preliminary explanations we proceed to a theory of propositional functions. By a propositional function of individuals we mean a symbol of the form ' $f(\hat{x}, \hat{y}, \hat{z}, \ldots)$ ' which is such that, were the names of any individuals substituted for ' $\hat{x}$ ', ' $\hat{y}$ ', ' $\hat{z}$ ', $\ldots$ in it, the result would always be a proposition. This definition needs to be completed by the explanation that two such symbols are regarded as the same function when the substitution of the same set of names in the one and in the other always gives the same proposition. Thus if ' $f(a, b, c)$ ', ' $g(a, b, c)$ ' are the same proposition for any set of $a, b, c,$ ' $f(\hat{x}, \hat{y}, \hat{z})$ ' and ' $g(\hat{x}, \hat{y}, \hat{z})$ ' are the same function, even if they are quite different to look at.

A function [1] ' $\phi\hat{x}$ ' gives us for each individual a proposition in the sense of a proposition-type (which may not have any instances, for we may not have given the individual a name). So the function collects together a set of propositions, whose logical sum and product we assert by writing respectively ' $(\exists x) \cdot \phi x$ ', ' $(x) \cdot \phi x$ '. This procedure can be extended to the case of several variables. Consider ' $\phi(\hat{x}, \hat{y})$ ' ; give y any constant value η, and ' $\phi(\hat{x}, \eta)$ ' gives a proposition when any individual name is substituted for $\hat{x}$, and is therefore a function of one variable, from which we can form the propositions

$$' (\exists x) \cdot \phi(x, \eta) ', ' (x) \cdot \phi(x, \eta) '.$$

Consider next ' $(\exists x) \cdot \phi(x, \hat{y})$ ' ; this, as we have seen, gives

---

[1] By ' function ' we shall in future always mean propositional function unless the contrary is stated.

a proposition when any name (e.g. ' η ') is substituted for ' y ', and is therefore a function of one variable from which we can form the propositions

$$(\exists y) : (\exists x) \cdot \phi(x, y) \text{ and } (y) : (\exists x) \cdot \phi(x, y).$$

As so far there has been no difficulty, we shall attempt to treat functions of functions in exactly the same way as we have treated functions of individuals. Let us take, for simplicity, a function of one variable which is a function of individuals. This would be a symbol of the form ' $f(\hat{\phi}\hat{x})$ ', which becomes a proposition on the substitution for ' $\hat{\phi}\hat{x}$ ' of any function of an individual. ' $f(\phi\hat{x})$ ' then collects together a set of propositions, one for each function of an individual, of which we assert the logical sum and product by writing respectively ' $(\exists\phi) \cdot f(\phi\hat{x})$ ', ' $(\phi) \cdot f(\phi\hat{x})$ '.

But this account suffers from an unfortunate vagueness as to the range of functions $\phi\hat{x}$ giving the values of $f(\phi\hat{x})$ of which we assert the logical sum or product. In this respect there is an important difference between functions of functions and functions of individuals which is worth examining closely. It appears clearly in the fact that the expressions ' function of functions ' and ' function of individuals ' are not strictly analogous ; for, whereas functions are symbols, individuals are objects, so that to get an expression analogous to ' function of functions ' we should have to say ' function of names of individuals '. On the other hand, there does not seem any simple way of altering ' function of functions ' so as to make it analogous to ' function of individuals ', and it is just this which causes the trouble. For the range of values of a function of individuals is definitely fixed by the range of individuals, an objective totality which there is no getting away from. But the range of arguments to a function of functions is a range of symbols, all symbols which become propositions by inserting in them the name of an individual. And this range of symbols, actual or possible, is not objectively fixed, but depends on our methods of constructing them and requires more precise definition.

This definition can be given in two ways, which may be distinguished as the subjective and the objective method. The subjective[1] method is that adopted in *Principia Mathematica* ; it consists in defining the range of functions as all those which could be constructed in a certain way, in the first instance by sole use of the ' / ' sign. We have seen how it leads to the impasse of the Axiom of Reducibility. I, on the other hand, shall adopt the entirely original objective method which will lead us to a satisfactory theory in which no such axiom is required. This method is to treat functions of functions as far as possible in the same way as functions of individuals. The signs which can be substituted as arguments in ' $\phi\hat{x}$ ', a function of individuals, are determined by their meanings ; they must be names of individuals. I propose similarly to determine the symbols which can be substituted as arguments in ' $f(\phi\hat{x})$ ' not by the manner of their construction, but by their meanings. This is more difficult, because functions do not mean single objects as names do, but have meaning in a more complicated way derived from the meanings of the propositions which are their values. The problem is ultimately to fix as values of $f(\phi\hat{x})$ some definite set of propositions so that we can assert their logical product and sum. In *Principia Mathematica* they are determined as all propositions which can be constructed in a certain way. My method, on the other hand, is to disregard how we could construct them, and to determine them by a description of their senses or imports ; and in so doing we may be able to include in the set propositions which we have no way of constructing, just as we include in the range of values of ϕx propositions which

[1] I do not wish to press this term ; I merely use it because I can find no better.

we cannot express from lack of names for the individuals concerned.

We must begin the description of the new method with the definition of an atomic function of individuals, as the result of replacing by variables any of the names of individuals in an atomic proposition expressed by using names alone; where if a name occurs more than once in the proposition it may be replaced by the same or different variables, or left alone in its different occurrences. The values of an atomic function of individuals are thus atomic propositions.

We next extend to propositional functions the idea of a truth-function of propositions. (At first, of course, the functions to which we extend it are only atomic, but the extension works also in general, and so I shall state it in general.) Suppose we have functions $\phi_1(\hat{x}, \hat{y})$, $\phi_2(\hat{x}, \hat{y})$, etc., then by saying that a function $\psi(\hat{x}, \hat{y})$ is a certain truth-function (e.g. the logical sum) of the functions $\phi_1(\hat{x}, \hat{y})$, $\phi_2(\hat{x}, \hat{y})$, etc., and the propositions p, q, etc., we mean that any value of $\psi(x, y)$, say $\psi(a, b)$, is that truth-function of the corresponding values of $\phi_1(x, y)$, $\phi_2(x, y)$, etc., i.e. $\phi_1(a, b)$, $\phi_2(a, b)$, etc., and the propositions p, q, etc. This definition enables us to include functions among the arguments of any truth-function, for it always gives us a unique function which is that truth-function of those arguments ; e.g. the logical sum of $\phi_1(\hat{x})$, $\phi_2(\hat{x})$, . . . is determined as $\psi(x)$, where $\psi(a)$ is the logical sum of $\phi_1 a$, $\phi_2 a$, . . ., a definite proposition for each a, so that $\psi(x)$ is a definite function. It is unique because, if there were two, namely $\psi_1(x)$ and $\psi_2(x)$, $\psi_1(a)$ and $\psi_2(a)$ would for each a be the same proposition, and hence the two functions would be identical.

We can now give the most important definition in this theory, that of a predicative function. I do not use this term in the sense of *Principia Mathematica*, 1st ed., for which I follow Mr Russell's later work in using ' elementary '. The notion of a predicative function, in my sense, is one which does not occur in *Principia*, and marks the essential divergence of the two methods of procedure. A *predicative function* of individuals is one which is any truth-function of arguments which, whether finite or infinite in number, are all either atomic functions of individuals or propositions.[1] This defines a definite range of functions of individuals which is wider than any range occurring in *Principia*. It is essentially dependent on the notion of a truth-function of an infinite number of arguments; if there could only be a finite number of arguments our predicative functions would be simply the elementary functions of *Principia*. Admitting an infinite number involves that we do not define the range of functions as those which could be constructed in a certain way, but determine them by a description of their meanings. They are to be truth-functions—not explicitly in their appearance, but in their significance—of atomic functions and propositions. In this way we shall include many functions which we have no way of constructing, and many which we construct in quite different ways. Thus, supposing $\phi(\hat{x}, \hat{y})$ is an atomic function, p a proposition,

$$\phi(\hat{x}, \hat{y}), \quad \phi(\hat{x}, \hat{y}) \ . \ \lor \ . \ p, \quad (y) \ . \ \phi(\hat{x}, y)$$

are all predicative functions. [The last is predicative because it is the logical product of the atomic functions $\phi(\hat{x}, y)$ for different values of y.]

For functions of functions there are more or less analogous definitions. First, an atomic function of (predicative[2]) functions of individuals and of individuals can only have one functional argument, say ϕ, but may have many individual

---

[1] Before ' propositions ' we could insert ' atomic ' without narrowing the sense of the definition. For any proposition is a truth-function of atomic propositions, and a truth-function of a truth-function is again a truth-function.

[2] I put ' predicative ' in parentheses because the definitions apply equally to the non-predicative functions dealt with in the next chapter.

arguments, x, y, etc., and must be of the form $\phi(x, y, \ldots, a, b, \ldots)$ where 'a', 'b', ... are names of individuals. In particular, an atomic function $f(\phi\hat{z})$ is of the form ϕa. A predicative function of (predicative) functions of individuals and of individuals is one which is a truth-function whose arguments are all either propositions or atomic functions of functions of individuals and of individuals,

e.g. $\phi a \,.\, \supset \,.\, \psi b : \lor : p$ (a function of ϕ, ψ),

$(x) \,.\, \phi x$, the logical product of the atomic functions ϕa, ϕb, etc.

It is clear that a function only occurs in a predicative function through its values. In this way we can proceed to define predicative functions of functions of functions and so on to any order.

Now consider such a proposition as $(\phi) \,.\, f(\phi\hat{x})$ where $f(\phi\hat{x})$ is a predicative function of functions. We understand the range of values of ϕ to be all predicative functions; i.e. $(\phi) \,.\, f(\phi\hat{x})$ is the logical product of the propositions $f(\phi\hat{x})$ for each predicative function, and as this is a definite set of propositions, we have attached to $(\phi) \,.\, f(\phi\hat{x})$ a definite significance.

Now consider the function of x, $(\phi) \,.\, f(\phi\hat{z}, x)$. Is this a predicative function? It is the logical product of the propositional functions of x, $f(\phi\hat{z}, x)$ for the different ϕ's which, since f is predicative, are truth-functions of ϕx and propositions possibly variable in ϕ but constant in x (e.g. ϕa). The ϕx's, since the ϕ's are predicative, are truth-functions of atomic functions of x. Hence the propositional functions of x, $f(\phi\hat{z}, x)$ are truth-functions of atomic functions of x and propositions. Hence they are predicative functions, and therefore their logical product $(\phi) \,.\, f(\phi\hat{z}, x)$ is predicative. More generally it is clear that by generalization, whatever the type of the apparent variable, we can never create non-predicative functions ; for the generalization is a truth-function of its instances, and, if these are predicative, so is it.

Thus all the functions of individuals which occur in *Principia* are in our sense predicative and included in our variable ϕ, so that all need for an axiom of reducibility disappears.

But, it will be objected, surely in this there is a vicious circle ; you cannot include $F\hat{x} = (\phi) \, . \, f(\phi\hat{z}, \hat{x})$ among the ϕ's, for it presupposes the totality of the ϕ's. This is not, however, really a vicious circle. The proposition Fa is certainly the logical product of the propositions $f(\phi\hat{z}, a)$, but to express it like this (which is the only way we can) is merely to describe it in a certain way, by reference to a totality of which it may be itself a member, just as we may refer to a man as the tallest in a group, thus identifying him by means of a totality of which he is himself a member without there being any vicious circle. The proposition Fa in its significance, that is, the fact it asserts to be the case, does not involve the totality of functions ; it is merely our symbol which involves it. To take a particularly simple case, $(\phi) \, . \, \phi a$ is the logical product of the propositions ϕa, of which it is itself one ; but this is no more remarkable and no more vicious than is the fact that $p \, . \, q$ is the logical product of the set $p, q, p \, . \, q$, of which it is itself a member. The only difference is that, owing to our inability to write propositions of infinite length, which is logically a mere accident, $(\phi) \, . \, \phi a$ cannot, like $p \, . \, q$, be elementarily expressed, but must be expressed as the logical product of a set of which it is also a member. If we had infinite resources and could express all atomic functions as $\psi_1 x, \psi_2 x$, then we could form all the propositions ϕa, that is, all the truth-functions of $\psi_1 a, \psi_2 a$, etc., and among them would be one which was the logical product of them all, including itself, just as $p.q$ is the product of $p, q, p \vee q, p.q$. This proposition, which we cannot express directly, that is elementarily, we express indirectly as the logical product of

them all by writing ' (ϕ) . ϕa '.   This is certainly a circuitous
process, but there is clearly nothing vicious about it.

In this lies the great advantage of my method over that of
Principia Mathematica. In *Principia* the range of ϕ is that
of functions which can be elementarily expressed, and since
(ϕ) . $f(\phi \, ! \, \hat{z}, x)$ cannot be so expressed it cannot be a value of
$\phi \, !$; but I define the values of ϕ not by how they can be
expressed, but by what sort of senses their values have, or
rather, by how the facts their values assert are related to their
arguments.   I thus include functions which could not even
be expressed by us at all, let alone elementarily, but only by a
being with an infinite symbolic system.   And any function
formed by generalization being actually predicative, there is
no longer any need for an Axiom of Reducibility.

It remains to show that my notion of predicative functions
does not involve us in any contradictions.   The relevant
contradictions, as I have remarked before, all contain some
word like ' means ', and I shall show that they are due to an
essential ambiguity of such words and not to any weakness
in the notion of a predicative function.

Let us take first Weyl's contradiction about ' heterological '
which we discussed in the last chapter.   It is clear that the
solution given there is no longer available to us.   For, as
before, if R is the relation of meaning between ' ϕ ' and $\phi \hat{x}$,
' x is heterological ' is equivalent to ' $(\exists \phi): \, xR \, (\phi \hat{z}) \, . \sim \phi x$ ',
the range of ϕ being here understood to be that of
predicative functions.   Then

$$(\exists \phi) : xR(\phi \hat{z}) \, . \sim \phi x,$$

which I will call Fx, is itself a predicative function.

So $\qquad\qquad\qquad$ ' F ' $R(F\hat{x})$

and $\qquad\qquad\qquad (\exists \phi) : \, ' F \, ' \, R(\phi \hat{x}),$

and therefore $\qquad\quad F(' \, F \, ') \, . \equiv . \sim F(' \, F \, '),$

which is a contradiction.

It will be seen that the contradiction essentially depends on deducing $(\exists \phi):\,{}'F\,'\,R(\phi \hat{x})$ from $'F\,'\,R(F\hat{x})$. According to *Principia Mathematica* this deduction is illegitimate because $F\hat{x}$ is not a possible value of $\phi \hat{x}$. But if the range of $\phi \hat{x}$ is that of predicative functions, this solution fails, since $F\hat{x}$ is certainly a predicative function. But there is obviously another possible solution—to deny $'F\,'\,R(F\hat{x})$ the premiss of the deduction. $'F\,'\,R(F\hat{x})$ says that $'F\,'$ means $F\hat{x}$. Now this is certainly true for some meaning of ' means ', so to uphold our denial of it we must show some ambiguity in the meaning of meaning, and say that the sense in which $'F\,'$ means $F\hat{x}$, i.e. in which ' heterological ' means heterological, is not the sense denoted by $'R\,'$, i.e. the sense which occurs in the definition of heterological. We can easily show that this is really the case, so that the contradiction is simply due to an ambiguity in the word ' meaning ' and has no relevance to mathematics whatever.

First of all, to speak of $'F\,'$ as meaning $F\hat{x}$ at all must appear very odd in view of our definition of a propositional function as itself a symbol. But the expression is merely elliptical. The fact which we try to describe in these terms is that we have arbitrarily chosen the letter $'F\,'$ for a certain purpose, so that $'Fx\,'$ shall have a certain meaning (depending on x). As a result of this choice $'F\,'$, previously non-significant, becomes significant ; it has meaning. But it is clearly an impossible simplification to suppose that there is a single object F, which it means. Its meaning is more complicated than that, and must be further investigated.

Let us take the simplest case, an atomic proposition fully written out, $'aSb\,'$, where $'a\,'$, $'b\,'$ are names of individuals and $'S\,'$ the name of a relation. Then $'a\,'$, $'b\,'$, $'S\,'$ mean in the simplest way the separate objects a, b, and S. Now suppose we define

$$\phi x \,.=.\, aSx \quad \text{Df.}$$

Then ' ϕ ' is substituted for ' aS ' and does not mean a single object, but has meaning in a more complicated way in virtue of a three-termed relation to both a and S. Then we can say ' ϕ ' means $aS\hat{x}$, meaning by this that ' ϕ ' has this relation to a and S. We can extend this account to deal with any elementary function, that is, to say that ' ϕ ! ' means $\phi ! \hat{x}$ means that ' ϕ ! ' is related in a certain way to the objects a, b, etc., involved in $\phi ! \hat{x}$.

But suppose now we take a non-elementary functional symbol, for example,

$$\phi_1 x : = : (y) . yRx \quad \text{Df.}$$

Here the objects involved in $\phi_1\hat{x}$ include all individuals as values of y. And it is clear that ' ϕ_1 ' is not related to them in at all the same way as ' ϕ ! ' is to the objects in its meaning. For ' ϕ ! ' is related to a, b, etc. by being short for an expression containing names of a, b, etc. But ' ϕ_1 ' is short for an expression not containing ' a ', ' b ', ..., but containing only an apparent variable, of which these can be values. Clearly ' ϕ_1 ' means what it means in quite a different and more complicated way from that in which ' ϕ ! ' means. Of course, just as elementary is not really a characteristic of the proposition, it is not really a characteristic of the function ; that is to say, $\phi_1\hat{x}$ and $\phi ! \hat{x}$ may be the same function, because $\phi_1 x$ is always the same proposition as $\phi ! x$. Then ' ϕ_1 ', ' ϕ ! ' will have the same meaning, but will mean it, as we saw above, in quite different senses of meaning. Similarly ' ϕ_2 ' which involves a functional apparent variable will mean in a different and more complicated way still.[1]

Hence in the contradiction which we were discussing, if ' R ', the symbol of the relation of meaning between ' ϕ '

[1] Here the range of the apparent variable in ' ϕ_2 ' is the set of predicative functions, not as in *Principia Mathematica* the set of elementary functions.

and $\phi\hat{x}$, is to have any definite meaning, ' ϕ ' can only be a symbol of a certain type meaning in a certain way ; suppose we limit ' ϕ ' to be an elementary function by taking R to be the relation between ' ϕ ! ' and $\phi ! \hat{x}$.

Then ' Fx ' or ' $(\exists\phi):xR(\phi\hat{z})$. $\sim \phi x$ ' is not elementary, but is a ' ϕ_2 '.

Hence ' F ' means not in the sense of meaning denoted by ' R ' appropriate to ' ϕ ! 's, but in that appropriate to a ' ϕ_2 ', so that we have $\sim : ' F ' R(F\hat{x})$, which, as we explained above, solves the contradiction for this case.

The essential point to understand is that the reason why

$$(\exists\phi) : ' F ' R(\phi\hat{x})$$

can only be true if ' F ' is an elementary function, is not that the range of ϕ is that of elementary functions, but that a symbol cannot have R to a function unless it (the symbol) is elementary. The limitation comes not from ' $\exists\phi$ ', but from ' R '. The distinctions of ' ϕ ! 's, ' ϕ_1 's, and ' ϕ_2 's apply to the symbols and to how they mean but not to what they mean. Therefore I always (in this section) enclosed ' ϕ ! ', ' ϕ_1 ' and ' ϕ_2 ' in inverted commas.

But it may be objected that this is an incomplete solution ; for suppose we take for R the sum of the relations appropriate to ' ϕ ! 's, ' ϕ_1 's, and ' ϕ_2 's. Then ' F ', since it still only contains $\exists\phi$,[1] is still a ' ϕ_2 ', and we must have in this case ' F ' $R(F\hat{x})$; which destroys our solution.

But this is not so because the extra complexity involved in the new R makes ' F ' not a ' ϕ_2 ', but a more complicated symbol still. For with this new R, for which ' ϕ_2 ' $R(\phi_2\hat{x})$, since ' $\phi_2 x$ ' is of some such form as $(\exists\phi) . f(\phi\hat{z}, x)$, in $(\exists\phi) . ' F '$ $R(\phi\hat{x})$ is involved at least a variable function $f(\phi\hat{z}, x)$ of functions of individuals, for this is involved in the notion of a

[1] The range of ϕ in $\exists\phi$ is that of predicative functions, including all ' ϕ_1 's, ' ϕ_2 's, etc., so it is not altered by changing R.

variable ' ϕ_2 ', which is involved in the variable ϕ taken in conjunction with R. For if anything has R to the predicative function $\phi\hat{x}$, $\phi\hat{x}$ must be expressible by either a ' ϕ ! ' or a ' ϕ_1 ' or a ' ϕ_2 '.

Hence $(\exists\phi)$. ' F ' $R(\phi\hat{x})$ involves not merely the variable ϕ (predicative function of an individual) but also a hidden variable f (function of a function of an individual and of an individual). Hence ' Fx ' or ' $(\exists\phi): xR(\phi\hat{x})$. $\sim \phi x$ ' is not a ' ϕ_2 ', but what we may call a ' ϕ_3 ', i.e. a function of individuals involving a variable function of functions of individuals. (This is, of course, not the same thing as a ' ϕ_3 ' in the sense of *Principia Mathematica*, 2nd edition.) Hence ' F ' means in a more complicated way still not included in R ; and we do not have ' F ' $R(F\hat{x})$, so that the contradiction again disappears.

What appears clearly from the contradictions is that we cannot obtain an all-inclusive relation of meaning for propositional functions. Whatever one we take there is still a way of constructing a symbol to mean in a way not included in our relation. The meanings of meaning form an illegitimate totality.

By the process begun above we obtain a hierarchy of propositions and a hierarchy of functions of individuals. Both are based on the fundamental hierarchy of individuals, functions of individuals, functions of functions of individuals, etc. A function of individuals we will call a function of type 1 ; a function of functions of individuals, a function of type 2 ; and so on.

We now construct the hierarchy of propositions as follows :

Propositions of order 0 (elementary), containing no apparent variable.

     ,,   ,,   1, containing an individual apparent variable.

Propositions of order 2, containing an apparent variable whose values are functions of type 1.

,,   ,, n, containing an apparent variable whose values are functions of type n—1.

From this hierarchy we deduce another hierarchy of functions, irrespective of their types, according to the order of their values.

Thus functions of order 0 (matrices) contain no apparent variable ;

,,   ,,   1 contain an individual apparent variable ;

and so on ; i.e. the values of a function of order n are propositions of order n. For this classification the types of the functions are immaterial.

We must emphasize the essential distinction between order and type. The type of a function is a real characteristic of it depending on the arguments it can take ; but the order of a proposition or function is not a real characteristic, but what Peano called a pseudo-function. The order of a proposition is like the numerator of a fraction. Just as from ' $x = y$ ' we cannot deduce that the numerator of x is equal to the numerator of y, from the fact that ' p ' and ' q ' are instances of the same proposition we cannot deduce that the order of ' p ' is equal to that of ' q '. This was shown above (p. 34) for the particular case of elementary and non-elementary propositions (Orders 0 and > 0), and obviously holds in general. Order is only a characteristic of a particular symbol which is an instance of the proposition or function.

We shall now show briefly how this theory solves the remaining contradictions of group B.[1]

---

[1] It may be as well to repeat that for the contradictions of group A my theory preserves the solutions given in *Principia Mathematica*.

(a) ' I am lying '.

This we should analyse as '$(\exists\,"p", p)$: I am saying "p". "p" means p. $\sim p$'. Here to get a definite meaning for *means* [1] it is necessary to limit in some way the order of 'p', Suppose 'p' is to be of the nth or lesser order. Then. symbolizing by ϕ_n a function of *type* n, 'p' may be $(\exists\phi_n)$. $\phi_{n+1}(\phi_n)$.

Hence $\exists$ 'p' involves $\exists\phi_{n+1}$, and 'I am lying' in the sense of 'I am asserting a false proposition of order n' is at least of order $n+1$ and does not contradict itself.

(b) (1) The least integer not nameable in fewer than nineteen syllables.

(2) The least indefinable ordinal.

(3) Richard's Paradox.

All these result from the obvious ambiguity of ' naming ' and ' defining '. The name or definition is in each case a functional symbol which is only a name or definition by meaning something. The sense in which it means must be made precise by fixing its order ; the name or definition involving all such names or definitions will be of a higher order, and this removes the contradiction. My solutions of these contradictions are obviously very similar to those of Whitehead and Russell, the difference between them lying merely in our different conceptions of the order of propositions and functions. For me propositions in themselves have no orders ; they are just different truth-functions of atomic propositions—a definite totality, depending only on what

---

[1] When I say " 'p' means p ", I do not suppose there to be a single object p meant by 'p'. The meaning of 'p' is that one of a certain set of possibilities is realized, and this meaning results from the meaning-relations of the separate signs in 'p' to the real objects which it is about. It is these meaning-relations which vary with the order of 'p'. And the order of 'p' is limited not because p in $(\exists p)$ is limited, but by ' means ' which varies in meaning with the order of 'p'.

atomic propositions there are. Orders and illegitimate totalities only come in with the symbols we use to symbolize the facts in variously complicated ways.

To sum up: in this chapter I have defined a range of predicative functions which escapes contradiction and enables us to dispense with the Axiom of Reducibility. And I have given a solution of the contradictions of group B which rests on and explains the fact that they all contain some epistemic element.

IV. Propositional Functions in Extension

Before we go on, let us look round and see where we have got to. We have seen that the introduction of the notion of a predicative function has given us a range for ϕ which enables us to dispense with the Axiom of Reducibility. Hence it removes the second and most important defect in the theory of *Principia Mathematica* ; but how do we now stand with regard to the other two difficulties, the difficulty of including all classes and relations in extension and not merely definable ones, and the difficulty connected with identity?

The difficulty about identity we can get rid of, at the cost of great inconvenience, by adopting Wittgenstein's convention, which enables us to eliminate ' $=$ ' from any proposition in which it occurs. But this puts us in a hopeless position as regards classes, because, having eliminated ' $=$ ' altogether, we can no longer use $x = y$ as a propositional function in defining finite classes. So that the only classes with which we are now able to deal are those defined by predicative functions.

It may be useful here to repeat the definition of a predicative function of individuals ; it is any truth-function of atomic functions and atomic propositions. We call such functions 'predicative' because they correspond, as nearly as a precise notion can to a vague one, to the idea that ϕa predicates the same thing of a as ϕb does of b. They include all the propositional functions which occur in *Principia Mathematica*, including identity as there defined. It is obvious, however, that we ought not to define identity in this way as agreement in respect of all predicative functions, because two things can clearly agree as regards all atomic functions and therefore as regards all predicative functions, and yet they are two things and not, as the proposed definition of identity would involve, one thing.

Hence our theory is every bit as inadequate as *Principia Mathematica* to provide an extensional logic ; in fact, if we reject this false definition of identity, we are unable to include among the classes dealt with even all finite enumerated classes. Mathematics then becomes hopeless because we cannot be sure that there is any class defined by a predicative function whose number is two ; for things may all fall into triads which agree in every respect, in which case there would be in our system no unit classes and no two-member classes.

If we are to preserve at all the ordinary form of mathematics, it looks as if some extension must be made in the notion of a propositional function, so as to take in other classes as well. Such an extension is desirable on other grounds, because many things which would naturally be regarded as propositional functions can be shown not to be predicative functions.

For example

$$F(x, y) = \text{Something other than } x \text{ and } y \text{ satisfies } \phi\hat{z}.$$

(Here, of course, 'other than' is to be taken strictly, and not in the *Principia Mathematica* sense of 'distinguishable from'.)

This is not a predicative function, but is made up of parts of two predicative functions :

(1) For $x \neq y$

$$F(x, y) \text{ is } \qquad \phi x . \phi y : \supset . Nc'\hat{z}(\phi z) \geqslant 3 : .$$

$$\phi x . \sim \phi y . \vee : \phi y . \sim \phi x : \supset : Nc'\hat{z}(\phi z) \geqslant 2 : .$$

$$\sim \phi x . \sim \phi y : \supset : Nc'z(\phi z) \geqslant 1.$$

This is a predicative function because it is a truth function of ϕx, ϕy and the constant proposition $Nc'\hat{z}(\phi z) \geqslant 1, 2, 3$, which do not involve x, y.

(2) For $x = y$

$$F(x, x) \text{ is } \qquad \phi(x) . \supset . Nc'\hat{z} (\phi z) \geqslant 2 :$$

$$\sim \phi x . \supset . Nc'\hat{z} (\phi z) \geqslant 1,$$

which is a predicative function.

But $F(x, y)$ is not itself a predicative function; this is perhaps more difficult to see. But it is easy to see that all functions of this kind cannot be predicative, because if they were we could find a predicative function satisfied by any given individual a alone, which we clearly cannot in general do.

For suppose fa (if not, take $\sim f\hat{x}$).

Let $\qquad\qquad a = \hat{x}(fx),$

$$\beta = a - (a).$$

Then $\phi x = $ 'There is nothing which satisfies fx except x, and members of β' applies to a and a alone. So such functions cannot always be predicative.

Just as $F(x, y)$ above, so also ' $x = y$ ' is made up of two predicative functions :

(1) For $x \neq y$

' $x = y$ ' may be taken to be $(\exists \phi) . \phi x . \sim \phi x :$ $(\exists \phi) . \phi y . \sim \phi y$, i.e. a contradiction.

(2) For $x = y$

$\qquad$ ' $x = y$ ' may be taken to be $(\phi) : . \phi x . \text{v} . \sim \phi x :$
$\qquad \phi y . \text{v} . \sim \phi y$, i.e. a tautology.

But ' $x = y$ ' is not itself predicative.

It seems, therefore, that we need to introduce non-predicative propositional functions. How is this to be done ? The only practicable way is to do it as radically and drastically as possible ; to drop altogether the notion that ϕa says about a what ϕb says about b ; to treat propositional functions like mathematical functions, that is, extensionalize them completely. Indeed it is clear that, mathematical functions being derived from propositional, we shall get an adequately extensional account of the former only by taking a completely extensional view of the latter.

So in addition to the previously defined concept of a predicative function, which we shall still require for certain purposes, we define, or rather explain, for in our system it must be taken as indefinable, the new concept of a propositional function in extension. Such a function of one individual results from any one-many relation in extension between propositions and individuals ; that is to say, a correlation, practicable or impracticable, which to every individual associates a unique proposition, the individual being the argument to the function, the proposition its value.

Thus ϕ (Socrates) may be Queen Anne is dead,

$\qquad \phi$ (Plato) may be Einstein is a great man ;

$\phi \hat{x}$ being simply an arbitrary association of propositions ϕx to individuals x.

A function in extension will be marked by a suffix e thus $\phi_e \hat{x}$.

Then we can talk of the totality of such functions as the range of values of an apparent variable ϕ_e.

Consider now $\qquad (\phi_e) . \phi_e x \equiv \phi_e y.$

This asserts that in any such correlation the proposition correlated with x is equivalent to that correlated with y.

If $x = y$ this is a tautology (it is the logical product of values of $p \equiv p$).

But if $x \neq y$ it is a contradiction. For in one of the correlations some p will be associated with x, and $\sim p$ with y.

Then for this correlation $f_e \hat{x}$, $f_e x$ is p, $f_e y$ is $\sim p$, so that $f_e x \equiv f_e y$ is self-contradictory and $(\phi_e) . \phi_e x \equiv \phi_e y$ is self-contradictory.

So $(\phi_e) . \phi_e x \equiv \phi_e y$ is a tautology if $x = y$, a contradiction if $x \neq y$.[1]

Hence it can suitably be taken as the definition of $x = y$.

$x = y$ is a function in extension of two variables. Its value is tautology when x and y have the same value, contradiction when x, y have different values.

We have now to defend this suggested range of functions for a variable ϕ_e against the charges that it is illegitimate and leads to contradictions. It is legitimate because it is an intelligible notation, giving a definite meaning to the symbols in which it is employed. Nor can it lead to contradictions, for it will escape all the suggested contradictions just as the range of predicative functions will. Any symbol containing the variable ϕ_e will mean in a different way from a symbol not containing it, and we shall have the same sort of ambiguity of 'meaning' as in Chapter III, which will remove the contradictions. Nor can any of the first group of contradictions be restored by our new notation, for it will still be impossible for a class to be a member of itself, as our functions in extension are confined to definite types of arguments by definition.

We have now to take the two notions we have defined,

[1] On the other hand $(\phi) . \phi x \equiv \phi y$ (ϕ predicative) is a tautology if $x = y$, but not a contradiction if $x \neq y$.

predicative functions and functions in extension, and consider when we shall want to use one and when the other.[1] First let us take the case when the arguments are individuals : then there is every advantage in taking the range of functions we use in mathematics to be that of functions in extension. We have seen how this enables us to define identity satisfactorily, and it is obvious that we shall need no Axiom of Reducibility, for any propositional function obtained by generalization, or in any manner whatever, is a function in extension. Further it will give us a satisfactory theory of classes, for any class will be defined by a function in extension, *e.g.* by the function which is tautology for any member of the class as argument, but contradiction for any other argument, and the null-class will be defined by the self-contradictory function. So the totality of classes can be reduced to that of functions in extension, and therefore it will be this totality which we shall require in mathematics, not the totality of predicative functions, which corresponds not to ' all classes ' but to ' all predicates ' or ' all properties '.

On the other hand, when we get to functions of functions the situation is rather different. There appears to be no point in considering any except predicative functions of functions ; the reasons for introducing functions in extension no longer apply. For we do not need to define identity between functions, but only identity between classes which reduces to equivalence between functions, which is easily defined. Nor do we wish to consider classes of functions, but classes of classes, of which a simpler treatment is also possible. So in the case of functions of functions we confine ourselves to such as are predicative.

Let us recall the definition of a predicative function of functions ; it is a truth-function of their values and constant

---

[1] Of course predicative functions are also functions in extension ; the question is which range we want for our variable function.

propositions.[1]   All functions of functions which occur in *Principia* are of this sort, but ' I believe (x) . ϕx ' as a function of $\phi \hat{x}$ is not.   Predicative functions of functions are extensional in the sense of *Principia*, that is if the range of $f(\phi \hat{x})$ be that of predicative functions of functions,

$$\phi_e x \equiv_x \psi_e x : \supset : f(\phi_e \hat{x}) \equiv f(\psi_e \hat{x}).$$

This is because $f(\phi_e \hat{x})$ is a truth-function of the values of $\phi_e x$ which are equivalent to the corresponding values of $\psi_e x$, so that $f(\phi_e \hat{x})$ is equivalent to $f(\psi_e \hat{x})$.

If we assumed this we should have a very simple theory of classes, since there would be no need to distinguish $\hat{x}(\phi_e x)$ from $\phi_e \hat{x}$.   But though it is a tautology there is clearly no way of proving it, so that we should have to take it as a primitive proposition.   If we wish to avoid this we have only to keep the theory of classes given in *Principia* based on " the derived extensional function ".   The range of predicative functions of functions is adequate to deal with classes of classes because, although, as we have seen, there may be classes of individuals which can only be defined by functions in extension, yet any class of classes can be defined by a predicative function, namely by $f(\alpha)$ where

$$f(\phi_e \hat{x}) = \Sigma_\psi (\phi_e x \equiv_x \psi_e x),$$

i.e. the logical sum of $\phi_e x \equiv_x \psi_e x$ for all the functions $\psi_e \hat{x}$ which define the members of the class of classes.   Of course, if the class of classes is infinite, this expression cannot be

---

[1] It is, I think, predicative functions of functions which Mr Russell in the Introduction to the Second Edition of *Principia* tries to describe as functions into which functions enter only through their values. But this is clearly an insufficient description, because $\phi \hat{x}$ only enters into $F(\phi \hat{x}) = $ ' I believe ϕa ' through its value ϕa, but this is certainly not a function of the kind meant, for it is not extensional.   I think the point can only be explained by introducing, as I have, the notion of a truth-function.   To contend, as Mr Russell does, that all functions of functions are predicative is to embark on a futile verbal dispute, owing to the ambiguity of the vague term functions of functions, which may be used to mean only such as are predicative or to include also such as $F(\phi \hat{x})$ above.

written down. But, nevertheless, there will be the logical sum of these functions, though we cannot express it.[1]

So to obtain a complete theory of classes we must take the range of functions of individuals to be that of functions in extension ; but the range of functions of functions to be that of predicative functions. By using these variables we obtain the system of *Principia Mathematica*, simplified by the omission of the Axiom of Reducibility, and a few corresponding alterations. Formally it is almost unaltered ; but its meaning has been considerably changed. And in thus preserving the form while modifying the interpretation, I am following the great school of mathematical logicians who, in virtue of a series of startling definitions, have saved mathematics from the sceptics, and provided a rigid demonstration of its propositions. Only so can we preserve it from the Bolshevik menace of Brouwer and Weyl.

V. The Axioms

I have shown in the last two chapters how to remedy the three principal defects in *Principia Mathematica* as a foundation for mathematics. Now we have to consider the two important difficulties which remain, which concern the Axiom of Infinity and the Multiplicative Axiom. The introduction of these two axioms is not so grave as that of the Axiom of Reducibility, because they are not in themselves such objectionable assumptions, and because mathematics is largely independent of the Multiplicative Axiom, and might reasonably be supposed to require an Axiom of Infinity. Nevertheless, we must try to determine the logical status of these axioms—whether they are tautologies or empirical

---

[1] A logical sum is not like an algebraic sum ; only a finite number of terms can have an algebraic sum, for an ' infinite sum ' is really a limit. But the logical sum of a set of propositions is the proposition that these are not all false, and exists whether the set be finite or infinite.

propositions or even contradictions. In this inquiry I shall include, from curiosity, the Axiom of Reducibility, although, since we have dispensed with it, it no longer really concerns us.

Let us begin with the Axiom of Reducibility, which asserts that all functions of individuals obtained by the generalization of matrices are equivalent to elementary functions. In discussing it several cases arise, of which I shall consider only the most interesting, that, namely, in which the numbers of individuals and of atomic functions of individuals are both infinite. In this case the axiom is an empirical proposition, that is to say, neither a tautology nor a contradiction, and can therefore be neither asserted nor denied by logic or mathematics. This is shown as follows :—

(*a*) The axiom is not a contradiction, but may be true.

For it is clearly possible that there should be an atomic function defining every class of individuals. In which case every function would be equivalent not merely to an elementary but to an atomic function.

(*b*) The axiom is not a tautology, but may be false.

For it is clearly possible that there should be an infinity of atomic functions, and an individual *a* such that whichever atomic function we take there is another individual agreeing with *a* in respect of all the other functions, but not in respect of the function taken. Then $(\phi) \cdot \phi ! x \equiv \phi ! a$ could not be equivalent to any elementary function of *x*.

Having thus shown that the Axiom of Reducibility is neither a tautology nor a contradiction, let us proceed to the Multiplicative Axiom. This asserts that, given any existent class *K* of existent classes, there is a class having exactly one member in common with each member of *K*. If by 'class' we mean, as I do, any set of things homogeneous in type not necessarily definable by a function which is not merely a function in extension, the Multiplicative Axiom seems to me the most evident tautology. I cannot see how this can be the subject of reasonable doubt, and I think it never would have been doubted unless it had been mis-interpreted. For with the meaning it has in *Principia*, where the class whose existence it asserts must be one definable by a propositional function of the sort which occurs in *Principia*, it becomes really doubtful and, like the Axiom of Reducibility, neither a tautology nor a contradiction. We prove this by showing

(*a*) It is not a contradiction.

For it is clearly possible that every class (in my sense) should be defined by an atomic function, so that, since there is bound to be a class in my sense having one member in common with each member of K, this would be also a class in the sense of *Principia*.

(*b*) It is not a tautology.

To show this we take not the Multiplicative Axiom itself but the equivalent theorem that any two classes are com-mensurable.

Consider then the following case : let there be no atomic functions of two or more variables, and only the following atomic functions of one variable :—

Associated with each individual a an atomic function $\phi_a\hat{x}$ such that

$$\phi_a x \ . \ \equiv_x . \ x = a.$$

One other atomic function $f\hat{x}$ such that $\hat{x}(fx)$, $\hat{x}(\sim fx)$ are both infinite classes.

Then there is no one-one relation, in the sense of *Principia*, having either $\hat{x}(fx)$ or $\hat{x}(\sim fx)$ for domain, and therefore these two classes are incommensurable.

Hence the Multiplicative Axiom, interpreted as it is in *Principia*, is not a tautology but logically doubtful. But, as I interpret it, it is an obvious tautology, and this can be claimed as an additional advantage in my theory. It will probably be objected that, if it is a tautology, it ought to be able to be proved, *i.e.* deduced from the simpler primitive propositions which suffice for the deduction of the rest of mathematics. But it does not seem to me in the least unlikely that there should be a tautology, which could be stated in finite terms, whose proof was, nevertheless, infinitely complicated and therefore impossible for us. Moreover, we cannot expect to prove the Multiplicative Axiom in my system, because my system is formally the same as that of *Principia*, and the Multiplicative Axiom obviously cannot be proved in the system of *Principia*, in which it is not a tautology.

We come now to the Axiom of Infinity, of which again my system and that of *Principia* give different interpretations. In *Principia*, owing to the definition of identity there used, the axiom means that there are an infinity of distinguishable individuals, which is an empirical proposition ; since, even supposing there to be an infinity of individuals, logic cannot determine whether there are an infinity of them no two of which have all their properties in common; but on my system, which admits functions in extension, the Axiom of Infinity asserts merely that there are an infinite number of individuals. This appears equally to be a mere question of fact ; but the profound analysis of Wittgenstein has shown that this is an illusion, and that, if it means anything, it must be either a tautology or a contradiction. This will be much easier to explain if we begin not with infinity but with some smaller number.

Let us start with ' There is an individual ', or writing it as simply as possible in logical notation,

$$' (\exists x) . x = x '$$

Now what is this proposition ? It is the logical sum of the tautologies $x = x$ for all values of x, and is therefore a tautology. But suppose there were no individuals, and therefore no values of x, then the above formula is absolute nonsense. So, if it means anything, it must be a tautology.

Next let us take ' There are at least two individuals ' or

$$' (\exists x, y) . x \neq y '.$$

This is the logical sum of the propositions $x \neq y$, which are tautologies if x and y have different values, contradictions if they have the same value. Hence it is the logical sum of a set of tautologies and contradictions ; and therefore a tautology if any one of the set is a tautology, but otherwise a contradiction. That is, it is a tautology if x and y can take different values (i.e. if there are two individuals), but otherwise a contradiction.

A little reflection will make it clear that this will hold not merely of 2, but of any other number, finite or infinite. That is, ' There are at least n individuals ' is always either a tautology or a contradiction, never a genuine proposition. We cannot, therefore, say anything about the number of individuals, since, when we attempt to do so, we never succeed in constructing a genuine proposition, but only a formula which is either tautological or self-contradictory. The number of individuals can, in Wittgenstein's phrase, only be shown, and it will be shown by whether the above formulæ are tautological or contradictory.

The sequence ' There is an individual ',

' There are at least 2 individuals ',

' There are at least n individuals ',

' There are at least $\aleph_0$ individuals ',

' There are at least $\aleph_1$ individuals ',

begins by being tautologous ; but somewhere it begins to be contradictory, and the position of the last tautologous term shows the number of individuals.

It may be wondered how, if we can say nothing about it, we can envisage as distinct possibilities that the number of individuals in the world is so-and-so. We do this by imagining different universes of discourse, to which we may be confined, so that by ' all ' we mean all in the universe of discourse ; and then that such-and-such a universe contains so-and-so many individuals is a real possibility, and can be asserted in a genuine proposition. It is only when we take, not a limited universe of discourse, but the whole world, that nothing can be said about the number of individuals in it.

We can do logic not only for the whole world but also for such limited universes of discourse ; if we take one containing n individuals,

$$Nc'\hat{x}(x = x) \geqslant n \text{ will be a tautology,}$$

$$Nc'\hat{x}(x = x) \geqslant n+1 \text{ a contradiction.}$$

Hence $Nc'\hat{x}(x = x) \geqslant n + 1$ cannot be deduced from the primitive propositions common to all universes, and therefore for a universe containing $n + 1$ individuals must be taken as a primitive proposition.

Similarly the Axiom of Infinity in the logic of the whole world, if it is a tautology, cannot be proved, but must be taken as a primitive proposition. And this is the course which we must adopt, unless we prefer the view that all analysis is self-contradictory and meaningless. We do not have to assume that any particular set of things, e.g. atoms, is infinite, but merely that there is some infinite type which we can take to be the type of individuals.

9

MATHEMATICAL LOGIC (1926)

I have been asked to speak about developments in Mathematical Logic since the publication of *Principia Mathematica*, and I think it would be most interesting if, instead of describing various definite improvements of detail, I were to discuss in outline the work which has been done on entirely different lines, and claims to supersede altogether the position taken up by Whitehead and Russell as to the nature of mathematics and its logical foundations.

Let me begin by recalling what Whitehead and Russell's view is : it is that mathematics is part of formal logic, that all the ideas of pure mathematics can be defined in terms which are not distinctively mathematical but involved in complicated thought of any description, and that all the propositions of mathematics can be deduced from propositions of formal logic, such as that if p is true, then either p or q is true. This view seems to me in itself plausible, for so soon as logic has been developed beyond its old syllogistic nucleus, we shall expect to have besides the forms ' All men are mortal ', ' Some men are mortal ', the numerical forms ' Two men are mortal ' and ' Three men are mortal ', and number will have to be included in formal logic.

Frege was the first to maintain that mathematics was part of logic, and to construct a detailed theory on that basis. But he fell foul of the famous contradictions of the theory of aggregates, and it appeared that contradictory consequences could be deduced from his primitive propositions. Whitehead and Russell escaped this fate by introducing their Theory of Types, of which it is impossible here to give an adequate account. But one of its implications must be explained if later developments are to be intelligible.

Suppose we have a set of characteristics given as all characteristics of a certain sort, say A, then we can ask about anything, whether it has a characteristic of the sort A. If it has, this will be another characteristic of it, and the question arises whether this characteristic, the characteristic of having a characteristic of the kind A, can itself be of the kind A, seeing that it presupposes the totality of such characteristics. The Theory of Types held that it could not, and that we could only escape contradiction by saying that it was a characteristic of higher order, and could not be included in any statement about all characteristics of lower order. And more generally that any statement about all characteristics must be regarded as meaning all of a certain order. This seemed in itself plausible, and also the only way of avoiding certain contradictions which arose from confusing these orders of characteristics. Whitehead and Russell also hold that statements about classes or aggregates are to be regarded as really about the characteristics which define the classes (a class being always given as the class of things possessing a certain character), so that any statement about all classes will be really about all characteristics, and will be liable to the same difficulties with regard to the order of these characteristics.

Such a theory enables us easily to avoid the contradictions of the Theory of Aggregates, but it has also the unfortunate consequence of invalidating an ordinary and important type of mathematical argument, the sort of argument by which we ultimately establish the existence of the upper bound of an aggregate, or the existence of the limit of a bounded monotonic sequence. It is usual to deduce these propositions from the principle of Dedekindian section, that if the real numbers are divided completely into an upper and a lower class, there must be a dividing number which is either the least of the upper class or the greatest of the lower. This in turn is proved by regarding real numbers as sections of rationals ; sections of rationals are a particular kind of classes of rationals, and hence a statement about real numbers will be a statement about a kind of classes of rationals, that is about a kind of characteristics of rationals, and the characteristics in question will have to be limited to be of a certain order.

Now suppose we have an aggregate E of real numbers ; that will be a class of characteristics of rationals. ξ, the upper bound of E, is defined as a section of rationals which is the sum of the members of E ; i.e. ξ is a section whose members are all those rationals which are members of any member of E, that is, all those rationals which have the characteristic of having any of the characteristics which give the members of E. So the upper bound ξ is a section whose defining characteristic is one of higher order than those of the members of E. Hence if all real numbers means all sections of rationals defined by characteristics of a certain order, the upper bound will, in general, be a section of rationals defined by a characteristic of higher order, and will not be a real number. This means that analysis as ordinarily understood is entirely grounded on a fallacious kind of argument, which when applied in other fields leads to self-contradictory results.

This unfortunate consequence of the Theory of Types Whitehead and Russell tried to avoid by introducing the Axiom of Reducibility, which asserted that to any characteristic of higher order there was an equivalent characteristic of the lowest order—equivalent in the sense that everything that has the one has the other, so that they define the same class. The upper bound, which we saw was a class of rationals defined by a characteristic of higher order, would then also be defined by the equivalent characteristic of lower order, and would be a real number. Unfortunately the axiom is certainly not self-evident, and there is no reason whatever to suppose it true. If it were true this would only be, so to speak, a happy accident, and it would not be a logical truth like the other primitive propositions.

In the Second Edition of *Principia Mathematica*, of which the first volume was published last year, Mr Russell has shown how mathematical induction, for which the Axiom of Reducibility seemed also to be required, can be established without it, but he does not hold out any hope of similar success with the Theory of Real Numbers, for which the ingenious method used for the whole numbers is not available. The matter is thus left in a profoundly unsatisfactory condition.

This was pointed out by Weyl, who published in 1918 a little book called *Das Kontinuum*, in which he rejected the Axiom of Reducibility and accepted the consequence that ordinary analysis was wrong. He showed, however, that various theorems, such as Cauchy's General Principle of Convergence, could still be proved.

Since then Weyl has changed his view and become a follower of Brouwer, the leader of what is called the intuitionist school, whose chief doctrine is the denial of the Law of Excluded Middle, that every proposition is either true or false.[1] This is denied apparently because it is thought impossible to know such a thing *a priori*, and equally impossible to know it by experience, because if we do not know either that it is true or that it is false we cannot verify that it is either true or false. Brouwer would refuse to agree that either it was raining or it was not raining, unless he had looked to see. Although it is certainly difficult to give a philosophical explanation of our knowledge of the laws of

---

[1] For instance, as the White Knight said : ' Everybody that hears me sing it—either it brings the *tears* into their eyes, or else—'. ' Or else what ? ' said Alice, for the Knight had made a sudden pause. ' Or else it doesn't, you know.'

logic, I cannot persuade myself that I do not know for certain
that the Law of Excluded Middle is true ; of course, it cannot
be proved, although Aristotle gave the following ingenious
argument in its favour. If a proposition is neither true nor
false, let us call it doubtful ; but then if the Law of Excluded
Middle be false, it need not be either doubtful or not doubtful,
so we shall have not merely three possibilities but four, that
it is true, that it is false, that it is doubtful, and that it is
neither true, false, nor doubtful. And so on *ad infinitum*.

But if it be answered ' Why not ? ', there is clearly nothing
more to be said, and I do not see how any common basis can be
found from which to discuss the matter. The cases in which
Brouwer thinks the Law of Excluded Middle false are ones
in which, as I should say, we could not tell whether the
proposition was true or false ; for instance, is $2^{\sqrt{2}}$ rational
or irrational ? We cannot tell, but Brouwer would say it was
neither. We cannot find integers m, n so that $\dfrac{m}{n} = 2^{\sqrt{2}}$;
therefore it is not rational : and we cannot show that it is
impossible to find such integers ; therefore it is not irrational.
I cannot see that the matter is not settled by saying that it is
either rational or irrational, but we can't tell which. The
denial of the Law of Excluded Middle renders illegitimate
the argument called a dilemma, in which something is shown
to follow from one hypothesis and also from the contradictory of that hypothesis, and it is concluded that it is true
unconditionally. Thus Brouwer is unable to justify much
of ordinary mathematics, and his conclusions are even more
sceptical than those of Weyl's first theory.

Weyl's second theory is very like Brouwer's, but he seems
to deny the Law of Excluded Middle for different reasons,
and in a less general way. He does not appear to deny that
any proposition is either true or false, but denies the derived
law that either every number has a given property, or at least

one number does not have it. He explains his denial first of all for real numbers in the following way. A real number is given by a sequence of integers, for instance as an infinite decimal ; this sequence we can conceive as generated either by a law or by successive acts of choice. If now we say there is a real number or sequence having a certain property, this can only mean that we have found a law giving one ; but if we say all sequences have a property, we mean that to have the property is part of the essence of a sequence, and therefore belongs to sequences arising not only by laws but from free acts of choice. Hence it is not true that either all sequences have the property or there is a sequence not having it. For the meaning of sequence is different in the two clauses. But I do not see why it should not be possible to use the word consistently. However this may be, nothing similar can be urged about the whole numbers which are not defined by sequences, and so another more fundamental reason is put forward for denying the Law of Excluded Middle. This is that general and existential propositions are not really propositions at all. If I say ' 2 is a prime number ', that is a genuine judgment asserting a fact ; but if I say ' There is a prime number ' or ' All numbers are prime ', I am not expressing a judgment at all. If, Weyl says, knowledge is a treasure, the existential proposition is a paper attesting the existence of a treasure but not saying where it is. We can only say ' There is a prime number ' when we have previously said ' This is a prime number ' and forgotten or chosen to disregard which particular number it was. Hence it is never legitimate to say ' There is a so-and-so ' unless we are in possession of a construction for actually finding one. In consequence, mathematics has to be very considerably altered ; for instance, it is impossible to have a function of a real variable with more than a finite number of discontinuities. The foundation on which this rests, namely the view that existential and general propositions are not genuine judgments, I shall come back to later.

But first I must say something of the system of Hilbert and his followers, which is designed to put an end to such scepticism once and for all. This is to be done by regarding higher mathematics as the manipulation of meaningless symbols according to fixed rules. We start with certain rows of symbols called axioms : from these we can derive others by substituting certain symbols called constants for others called variables, and by proceeding from the pair of formulae p, if p then q, to the formula q.

Mathematics proper is thus regarded as a sort of game, played with meaningless marks on paper rather like noughts and crosses ; but besides this there will be another subject called metamathematics, which is not meaningless, but consists of real assertions about mathematics, telling us that this or that formula can or cannot be obtained from the axioms according to the rules of deduction. The most important theorem of metamathematics is that it is not possible to deduce a contradiction from the axioms, where by a contradiction is meant a formula with a certain kind of shape, which can be taken to be $0 \neq 0$. This I understand Hilbert has proved, and has so removed the possibility of contradictions and scepticism based on them.

Now, whatever else a mathematician is doing, he is certainly making marks on paper, and so this point of view consists of nothing but the truth ; but it is hard to suppose it the whole truth. There must be some reason for the choice of axioms, and some reason why the particular mark $0 \neq 0$ is regarded with such abhorrence. This last point can, however, be explained by the fact that the axioms would allow anything whatever to be deducted from $0 \neq 0$, so that if $0 \neq 0$ could be proved, anything whatever could be proved, which would end the game for ever, which would be very boring for posterity. Again, it may be asked whether it is really possible to prove that the axioms do not lead to contradiction, since nothing can be proved unless some principles are taken for granted and assumed not to lead to contradiction. This objection is admitted, but it is contended that the principles used in the metamathematical proof that the axioms of mathematics do not lead to contradiction, are so obviously true that not even the sceptics can doubt them. For they all relate not to abstract or infinitely complex things, but to marks on paper, and though anyone may doubt whether a subclass of a certain sort of infinite series must have a first term, no one can doubt that if $=$ occurs on a page, there is a place on the page where it occurs for the first time.

But, granting all this, it must still be asked what use or merit there is in this game the mathematician plays, if it is really a game and not a form of knowledge ; and the only answer which is given is that some of the mathematician's formulae have or can be given meaning, and that if these can be proved in the symbolic system their meanings will be true. For Hilbert shares Weyl's opinion that general and existential propositions are meaningless, so that the only parts of mathematics which mean anything are particular assertions about finite integers, such as ' 47 is a prime ' and conjunctions and disjunctions of a finite number of such assertions like ' There is a prime between 50 and 100 ', which can be regarded as meaning ' Either 51 is a prime or 52 is a prime, etc., up to, or 99 is a prime '. But as all such propositions of simple arithmetic can be easily proved without using higher mathematics at all, this use for it cannot be of great importance. And it seems that although Hilbert's work provides a new and powerful method, which he has successfully applied to the Continuum problem, as a philosophy of mathematics it can hardly be regarded as adequate.

We see then that these authorities, great as are the differences between them, are agreed that mathematical analysis as ordinarily taught cannot be regarded as a body of truth, but is either false or at best a meaningless game with marks on paper ; and this means, I think, that mathematicians in this country should give some attention to their opinions, and try to find some way of meeting the situation.

Let us then consider what sort of a defence can be made for classical mathematics, and Russell's philosophy of it.

We must begin with what appears to be the crucial question, the meaning of general and existential propositions, about which Hilbert and Weyl take substantially the same view. Weyl says that an existential proposition is not a judgment, but an abstract of a judgment, and that a general proposition is a sort of cheque which can be cashed for a real judgment when an instance of it occurs.

Hilbert, less metaphorically, says that they are ideal propositions, and fulfil the same function in logic as ideal elements in various branches of mathematics. He explains their origin in this sort of way ; a genuine finite proposition such as ' There is a prime between 50 and 100 ', we write ' There is a prime which is greater than 50 and less than 100 ', which appears to contain a part, ' 51 is a prime, or 52 is a prime, etc., *ad inf.*,' and so be an infinite logical sum, which, like an infinite algebraic sum, is first of all meaningless, and can only be given a secondary meaning subject to certain conditions of convergence. But the introduction of these meaningless forms so simplifies the rules of inference that it is convenient to retain them, regarding them as ideals, for which a consistency theorem must be proved.

In this view of the matter there seem to me to be several difficulties. First it is hard to see what use these ideals can be supposed to be ; for mathematics proper appears to be reduced to elementary arithmetic, not even algebra being admitted, for the essence of algebra is to make general assertions. Now any statement of elementary arithmetic can be easily tested or proved without using higher mathematics, which if it be supposed to exist solely for the sake of simple arithmetic seems entirely pointless. Secondly, it is hard to see how the notion of an ideal can fail to presuppose the possibility of general knowledge. For the justification of ideals lies in the fact that *all* propositions not containing ideals which can be proved by means of them are true. And so Hilbert's metamathematics, which is agreed to be genuine truth, is bound to consist of general propositions about all possible mathematical proofs, which, though each proof is a finite construct, may well be infinite in number. And if, as Weyl says, an existential proposition is a paper attesting the existence of a treasure of knowledge but not saying where it is, I cannot see how we explain the utility of such a paper, except by presupposing its recipient capable of the existential knowledge that there is a treasure somewhere.

Moreover, even if Hilbert's account could be accepted so long as we confine our attention to mathematics, I do not see how it could be made plausible with regard to knowledge in general. Thus, if I tell you ' I keep a dog ', you appear to obtain knowledge of a fact ; trivial, but still knowledge. But ' I keep a dog ' must be put into logical symbolism as ' There is something which is a dog and kept by me ' ; so that the knowledge is knowledge of an existential proposition, covering the possibly infinite range of ' things '. Now it might possibly be maintained that my knowledge that I keep a dog arose in the sort of way Hilbert describes by my splitting off incorrectly what appears to be part of a finite proposition, such as ' Rolf is a dog and kept by me ', but your knowledge cannot possibly be explained in this way, because the existential proposition expresses all you ever have known, and probably all you ever will know about the matter.

Lastly, even the apparently individual facts of simple

arithmetic seem to me to be really general. For what are these numbers, that they are about? According to Hilbert marks on paper constructed out of the marks 1 and $+$. But this account seems to me inadequate, because if I said 'I have two dogs', that would also tell you something; you would understand the word 'two', and the whole sentence could be rendered something like 'There are x and y, which are my dogs and are not identical with one another'. This statement appears to involve the idea of existence, and not to be about marks on paper; so that I do not see that it can be seriously held that a cardinal number which answers the question 'How many?' is merely a mark on paper. If then we take one of these individual arithmetical facts, such as $2 + 2 = 4$, this seems to me to mean 'If the p's are two in number, and the q's also, and nothing is both a p and a q, then the number of things which are either p's or q's is four.' For this is the meaning in which we must take $2 + 2 = 4$ in order to use it, as we do, to infer from I have two dogs and two cats to I have four pets. This apparently individual fact, $2 + 2 = 4$, then contains several elements of generality and existentiality, firstly because the p's and q's are absolutely general characteristics, and secondly because the parts of the proposition, such as 'if the p's are two in number', involve as we have seen the idea of existence.

It is possible that the whole assertion that general and existential propositions cannot express genuine judgments or knowledge is purely verbal; that it is merely being decided to emphasize the difference between individual and general propositions by refusing to use the words judgment and knowledge in connection with the latter. This, however, would be a pity, for all our natural associations to the words judgment and knowledge fit general and existential propositions as well as they do individual ones; for in either case we can feel greater or lesser degrees of conviction about the matter, and in either case we can be in some sense right or wrong. And the suggestion which is implied, that general and existential knowledge exists simply for the sake of individual knowledge, seems to me entirely false. In theorizing what we principally admire is generality, and in ordinary life it may be quite sufficient to know the existential proposition that there is a bull somewhere in a certain field, and there may be no further advantage in knowing that it is this bull and here in the field, instead of merely a bull somewhere.

How then are we to explain general and existential propositions? I do not think we can do better than accept the view which has been put forward by Wittgenstein as a consequence of his theory of propositions in general. He explains them by reference to what may be called atomic propositions, which assert the simplest possible sort of fact, and could be expressed without using even implicitly any logical terms such as or, if, all, some. ' This is red ' is perhaps an instance of an atomic proposition. Suppose now we have, say, n atomic propositions; with regard to their truth or falsity, there are 2^n mutually exclusive ultimate possibilities. Let us call these the truth-possibilities of the n atomic propositions; then we can take any sub-set of these truth-possibilities and assert that it is a possibility out of this sub-set which is, in fact, realized. We can choose this sub-set of possibilities in which we assert the truth to lie in 2^{2^n} ways; and these will be all the propositions we can build up out of these n atomic propositions. Thus to take a simple instance, ' If p, then q ' expresses agreement with the three possibilities, that both p and q are true, that p is false and q true, and that p is false and q false, and denies the remaining possibility that p is true and q false.

We can easily see that from this point of view there is a redundancy in all ordinary logical notations, because we can write in many different ways what is essentially the same proposition, expressing agreement and disagreement with the same sets of possibilities.

Mr Wittgenstein holds that all propositions express agreement and disagreement with truth-possibilities of atomic propositions, or, as we say, are truth-functions of atomic propositions; although often the atomic propositions in question are not enumerated, but determined as all values of a certain propositional function. Thus the propositional function ' x is red ' determines a collection of propositions which are its values, and we can assert that all or at least one of these values are true by saying ' For all x, x is red ' and ' There is an x such that x is red ' respectively. That is to say, if we could enumerate the values of x as $a, b \ldots z$, ' For all x, x is red ' would be equivalent to the proposition ' a is red and b is red and $\ldots$ and z is red '. It is clear, of course, that the state of mind of a man using the one expression differs in several respects from that of a man using the other, but what might be called the logical meaning of the statement, the fact which is asserted to be, is the same in the two cases.

It is impossible to discuss now all the arguments which might be used against this view, but something must be said about the argument of Hilbert, that if the variable has an infinite number of values, if, that is to say, there are an infinite number of things in the world of the logical type in question, we have here an infinite logical sum or product which, like an infinite algebraic sum or product, is initially meaningless and can only be given a meaning in an indirect way. This seems to me to rest on a false analogy ; the logical sum of a set of propositions is the proposition that one of the set at least is true, and it doesn't appear to matter whether the set is finite or infinite. It is not like an algebraic sum to which finitude is essential, since this is extended step by step from the sum of two terms. To say that anything possibly involving an infinity of any kind must be meaningless is to declare in advance that any real theory of aggregates is impossible.

Apart from providing a simple account of existential and general propositions, Wittgenstein's theory settles another question of the first importance by explaining precisely the peculiar nature of logical propositions. When Mr Russell first said that mathematics could be reduced to logic, his view of logic was that it consisted of all true absolutely general propositions, propositions, that is, which contained no material (as opposed to logical) constants. Later he abandoned this view, because it was clear that some further characteristic besides generality was required. For it would be possible to describe the whole world without mentioning any particular thing, and clearly something may by chance be true of anything whatever without having the character of necessity which belongs to the truths of logic.

If, then, we are to understand what logic, and so on Mr Russell's view mathematics is, we must try to define this further characteristic which may be vaguely called necessity, or from another point of view tautology. For instance, 'p is either true or false' may be regarded either as necessary truth or as a mere tautology. This problem is incidentally solved by Wittgenstein's theory of propositions. Propositions, we said, expressed agreement and disagreement with the truth-possibilities of atomic propositions. Given n atomic propositions, there are 2^n truth-possibilities, and we can agree with any set of these and disagree with the remainder. There will then be two extreme cases, one in which we agree with all the possibilities, and disagree with none, the other in which we agree with none and disagree with all. The former is called a tautology, the latter a contradiction.

The simplest tautology is 'p or not p' : such a statement adds nothing to our knowledge, and does not really assert a fact at all; it is, as it were, not a real proposition, but a degenerate case. And it will be found that all propositions of logic are in this sense tautologies ; and this is their distinguishing characteristic. All the primitive propositions in *Principia Mathematica* are tautologies except the Axiom of Reducibility, and the rules of deduction are such that from tautologies only tautologies can be deduced, so that were it not for the one blemish, the whole structure would consist of tautologies. We thus are brought back to the old difficulty, but it is possible to hope that this too can be removed by some modification of the Theory of Types which may result from Wittgenstein's analysis.

A Theory of Types must enable us to avoid the contradictions ; Whitehead and Russell's theory consisted of two distinct parts, united only by being both deduced from the rather vague ' Vicious-Circle Principle '. The first part distinguished propositional functions according to their arguments, i.e. classes according to their members; the second part created the need for the Axiom of Reducibility by requiring further distinctions between orders of functions with the same type of arguments.

We can easily divide the contradictions according to which part of the theory is required for their solution, and when we have done this we find that these two sets of contradictions are distinguished in another way also. The ones solved by the first part of the theory are all purely logical ; they involve no ideas but those of class, relation and number, could be stated in logical symbolism, and occur in the actual development of mathematics when it is pursued in the right direction. Such are the contradiction of the greatest ordinal, and that of the class of classes which are not members of themselves. With regard to these Mr Russell's solution seems inevitable.

On the other hand, the second set of contradictions are none of them purely logical or mathematical, but all involve some psychological term, such as meaning, defining, naming or asserting. They occur not in mathematics, but in thinking about mathematics ; so that it is possible that they arise not from faulty logic or mathematics, but from ambiguity in the psychological or epistemological notions of meaning and asserting. Indeed, it seems that this must be the case, because examination soon convinces one that the psychological term is in every case essential to the contradiction, which could not be constructed without introducing the relation of words to their meaning or some equivalent.

If now we try to apply to the question Wittgenstein's theory of generality, we can, I think, fairly easily construct a solution along these lines. To explain this adequately would require a paper to itself, but it may be possible to give some idea of it in a few words. On Wittgenstein's theory a general proposition is equivalent to a conjunction of its instances, so that the kind of fact asserted by a general proposition is not essentially different from that asserted by a conjunction of atomic propositions. But the symbol for a general proposition means its meaning in a different way from that in which the symbol for an elementary proposition means it, because the latter contains names for all the things it is about, whereas the general proposition's symbol contains only a variable standing for all its values at once. So that though the two kinds of symbol could mean the same thing, the senses of meaning in which they mean it must be different. Hence the orders of propositions will be characteristics not of what is meant, which is alone relevant in mathematics, but of the symbols used to mean it.

First-order propositions will be rather like spoken words ; the same word can be both spoken and written, and the same proposition can theoretically be expressed in different orders. Applying this *mutatis mutandis* to propositional functions, we find that the typical distinctions between functions with the same arguments apply not to what is meant, but to the relation

240

of meaning between symbol and object signified. Hence they can be neglected in mathematics, and the solution of the contradictions can be preserved in a slightly modified form, because the contradictions here relevant all have to do with the relation of meaning.

In this way I think it is possible to escape the difficulty of the Axiom of Reducibility, and remove various other more philosophical objections, which have been made by Wittgenstein, thus rehabilitating the general account of the Foundations of Mathematics given by Whitehead and Russell. But there still remains an important point in which the resulting theory must be regarded as unsatisfactory, and that is in connection with the Axiom of Infinity.

According to the authors of *Principia Mathematica* there is no way of proving that there are an infinite number of things in any logical type ; and if there are not an infinite number in any type, the whole theory of infinite aggregates, sequences, differential calculus and analysis in general breaks down. According to their theory of number, if there were only ten individuals, in the sense of number appropriate to individuals all numbers greater than ten would be identical with the null-class and so with one another. Of course there would be 2^{10} classes of individuals, and so the next type of numbers would be all right up to 2^{10}, and so by taking a high enough type any finite number can be reached.

But it will be impossible in this way to reach $\aleph_0$. There are various natural suggestions for getting out of this difficulty, but they all seem to lead to reconstituting the contradiction of the greatest ordinal.

It would appear then impossible to put forward analysis except as a consequence of the Axiom of Infinity ; nor do I see that this would in general be objectionable, because there would be little point in proving propositions about infinite series unless such things existed. And on the other hand

241

the mathematics of a world with a given finite number of members is of little theoretical interest, as all its problems can be solved by a mechanical procedure.

But a difficulty seems to me to arise in connection with elementary propositions in the theory of numbers which can only be proved by transcendental methods, such as Dirichlet's evaluation of the class number of quadratic forms. Let us consider such a result of the form ' Every number has the property p ', proved by transcendental methods only for the case of an infinite world ; besides this, if we knew the world only contained say, 1,000,000 things, we could prove it by testing the numbers up to 1,000,000. But suppose the world is finite and yet we do not know any upper limit to its size, then we are without any method of proving it at all.

It might be thought that we could escape this conclusion by saying that although no infinite aggregate may exist, the notion of an infinite aggregate is not self-contradictory, and therefore permissible in mathematics. But I think this suggestion is no use, for three reasons : firstly, it appears as a result of some rather difficult, but I think conclusive, reasoning by Wittgenstein that, if we accept his theory of general and existential propositions (and it was only so that we could get rid of the Axiom of Reducibility), it will follow that if no infinite aggregate existed the notion of such an aggregate would be self-contradictory ; secondly, however that may be, it is generally accepted that the only way of demonstrating that postulates are compatible, is by an existence theorem showing that there actually is and not merely might be a system of the kind postulated ; thirdly, even if it were granted that the notion of an infinite aggregate were not self-contradictory, we should have to make large alterations in our system of logic in order to validate proofs depending on constructions in terms of things which might exist but don't. The system of *Principia* would be quite inadequate.

What then can be done ? We can try to alter the proofs of such propositions, and it might therefore be interesting to try to develop a new mathematics without the Axiom of Infinity ; the methods to be adopted might resemble those of Brouwer and Weyl. These authorities, however, seem to me to be sceptical about the wrong things in rejecting not the Axiom of Infinity, but the clearly tautologous Law of Excluded Middle. But I do not feel at all confident that anything could be achieved on these lines which would replace the transcendental arguments at present employed.

Another possibility is that Hilbert's general method should be adopted, and that we should use his proof that no contradiction can be deduced from the axioms of mathematics including an equivalent of the Axiom of Infinity. We can then argue thus : whether a given number has or has not the property p can always be found out by calculation. This will give us a formal proof of the result for this particular number, which cannot contradict the general result proved from the Axiom of Infinity which must therefore be valid.

But this argument will still be incomplete, for it will only apply to numbers which can be symbolized in our system. And if we are denying the Axiom of Infinity, there will be an upper limit to the number of marks which can be made on paper, since space and time will be finite, both in extension and divisibility, so that some numbers will be too large to be written down, and to them the proof will not apply. And these numbers being finite will be existent in a sufficiently high type, and Hilbert's theory will not help us to prove that they have the property p.

Another serious difficulty about the Axiom of Infinity is that, if it is false, it is difficult to see how mathematical analysis can be used in physics, which seems to require its mathematics to be true and not merely to follow from a possibly false hypothesis. But to discuss this adequately would take us too far.

As to how to carry the matter further, I have no suggestion to make ; all I hope is to have made it clear that the subject is very difficult, and that the leading authorities are very sceptical as to whether pure mathematics as ordinarily taught can be logically justified, for Brouwer and Weyl say that it cannot, and Hilbert proposes only to justify it as a game with meaningless marks on paper. On the other hand, although my attempted reconstruction of the view of Whitehead and Russell overcomes, I think, many of the difficulties, it is impossible to regard it as altogether satisfactory.

10

EPILOGUE (1925)

Having to write a paper for the Society I was as usual at a loss for a subject ; and I flattered myself that this was not merely my personal deficiency, but arose from the fact that there really was no subject suitable for discussion. But, happening to have recently lectured on the Theory of Types, I reflected that in such a sentence the word ' subject ' must be limited to mean subject of the first order and that perhaps there might be a subject of the second order which would be possible. And then I saw that it lay ready before me, namely, that I should put forward the thesis that there is no discussable subject (of the first order).

A serious matter this if it is true. For for what does the Society exist but discussion ? And if there is nothing to discuss—but that can be left till afterwards.

I do not wish to maintain that there never has been anything to discuss, but only that there is no longer ; that we have really settled everything by realizing that there is nothing to know except science. And that we are most of us ignorant of most sciences so that, while we can exchange information, we cannot usefully discuss them, as we are just learners.

Let us review the possible subjects of discussion. They fall, as far as I can see, under the heads of science, philosophy, history and politics, psychology and æsthetics ; where, not to beg any question, I am separating psychology from the other sciences.

Science, history, and politics are not suited for discussion except by experts. Others are simply in the position of requiring more information ; and, till they have acquired all available information, cannot do anything but accept on authority the opinions of those better qualified. Then there is philosophy ; this, too, has become too technical for the layman. Besides this disadvantage, the conclusion of the greatest modern philosopher is that there is no such subject as philosophy ; that it is an activity, not a doctrine ; and that, instead of answering questions, it aims merely at curing headaches. It might be thought that, apart from this technical philosophy whose centre is logic, there was a sort of popular philosophy which dealt with such subjects as the relation of man to nature, and the meaning of morality. But any attempt to treat such topics seriously reduces them to questions either of science or of technical philosophy, or results more immediately in perceiving them to be non-sensical.

Take as an example Russell's recent lecture on " What I Believe ". He divided it into two parts, the philosophy of nature and the philosophy of value. His philosophy of nature consisted mainly of the conclusions of modern physics, physiology, and astronomy, with a slight admixture of his own theory of material objects as a particular kind of logical construction. Its content could therefore only be discussed by someone with an adequate knowledge of relativity, atomic theory, physiology, and mathematical logic. The only remaining possibility of discussion in connection with this part of his paper would be about the emphasis he laid on certain points, for instance, the disparity in physical size between stars and men. To this topic I shall return.

His philosophy of value consisted in saying that the only questions about value were what men desired and how their desires could be satisfied, and then he went on to answer these questions. Thus the whole subject became part of psychology, and its discussion would be a psychological one.

Of course his main statement about value might be disputed, but most of us would agree that the objectivity of good was a thing we had settled and dismissed with the existence of God. Theology and Absolute Ethics are two famous subjects which we have realized to have no real objects.

Ethics has then been reduced to psychology, and that brings me to psychology as a subject for discussion. Most of our meetings might be said to deal with psychological questions. It is a subject in which we are all more or less interested for practical reasons. In considering it we must distinguish psychology proper, which is the study of mental events with a view to establishing scientific generalizations, from merely comparing our own experience from personal interest. The test is whether we should want to know of this experience as much if it were a stranger's as we do when it is our friend's ; whether we are interested in it as scientific material, or merely from personal curiosity.

I think we rarely, if ever, discuss fundamental psychological questions, but far more often simply compare our several experiences, which is not a form of discussing. I think we realize too little how often our arguments are of the form :—A. : " I went to Grantchester this afternoon." B. : " No I didn't." Another thing we often do is to discuss what sort of people or behaviour we feel admiration for or ashamed of. E.g., when we discuss constancy of affection, it consists in A. saying he would feel guilty if he weren't constant, B saying *he* wouldn't feel guilty in the least. But that, although a pleasant way of passing the time, is not discussing anything whatever, but simply comparing notes.

Genuine psychology, on the other hand, is a science of which we most of us know far too little for it to become us to venture an opinion.

Lastly, there is æsthetics, including literature. This always excites us far more than anything else ; but we don't really discuss it much. Our arguments are so feeble ; we are still at the stage of " Who drives fat oxen must himself be fat ", and have very little to say about the psychological problems of which æsthetics really consists, e.g., why certain combinations of colours give us such peculiar feelings. What we really like doing is again to compare our experience ; a practice which in this case is peculiarly profitable because the critic can point out things to other people, to which, if they attend, they will obtain feelings which they value which they failed to obtain otherwise. We do not and cannot discuss whether one work of art is better than another ; we merely compare the feelings it gives us.

I conclude that there really is nothing to discuss ; and this conclusion corresponds to a feeling I have about ordinary conversation also. It is a relatively new phenomenon, which has arisen from two causes which have operated gradually through the nineteenth century. One is the advance of science, the other the decay of religion ; which have resulted in all the old general questions becoming either technical or ridiculous. This process in the development of civilization we have each of us to repeat in ourselves. I, for instance, came up as a freshman enjoying conversation and argument more than anything else in the world ; but I have gradually come to regard it as of less and less importance, because there never seems to be anything to talk about except shop and people's private lives, neither of which is suited for general conversation. Also, since I was analysed, I feel that people know far less about themselves than they imagine, and am not nearly so anxious to talk about myself as I used to be, having had enough of it to get bored. There still are literature and art ; but about them one cannot argue, one can only compare notes, just as one can exchange information about history or economics. But about art one exchanges not information but feelings.

This brings me back to Russell and " What I believe ". If I was to write a *Weltanschauung* I should call it not " What

I believe '' but " What I feel ''. This is connected with Wittgenstein's view that philosophy does not give us beliefs, but merely relieves feelings of intellectual discomfort. Also, if I were to quarrel with Russell's lecture, it would not be with what he believed but with the indications it gave as to what he felt. Not that one can really quarrel with a man's feelings, one can only have different feelings oneself, and perhaps also regard one's own as more admirable or more conducive to a happy life. From this point of view, that it is a matter not of fact but of feeling, I shall conclude by some remarks on things in general, or, as I would rather say, not things but *life* in general.

Where I seem to differ from some of my friends is in attaching little importance to physical size. I don't feel the least humble before the vastness of the heavens. The stars may be large, but they cannot think or love ; and these are qualities which impress me far more than size does. I take no credit for weighing nearly seventeen stone.

My picture of the world is drawn in perspective, and not like a model to scale. The foreground is occupied by human beings and the stars are all as small as threepenny bits. I don't really believe in astronomy, except as a complicated description of part of the course of human and possibly animal sensation. I apply my perspective not merely to space but also to time. In time the world will cool and everything will die ; but that is a long time off still, and its present value at compound discount is almost nothing. Nor is the present less valuable because the future will be blank. Humanity, which fills the foreground of my picture, I find interesting and on the whole admirable. I find, just now at least, the world a pleasant and exciting place. You may find it depressing ; I am sorry for you, and you despise me. But I have reason and you have none ; you would only have a reason for despising me if your feeling corresponded to the fact in a way mine didn't. But neither can correspond to the fact. The fact is not in itself good or bad ; it is just that it thrills me but depresses you. On the other hand, I pity you with reason, because it is pleasanter to be thrilled than to be depressed, and not merely pleasanter but better for all one's activities.

28th February, 1925.

BIBLIOGRAPHY OF
RAMSEY'S WORKS

Items marked *PP* are reprinted in this volume. Items marked *FM* or *F* were either reprinted or first published in *The Foundations of Mathematics and other Logical Essays*, edited by R. B. Braithwaite, Routledge and Kegan Paul, London 1931 (*FM*) or in *Foundations: Essays in Philosophy, Logic, Mathematics and Economics*, edited by D. H. Mellor, Routledge and Kegan Paul, London 1978 (*F*).

1922

' Mr Keynes on Probability ', *The Cambridge Magazine* **11**, no. 1 (Decennial Number, 1912–21), pp. 3–5. January. [Reprinted in *The British Journal for the Philosophy of Science* **40**, June 1989].

'The Douglas Proposal ', *The Cambridge Magazine* **11**, no. 1 (Decennial Number 1912–21), 74–6, January.

Review of W. E. Johnson's *Logic, Part II* in *The New Statesman* **19**, 469–70, 29th July.

1923

Critical notice of L. Wittgenstein's *Tractatus Logico-Philosophicus* in *Mind* **32**, 465–78, October. [*FM* pp. 27–86.]

1924

Review of C. K. Odgen's and I. A. Richard's *The Meaning of Meaning* in *Mind* **33**, 108–9, January.

1925

' The New Principia ' (review of Volume 1 of the 2nd edition of A. N. Whitehead's and B. Russell's *Principia Mathematica*), in *Nature* **116**, 127–8, 25th July.

Review of the same book in *Mind* **34**, 506–7, October.

' Universals ', *Mind* **34**, 401–17, October. [*FM* 112–134, *F* 17–39, *PP* 8–30.]

' The Foundations of Mathematics ', *Proceedings of the London Mathematical Society* **25**, 338–84, read 12th November. [*FM* 1–61, *F* 152–212, *PP* 164–224.]

BIBLIOGRAPHY OF RAMSEY'S WORKS

1926

' Mathematics: Mathematical Logic ', *The Encyclopaedia Britannica*, Supplementary Volumes of the 13th edition, Volume **2**, 830–2.

' Universal and the " Method of analysis " ' (contribution to a symposium with H. W. B. Joseph and R. B. Braithwaite), *Aristotelian Society Supplementary Volume* **6**, 17–26, July. [Part reprinted as ' Note on the preceding paper ' in *FM* 135–7 and in *PP* 31–3.]

' Mathematical Logic ', *The Mathematical Gazette* **13**, 185–94, October (read before the British Association in August). [*FM* 62–81, *F* 213–32, *PP* 225–44.]

1927

' A Contribution to the Theory of Taxation ', *The Economic Journal* **37**, 47–61, March. [*F* 242–60.]

' Facts and Propositions ' (contribution to a symposium with G. E. Moore), *Aristotelian Society Supplementary Volume* **7**, 153–70, July. [*FM* 138–55, *F* 40–57, *PP* 34–51.]

1928

' A Mathematical Theory of Saving ', *The Economic Journal* **38**, 543–9, December. [*F* 261–81.]

' On a Problem of Formal Logic ', *Proceedings of the London Mathematical Society* **30**, 338–84, read 13th December. [*FM* 82–111, Part I reprinted as ' Ramsey's theorem ' in *F* 223–41.]

1929

' Mathematics, Foundations of ', *Encyclopaedia Britannica* 14th edition, Volume **15**, 82–4.

' Russell, Bertrand Arthur William ' (in part), *The Encyclopaedia Britannica* 14th edition, Volume **19**, 678.

POSTHUMOUSLY PUBLISHED PAPERS

1931

' Epilogue ' (a paper read to the Apostles, a Cambridge discussion Society, in 1925), *FM* 287–92, *PP* 245–50.

' Truth and Probability ' (parts read to the Moral Sciences Club, Cambridge, in 1926), *FM* 156–98, *F* 58–100, *PP* 52–94.

' Reasonable Degree of Belief ' (1928), *FM* 199–203, *PP* 97–101.

' Statistics ' (1928), *FM* 204–5, *PP* 102–3.

'Chance' (1928), *FM* 206–11, *PP* 104–9.
'Theories' (1929), *FM* 212–36, *F* 101–25, *PP* 112–36.
'General Propositions and Causality' (1929), *FM* 237–55, *F* 133–51, *PP* 145–63.
'Probability and Partial Belief' (1929), *FM* 256–7, *PP* 95–6.
'Knowledge' (1929), *FM* 258–9, *F* 126–7, *PP* 110–1.
'Causal Qualities' (1929), *FM* 260–2, *PP* 137–9.
'Philosophy' (1929), *FM* 263–9, *PP* 1–7.

1978
'Universals of Law and of Fact' (1928), *F* 128–32, *PP* 140–4.

1980
Grundlagen: Abhandlungen zur Philosophie, Logik, Mathematik und Wirtschaftswissenschaft [translation of *F*], translated and edited by I. U. Dalferth and J. Kalkaj, Fromman-Holzboog, Stuttgart-Bad Cannstatt.

1987
'The "Long" and the "Short" of it *or* a Failure of Logic' (precursor of part of 'The Foundations of Mathematics'), *American Philosophical Quarterly* **24,** 357–9.

1990
'Weight or the Value of Knowledge', *The British Journal for the Philosophy of Science* **41,** 1–3.

INDEX

INDEX